TWIGG & COGLEE PUBLISHERS
twigcog.com

FAITHFUL SLAVE
A POST DOGMATIC PARADIGM

By Daniel J. Quigley

Faithful Slave: A Post-Dogmatic Paradigm
Written by Daniel J. Quigley, PMP
Cover Art by Daniel J. Quigley and Stacey D. Quigley
Cover Background: Masterpiece of Light and Shadow,
by Athanasius Kirscher

© 2022 All Rights Reserved
Published in Canada by Twigg & Coglee Publishers
Printed in the United States of America 22-11-13
1st Ed. Hardcover Includes Bibliographical References
ISBN 978-1-7386799-2-8
ISBN 978-1-7386799-0-4
ISBN 978-1-7386799-1-1

postdogma.org
twigcog.com

CONTENTS

PREFACE

Those who are able to see beyond the shadows and lies of their culture will never be understood let alone believed by the masses.
Plato

In my mid-life years, when most people are settling into who they are and determining their preferred lifestyle, I went through an eruption of change so dramatic I was forced to acknowledge I was wrong about everything I thought most true. This was especially difficult for me because I held my convictions with the tenacity of a junkyard dog. I was convinced my conclusions were formulated by comprehensive research and validated by sound logic. But I was wrong.

The realization was humiliating. But humility is not a terrible condition. Humility opened my eyes to new perspectives, my heart to different feelings, and doors to unimagined possibilities.

Disgorging the faith which once defined me was painful. But the blessings which followed have been of such transcendent value I encountered a powerful force I was not familiar with: gratitude. Certainly, I felt grateful in my past. But they were isolated moments, peppered over a sea of heartfelt contempt. I was unjustifiably angry with my lot in life. The successes of others had me seething with jealousy. I was burdened with a sense of injustice for all matters occurring within my purview. Life was not fair.

It was an extrication from religion, and it was not instantaneous or smooth. It was a bumpy ride with painful turns. But up to that point, taking the easiest path and avoiding discomfort had not worked in my favor. As painful as growth is, I can't imagine anything more painful than living a miserable life.

I was not a particularly good student while in grade school, so I don't think I could represent myself as studious. If I were to be completely honest, I would admit I'm a slow learner. From my earliest school years to this present moment, I learn slower from a need to know *why*. Memorizing the material is not enough. I need the overall picture – the underlying concept. If you teach me the concept, I'll buy in and will not forget.

School was taught differently, though. I struggled with mathematics and thought that was evidence of a lower intellect. I fought agonizing battles to keep my mind wandering from the algebraic formulas my teacher expected me to memorize. I would lose those battles time and again. I remember asking teachers what I thought were the right questions only to have my inquiries cast aside with a glare. *How dare you ask why. It just is. Learn it.* What seemed a handicap in grade school would later become an advantage in my professional career – a strength I could regard as a super-power. The desire to understand the bigger picture was the desire which pushed me to solve problems and thus prove myself as a resource. It was that desire which later added a studious element to my learning.

When I left my religion, I was also left with many unanswered questions and for each of those I needed to know *why*. *Why did I believe what I believed? Why was I so insistent? Why are beliefs held so personally? Why are certain people effective at convincing others? What is the meaning of life? Why do I think my new trajectory is better?* I offer this work to you, constructed upon my journey to answering those questions. This project was constructed upon that first question. *Why did I believe what I believed?* My adventure to find that answer would entirely change the way I saw the world.

I was one of Jehovah's Witnesses, a religion not easily left behind. It is a religion which encompasses a believer's life and isolates them from the world. Stepping away from it is a significant life-change and often results in a dissident being separated from all friends and family and stripped of their foundations for belief. Disoriented from having those foundations removed and the shredding of my family, I joined a number of support groups for people who left their various religions.

Through my time in those support groups I learned my suffering was not unique. I learned that what I shared could provide strength to those who lost theirs, and an opportunity to heal. I feel somewhat selfish that when I learned of their healing, it healed me as well. It validated my own suffering. It solidified that what I had felt was real. Never have I felt such a wholesome and humbling purpose than offering missing pieces of the puzzle to those who need them.

It became apparent to me there was a need for something dialed into the needs of religious dissidents. Something more comprehensive than books on psychology, philosophy, sociology or a personal memoir on their own.

It seems to me healing requires something different for each person. For some, healing requires a higher perspective of their situation. Others need more – perhaps a complete re-tooling of their habits. There are certain concepts which seem universally important. I found most religious dissidents are plagued with the unsettling realization they are considered disloyal and deserving of death by every person they loved. That bothered me most. And for anyone who has followed in a similar path, I hope they can find confidence knowing in the face of powerful opposition they proved themselves heroic. Those efforts did not go unnoticed. If there was any doubt, I hope they find assurance that their courageous stand for truth was just that.

I mulled over the concept for a couple years unsure how to approach such a thing. What kind of format would be appropriate? Who could be considered qualified for an undertaking with numerous fields of study?

The project finally got underway after a conversation with my sister. She expressed anger toward me having found it difficult listening to my criticisms of beliefs I spent my life promoting. *How could you spend so much time being the greatest advocate for this religion, and now you're the opposite?* That was a solid point, and I didn't have a response at the time.

She felt I had turned against those who had cared for me most. I did not feel that was true. I had not turned against them in any way. Neither did I hate them or hate anyone. I had grown to love them more. But I did not have those words in that moment. The short conversation with my sister or ten more like it could never explain what had taken me years to explore. So I decided to get to work and write that response.

With the words on these pages I hope to articulate why it was important for me to leave. I hope this can offer some form of help. Perhaps it will help people leaving authoritarian religions to relate to my struggles and to hold hope there are brighter days ahead. Perhaps a religious parent can read from this that their child is not of poor character for doubting their religion.

It seems to me when children stand for their individual beliefs, even if they are mistaken, such is a sign of powerful morals. Should parents not feel proud they raised an individual who cared so much about truth? Perhaps someone can find a measure of healing with the reassurance they are not alone. Perhaps others can find a way to forgive those who have failed to accept what they feel is precious and true.

I am not a psychologist, historian, theologian, or sociologist. By profession, I am a project manager. In that profession I coordinate the activities of numerous professional disciplines to bring about a final product. That might best describe what this book is: the arrangement of professional opinions and academic resources – the hard work and brilliance of others, compiled and condensed into something which would have helped – well me – when I first left my religion and when I found myself listless, searching for answers and direction.

Within these pages I don't shy from the most difficult topics including politics, death, religion, sexual abuse, and morality – essentially every subject we're not supposed to talk about. It is not intended to be a hit piece on any religion, although I hold nothing back when I feel criticism is due. There are positive aspects of religion, and if I didn't highlight those along with the harmful, a work like this would not be honest.

Honesty is imperative – yet another lesson I learned late in my life. Above all things I hope to express with honesty what I have come to believe.

INTRODUCTION

The hardest thing to explain is the glaringly evident which everyone had decided not to see.

Ayn Rand

My mission and vision for this project is to be effective – I wanted to effectively assist people cross the threshold from a dogmatic mindset to one that is healthily post-dogmatic.

As I started to write and to share the blogs, posts and articles which would comprise the body of this work, the grief of many in semi-related support groups reshaped this toward something palatable for exMuslims exChristians, and exCatholics. These groups might appear fragmented when first encountering them. But they have proven to be a tolerant and welcoming great crowd, quick to aid their fellow former faith friends. Thus I tried to be mindful of dissidents from all faith groups.

When testing these concepts, I received questions from others on the outside – those unfamiliar with authoritarian religion, who were perplexed as to how an otherwise intelligent person could find themselves trapped in the beliefs of others. I realized how the dogmatism I experienced in religion was not dissimilar to that exhibited within other facets of humanity. So again, I considered another demographic and how to ensure those without a religious background could relate and could benefit.

As a result, those on the outside looking in might think it silly I spend time explaining common academic principles. But for those of us who were held back from education, those concepts are less common. Those from within religion might feel I over-explain common Biblical concepts. I hope you will understand the variety I have striven to speak to and why I likely should have listened to my editor who told me to do no such thing.

In the end, I would have to admit the primary reader for which this is targeted is me – when I first stepped outside the confines of my faith. This book addresses the issues I needed to work on, and these were the answers I was looking for.

This work comes in reference to the religion of Jehovah's Witnesses, but I have found the concepts very much universal among monotheistic faiths. Jehovah's Witnesses embody many features of Islam, Protestant Christianity, Judaism, and Catholicism.

Despite their numbers being a small fraction of Catholics or Muslims, Jehovah's Witnesses hold staggering influence over the lives of tens of millions. Some might argue Jehovah's Witnesses are more closely aligned with Islam than with mainstream Christianity. I would say they fit in the middle somewhere, and thus provide an informative case study. *They are just like every other religion. Only more so.*

Rather than launching an uninterrupted series of attacks on religion, I take the time to earnestly consider the benefits and how those could be nurtured. I offer a means to keep religion in relevance – concepts which I feel are critical for humanity.

The nature of the subject is sensitive and taking any position within it is bound to insult some. That is not my intent. But I believe engaging in these discussions is important enough to risk hurt feelings. I have done my best to protect the truth to the best of my ability and where I have erred, I would be happy to correct. Because I value the interchange of thought, I set up a website with conversation features. All are welcomed to voice their questions, comments, and concerns at Postdogma.org

When not otherwise stated, I will quote the Bible from the New International Version because it was the most accessible and commonly used version I was aware of. When referencing NWT, I am referring to the New World Translation 2013 English version, published by the Watchtower Bible and Tract Society.

The organization of Jehovah's Witnesses is represented by multiple legal entities: The Watchtower Bible and Tract Society of Pennsylvania, The Watchtower Bible and Tract Society of New York, The Christian Congregation of Jehovah's Witnesses, and others. I will refer to the organized body as *the Watchtower,* or as *the Organization,* as Jehovah's Witnesses do.

The body of this work is divided into three sections entitled *Humility,* *Honesty,* and *Integrity.* Admittedly, I throw some softballs in the first section because my intent is not to be argumentative. *Humility* intends to prepare the minds of readers for concepts they may not have considered. Depending on the predisposition or culture of the reader, those may take time to appreciate, so I tried to leave a wide enough berth for any amount of mental appraisal required. In the second section, *Honesty,* I challenge a selection of common monotheistic beliefs. Beliefs which I am convinced reduce the quality of life and quality of thoughts of billions. In the third section, *Integrity,* I build upon the excavation of those previously challenged concepts.

When I first started my journey to find truth after religion, I was dismayed to find that the scholars who so artfully dismantled my earlier beliefs had nothing to offer in their stead. And of course that is true. I'm glad they did not. They never pretended to have expertise in evangelism. And nobody wants to escape the clutches of one belief system just to adopt the next. Still though, my structure had been lost and structure was what I needed.

I try to offer some structure with this work. Something for fresh-freed slaves to build from. A foundation I would think few could disagree with. If anything I close this out with a new take on timeless concepts – a reason for hope, and a means to build bridges across polarized divisions.

HUMILITY

1.

Listen to
everyone, read
everything;
believe
absolutely
nothing unless
you can prove it
in your own
right.

Milton William Cooper

What do you believe?

What belief has become so precious in your heart you were enraged when others failed to validate your assumptions?

We might feel personally betrayed when a loved one leaves our religion. We might be concerned how it would affect our standing. *How could they turn their back on God? How could they hurt the people who worked hard to care for them? What could I have done differently to prevent this?*

Belief is a sensitive subject. Listening to others reject what has become precious in our hearts can have an infuriating effect. What then would motivate a person to take a stand against their convictions and face the wrath and intolerance of every person they care most about? People have been burned at the stake for their beliefs. Is there a truth so precious it is worth the ultimate sacrifice? Is there a lie so potent we would rather watch a loved one writhe on the stake than listen to?

What makes religious discussions so volatile?

We shy from conversations which are likely to become pressure cookers. We have learned there is value in keeping peace. But in this increasingly polarized world avoidance of important issues doesn't relieve the pressure. It turns up the heat. We need to have frank discussions about our beliefs. Are we able to admit we might be wrong? Are we able to question the unquestionable?

The ripples of our thoughts can reach further than we ever imagined. We can't pretend our beliefs are isolated possessions, or that our loved ones aren't affected by what we choose to accept. Should this motivate us to pay careful attention to what we absorb and what we cling to?

The sheer volume of information at our disposal has presented a problem perhaps few anticipated before the internet. How can we surf through the tsunami of data and sort between accurate and inaccurate? How can we determine whether an idea is credible and worthy to integrate into the infrastructure of our beliefs?

We can't live without beliefs. We require some degree of confidence in something. We must believe eating will sustain us. We must believe clothing and shelter are necessary. We must believe our actions have consequences and we are worthy of the life we have been given. But how can we be sure if even those are true? How can we trust anything anyone tells us?

Everybody wants to know the truth. At the very least, they don't want to be deceived. Even those more willing to be ignorant prefer not to be deceived. Ironically though, the humiliation of being deceived is a prospect so horrifying for some, they will remain faithful to deceit to avoid the feeling. A pattern which seems to guarantee ignorance.

Since the earliest moments of our awareness, we were offered a perception of the world by others. Our mothers explained things in terms they felt would make most sense to our developing minds. They told stories that served as warnings for our safety and to correct unwanted behaviors. *Santa Clause will put you on the naughty list* or *chewing gum will stay in your stomach for seven years.*

This trend continues when children reach school. Some teachers will relate reductionist tales like *Columbus discovered America,* having omitted crucial details. Other times, the curriculum may use rules which will later expire like *I before E except after C,* or *you can't start a sentence with a preposition.* And some people remain stuck on those untruths throughout their lives. Perhaps you still think chewing gum remains in your stomach for years.

The difference between accepting a belief and rejecting it could be fatal. Imagine being a Christian in 1977 San Francisco when you finally find a church which promotes your progressive values of civil rights and racial equality. It operates homes for the elderly, a soup kitchen, an orphanage, and services for the disabled. Imagine when the reverend, a charismatic man named Jim Jones, floats the idea of a utopian community in Guyana and you believe in the mission. You board the plane, and – if you didn't know how this story ends – yourself, your family, and 900 other people are talked into drinking "Kool-Aid" laced with cyanide and perish because of those beliefs.

We can trace many of the world's greatest atrocities to religion. The Spanish Inquisition saw the brutal torture of dissidents at the hands of the Catholic Church in the 12th and 13th centuries. Around the same time in history, the Aztecs ritually sacrificed 20,000 people every year to appease their gods, and the Crusades saw Christians launch multiple campaigns to rid the *Holy Land* of Muslims. The Salem Witch Hunt, the genocide of American natives, The Jonestown Massacre, ISIS, and Boko Haram all paint religion with a very dark brush.[1]

But atrocity is not the exclusive possession of religion. Ethnic tensions, political assertion, economic fears, and the timeless allure of greed are also major contributors to world terror. Political entities may have used religion as a tool to motivate people into horrific acts. But it can hardly be said that religion was the cause of all conflict.

Some atrocities proceeded without the contribution of religion. The Holodomor was a man-made famine that killed millions of Ukrainians and Russians at the hands of Stalin's Communist rulership. Also under the banner of Communism, the Khmer Rouge led a revolution in Cambodia in the 1970s. They instituted an anti-intellectual reform of Marxism, purged any perceived voices of dissent, and ultimately lead to the death of a quarter of the population.[2] Two million Cambodians died because of an arrogant insistence on unverified beliefs.

There is a common denominator among atrocious movements. A misguided ideology. An unbending belief which forbids critique or alternate opinion. A concept that can build to such momentum even its founders can no longer bridle its ferocity. I submit that common denominator is *dogma*.

dog·ma

a. something held as an established opinion
   especially: a definite authoritative tenet.
b. a code of such tenets
c. a point of view or tenet put forth as authoritative without adequate grounds

Merriam-Webster's Dictionary

Stubborn beliefs.

I have arrived at a number of conclusions in this book with the above being the first. While trying not to sound too assured, too stubborn in my beliefs, I invite you to consider several more.

The next is this: Formulating a belief or a *conclusion* is a necessity. When a conclusion has been reached, thinking humans are free to focus their thoughts elsewhere. The formulation of conclusions is a necessary function of scientific research. The difference between *conclusions* and *dogma* is the degree to which a person is committed to the concept. Many people reach conclusions and adjust those when new information is presented. People who hold to dogma, however, are unwilling to adjust their beliefs even when solid evidence is presented to the contrary.

Within this use of the term, we could describe the contrast between dogma and conclusions using the analogy of a scaffold. A scaffold is a temporary structure, intended to give access to something otherwise unreachable. It is removed when a task is complete, or a more permanent structure is established. Like a scaffold, a conclusion is a belief which can be adjusted, removed, or replaced as required.

Dogma would be a different entity altogether. Dogma could be likened to an indestructible building material. Once placed it could never be removed or altered. It might sound like a good idea at the outset, but with enough of this material in place, building anything new becomes impossible.

Just because someone reaches a conclusion does not mean they established a fact. Without access to every conceivable form of information, we will always be uninformed. And while uninformed we will never have absolute truth. We will never know anything for certain. We don't even know if we exist.

Even within the precise world of mathematics, hard facts are elusive. We can only distill concepts to a point where the problems are so large, we can no longer prove them. These are called *assumptions* or *axioms*. We can measure the effects of these axioms. We can reasonably conclude they exist, even if we can't prove them.[3] *Proof* in the common use of the term really is a non-existent phenomenon. We only have evidence, and evidence can be misleading.

There are gaps in our knowledge regardless of our education. To function in any manner, we *must* make assumptions. Do you remember the adage, *never assume, because when you ASSUME you make an ASS out of U and ME?* That adage is misleading, just like *I before E except after C.* We *always* have to assume. We have to assume because we don't know the things. Acknowledging we don't know things and that we must employ assumptions is an invaluable skill. It is an advancement in logical development. The *never assume rule* is a scaffold that teaches us not to trust *all* assumptions. When that lesson is learned, *the never assume rule* can expire. Failing to expire the *never assume* rule suggests we don't *assume* because we *know* the things. But do we?

Project managers are taught to recognize their assumptions, list those assumptions, analyze them, and calculate their probability. Only by careful recognition of assumptions can a project be successfully planned. Assumptions in this function are a critical utility.[4] They provide a means to navigate the future without knowing precisely what will happen.

When an *assumption* or *conclusion* hardens in our minds in the form of a concrete *fact,* we find ourselves encased in closed-mindedness. When we are adamant that something is *the truth*, we are unwilling to explore further. We have closed ourselves off like a prisoner laying the bricks of their own prison – content never to see beyond those walls – closed to alternative ideas.

It seems important to remain cognizant our beliefs fall along varying degrees of certainty. If we understand those beliefs are only *relatively* certain – that they are subject to revision – we can resist the urge to become emotionally attached. We need to break down the building blocks of our belief structure if we value knowing more.

The greatest minds in history were aware of their limited knowledge. Their humble and honest disposition appears foundational for their enlightenment. Sir Isaac Newton's laws were incomplete, and he acknowledged that. Newton is one of the most influential scientists of all time having laid the foundation for classical mechanics. Despite his unmatched comprehension he wrote: "we have explained the phenomena of the heavens and of our sea by the power of gravity, but have not yet assigned the cause of this power [...] I have not been able to discover the cause of those properties of gravity from phenomena, and I frame no hypotheses."[5] That last sentence famously coining the term *hypothesis non fingo*, which I'm sure could be translated to: *I don't know the things*.

"I know that I know nothing," said Plato quoting Socrates. "To know is to know that you know nothing. That is the meaning of true knowledge." - Confucius. "The more I read, the more I acquire, the more certain I am that I know nothing." – Voltaire. I doubt it is a coincidence those who are regarded as the world's deepest thinkers are also those who maintained a humble mind. I am convinced the admission of not knowing the things was pivotal for them to comprehend and advance new ideas.

The therapist known on YouTube as Theramintrees paints a picture of those on the opposite side of the spectrum – ideologues who insist on dogma. They are assured of their opinions and demand everyone accept their beliefs uncritically. Simple-minded ideologues are experts in all fields. They know everything. They cannot learn from anyone. They can rarely manage a constructive conversation, often reacting emotionally. What could they possibly learn from a different perspective – the wrong perspective – the other side of their cell wall? Ideologues may use a superficial form of dialogue to feign communication. They may pretend to listen to another's point, only to search out a means to contradict or to falsify. They may employ a more aggressive approach of hurling insults and insisting on *strawman*, or *ad hominem* arguments which misrepresent their opponent's conclusions or character.

The intent of the ideologue is to make the world simple so they can comprehend it. *Why see the world in a wide spectrum of colors when it's more easily computed as black and white?* Instead of accepting a variety of perspectives, they insist thoughts are either right or wrong. Of course the ideologue is always right. They intend to separate and divide people into camps. People are either with them, or against. That perspective is easier to understand. But oversimplification can be dangerous. It is the basis for prejudice and functions as a powerful obstruction to communication. Simple-minded approaches lead to mischaracterizations, fear, hatred, and violence. "When ideologies are rendered untouchable, they guarantee conflict" (TheraminTrees).[6]

I grew up and spent three solid decades in the fundamental Christian[i] religion known as Jehovah's Witnesses. This helped me become acutely aware of dogma's effects, both on individual minds, and the culture of groups. I displayed blind obedience to authority, stubborn attachment to beliefs, and the embarrassing stunted growth which resulted from both.

I later found human growth requires an undying curiosity that is quenched only with real experiences and honest assessment. A dogmatic religious stance does not allow honest inflection. It won't allow critical

---

[i] Jehovah's Witnesses self-define as Christian. Others would not classify them Christian because JWs do not consider Jesus a deity.

assessment of tenets. It asserts it has found the truth, and its truth is from a higher source – an unverified, and unfalsifiable claim. Critical assessment of its belief is seen as disrespect. *No human can challenge the wisdom of God.* It cannot grasp there is no challenge to God. The challenge is whether this "wisdom" came from God. I am familiar with that dogmatic and defensive mode of thought because it was my own. That was the tenacious nature with which I guarded my beliefs.

I would unknowingly use logical fallacies like *equivocation fallacy.* After laying down the claim that my beliefs were grounded in verifiable evidence, I would struggle to define my faith in certain situations. When asked how I knew God imparts wisdom to certain people I couldn't explain it. I just *knew.* My reason for belief was no longer evidential. It shifted to a *feeling* which couldn't be independently measured. The definition of *faith* had changed. That wasn't very honest.

> *Those who cannot change their minds cannot change anything.*
> George Bernard Shaw

What is especially hard to admit is when cornered with difficult logical arguments I would boldly lie. I was misaligned with reality and so I distorted reality to fit the stained glass I saw through. I didn't know I was lying. Because I wasn't lying to others. I was lying to myself.

I'm not saying that all unexplained feelings are false. There could indeed be entities we sense yet cannot externally verify. Those could be real. But such a personal experience hardly warrants the forcing of others to accept those beliefs or to feel a heated sense of disrespect.

Some find themselves angrily defending the Bible or Quran. But if God supplied humans with wisdom by means of a book or an organized religion, why would criticism indicate disrespect? With the plethora of religious beliefs, and the unending publishing of religious materials, does it not stand to reason God would *expect* individuals to sort through it? Most people recognize false beliefs are dangerous – wouldn't God expect our diligent effort to avoid those? Wouldn't God want us to chip away at, and critically inspect our own beliefs? I would think God would be proud of people for digging thoroughly for truth – for critically examining what they hear. If we did not use a critical approach, we would be boxed into whichever faith was presented first. Which is the path most religious people take: The religion of their parents.

Still, I hardly believe it is fair or realistic to pin the world's problems on religion. Religion has not been a consistent failure throughout history. It has proven itself a crucial unifying force and an integral component for building civilization's largest empires. It contributes to the shaping of shared values which in turn provides the necessary unity for constructive, coordinated efforts.[7]

Modern psychological studies suggest religious people tend to be happier than non-religious. If there are positive aspects of religion, I think those deserve our consideration. It would not be a truly critical process to analyze religion by painting an overly positive or overly negative portrait. I posit religion is not the problem. Dogma is the problem with religion.

It appears to me that authoritative monotheistic religion is disproportionately susceptible to dogma. I only hold a fleeting understanding of other forms of religion. Monotheism is my only frame of reference. From that experience it appears monotheism struggles with dogma because it asserts its beliefs and writings originate from a singular truth. To maintain this assertion they must project they *know*. Because they *know* the truth, they needn't bother looking beyond their cell walls. In many cases they don't feel the need for windows to see through.

Religion is not the only entity susceptible to dogma. One could argue political policy is driven by populist movements and bares little foundation in logic. The popularity contest which democracy has become does not incentivize critical thought. The process is driven by emotion which tends to stifle or reject constructive innovation, and yet it is stubbornly clung to without any sense of scientific challenge or test. Businesses may become entrenched in dogmatic ideologies and find themselves hemorrhaging money due to the stubborn beliefs of their leadership. When scientists forego humility of mind and arrogantly assert they are right, they choke advancement with their dogma.[8] Would they not then cease to be scientists?

What if that changed? What if we could construct religion or political systems in a manner which excludes dogma, and facilitates honest development of spiritual beliefs by function of verifiable evidence and open exchange of thought? What if we could recognize nonsensical stories for what they are? What if, like science, we built religious and political systems to test theories, conduct experiments, critically examine conclusions as a group, and remain poised to adjust as evidence demands? What if religion and science were the same entity?

If anyone can refute me—show me I'm making a mistake or looking at things from the wrong perspective—I'll gladly change. It's the truth I'm after, and the truth never harmed anyone. What harms us is to persist in self-deceit and ignorance.
Marcus Aurelius

1.1 LET'S TALK ABOUT THE BIG THINGS

Pure Truth cannot be assimilated by the crowd; it must be communicated by contagion.

Henri Frederic Amiel

As a feature of our culture, we avoid talking to others about important matters. Religion and politics are taboo subjects for everyday conversations. I find it tragic that topics are dismissed which could drastically improve the lives of everyone. How could we possibly improve the quality of existence and evolve our civilization if we don't discuss difficult issues? Could it really be we are too polite? Since when does a society care so deeply about social etiquette, they will forsake an opportunity to improve their well-being? Who decided agreeableness holds a greater value than happiness, truth, and prosperity?

One reason difficult topics are avoided are their tendency to descend into heated rhetoric. An unyielding attitude hardened around the simple-minded slogans of dogma is hardly the environment for respectful, ideological interchange. Exploratory discussions require an open mind from the outset.

Another common reason for avoiding deep conversations is the culture of offense. There is a tendency in many circles to regard the taking of offense as legitimate cause for alarm. But being offended is not harmful. Being offended is an emotional reaction, and not all emotional reactions are rational. This is the case for people who suffer from phobias. They experience an irrational emotional response. When a person suffers from a phobia, the therapy they receive to treat said phobia does not rely on insulating the sufferer from the object of their phobia. To overcome a phobia is to come to terms with the object, most often by exposing them to it.[9]

Similarly, if someone finds themselves easily offended, they don't help themselves by isolating from the ideals or groups that offend them. Even if there is legitimate cause for offense, complete isolation from offense works to preserve it. Cesare Pavese lived most of his life in Fascist Italy. He fled for the hills when Nazis stationed in his town. But he would later write: "We do not free ourselves from something by avoiding it, but only by living through it."[10]

It has been my experience that finding a safe place from offense and remaining within the comfortable boundaries of like-minded people only *feels* safer. Within those safe places my outrage grew, fueled by the reassurance of peers. Irrational emotional responses were reinforced. It stunted my emotional growth, deprived me of connectivity, and left me ignorant of important issues. Now a similar chasm appears to divide humanity into opposing camps, and with division, we find conflict.

University campuses have set up safe places. Social anxiety can be a crippling ordeal, and some have found that having a brief reprieve from judgment, unsolicited opinions, and having to explain themselves as marginalized people, is all they need to compose before venturing back into the fray.[11] But the result has not always been unity or intellectual advancement. Free speech can be stifled, if not entirely demonized. The divisions between ideologies don't dissolve. When left unchallenged, divisions widen.[12] In those circumstances, students are robbed of the opportunity to confront opposing ideas and to expand their perception of the world. They're robbed of the opportunity to develop necessary skills, to think critically, to control their emotions, to develop their neural networks and prepare intelligent responses.[13]

That said, one only needs to be a parent to understand that protecting our children from relentless insults and intolerance is a crucial function of our role. Taking a dogmatic stance against safe places isn't helpful. I'm convinced we could use pragmatism while understanding the need for safety and protection from the elements.[14]

Social media is a significant factor in inhibiting productive conversations. While it may appear on the outset to connect people, the net result has been isolation – where social skills deteriorate. It functions to encapsulate like-minded people into insular groups. Algorithms intended to provide a positive experience filter out opposing viewpoints that would benefit the user. This creates cults of like-minded people, isolated from, and intolerant toward others. These groups become a vacuum of critical thought and an echo chamber for narrow-minded ideology. Or so has been the running theory.

The *echo-chamber* theory hasn't stood up to all recent analyses. In his book *Breaking the Social Media Prism*, social scientist Chris Bail argued it wasn't echo chambers that polarized people. Rather than functioning to isolate people from opposing views, he argues that social media platforms serve more to distort political and personal views and offer a stage for extremism. Social media does indeed widen divisions. But Bail argued if social media encouraged people to discuss political issues *one-on-one,* it could play a role in alleviating polarization.[15]

While I have an overall positive outlook for humanity, current divisions worry me that we may require painful corrections. In its current state, we are primed for the widening of those rifts. The opportunity to connect with, and learn from each other has increased with the internet. But that opportunity seems squandered in favor of quick-fix communication and sensationalized news. People trade deeper understanding for overly simplified slogans, then collect into their cults and entrench those slogans into dogma.

Have you noticed how offense and dogma reciprocate each other's cause and effect? When someone is offended and isolates themselves, they develop narrow and unbending beliefs: dogma. In turn, those who adhere to dogma, are offended by those who do not show respect for said dogma. Without a means to break the cycle, we're looking at a dangerous mix – a self-perpetuating powder keg with the potential for harm.

There is hope. The solution to polarization is within our grasp. The Better Angels Society hosts workshops and debates in the U.S. encouraging participants from both sides of the political aisle to engage with the other. Their report found that "more than 70 percent of participants in community-based debates say that the experience caused them to have 'more understanding of other viewpoints.' About the same proportion say that they 'learned something that might be helpful to others,' and more than three of four participants report that they want to follow up on relationships begun in the debate."[16] Imagine both a liberal and a conservative wanting to hear from the other.

Engaging constructively with people who hold opposing views requires patience. It also requires skills related to openness, tact, listening, problem-solving, and empathy. Those skills increase with each discussion, making them crucial for our emotional development. Andrew Sherman, Head of GEMS World Academy in Chicago, argued that "difficult conversations [are] as important to teach as math or science."[17]

That doesn't mean the solution will be instant. There are monumental roadblocks. A cancel culture is growing where conflicting ideals are immediately expunged. Both religious and political entities have made it a matter of offense to hold alternate ideas.

Religions have created a crime known as *apostasy*. It represents those who speak out about their religion or former religion. The word does not have a root in the Bible and its explicit doctrine in the Quran is contested. Apostasy is an invention of religious bodies to control dissent. Despite not having a clear scriptural basis, apostasy still ranks the most heinous of all sins in the eyes of Judaism, Christianity, and Islam. Throughout history, and in certain parts of the modern world, apostasy is a state crime. As of 2019, there were 12 countries that carried the death sentence for apostasy.[18] With the very real dangers of being labeled an apostate it is little wonder open discussion of religion has been discouraged. It is no exaggeration that religious debate has been a dangerous endeavor throughout history.

Even where the dangers of physical violence are unlikely, the risk of religious ostracism and emotional outrage are enough to keep religious discussion closed from most public arenas. Conversations about a higher power or a greater good, though infinitely valuable, continue to evade our social norms.

Adding to this are external forces with an interest in polarization. Policy changes have staggering financial implications. The incentive for corporations and elected officials to influence the population should not be ignored. The result of their influence is a barrage of propaganda, making the extraction of accurate intelligence difficult and tedious.[19]

The term *Fake News* and the vilifying of mainstream media have called into question the trustworthiness of the information we receive. And so they should. But with this vilification come few legitimate alternatives.

Information needs to be viewed with a critical eye, but is it? We all know we can't believe everything we read on the internet, but how many believe everything they read on their favorite website or social media page? It might be worth imagining what the world would be like without the internet. Like the 80s when information was dangled out of reach and controlled by conglomerates. Or is it worse now because the internet dangles information out of reach and is controlled by conglomerates?

Trying to have political conversations around the water-cooler is a precarious thing. Political polarization pits two otherwise cordial humans into a frenzied ideological battle, perpetuated by that same offense-dogma cause-effect mechanism shared with religion. It might be important to discuss these issues, but we also recognize how emotionally charged people can become.

Being emotionally involved in policy decisions could be valuable, but it strikes me how hunkered some become over an issue they could not possibly understand. Not because they're mentally incapable of understanding, but because the information available is prohibitively inadequate. It's one thing to discuss peer-reviewed studies on homelessness or taxation incentives. It's quite another to argue incessantly about a subject without any data. Does anyone benefit from an argument between people who don't know what they're talking about? It's bound to get emotional.

But then, perhaps a stupid conversation is better than none. If two people who only know 1% engage constructively, they could both walk away knowing 2%. I have come to believe few things will provide better clarity and intelligence than frank dialogue. I have been witness to, and involved in, many mature conversations with opposing viewpoints and invariably felt enriched on the other side. I hold no doubt we can have political and religious conversations, and we can do so in casual settings. It seems to me, however, finding success in those conversations requires one admission as part of the framework: *I don't know the things.*

We can put an idea on the table and prepare to defend that position – present an assertion and allow others to challenge. Encourage them to find fault. Let them chisel and refine the concept. That is what I'm attempting with this book. Subjecting our thoughts to criticism is to our benefit because it prompts us to remove incorrect or unnecessary parts. Of course, that won't be effective if we're sensitive to offense. To benefit from criticism, one would *seek* correction.

> *Conversation – whether with other people or with ourselves – remains our only means of making intellectual and moral progress.*
> Sam Harris

In Arthur Brooks' book, *Love Your Enemies,* he argues we don't find unity by shying from difficult conversations. By voicing our disagreement with others, we bridge the gap, and by listening to the arguments of others we learn, and we find the secret to excellence. We are given the opportunity to correct the dangerous beliefs of others – and of our own. "Ignoring voices of hate is a mistake. If we do, the ideas go unchallenged by people of goodwill. And if these people have views that are truly worthy of contempt? Remember that their views might be, but that no person is. Repudiate their views, confidently and concisely, with respect."[20]

Imagine the openness and refreshing dialogue we could experience if we separated from dogmatic stubbornness. How useful would it be to understand why the other person holds their view? It could be they have been given false information. It is just as likely we have. The best way to find out is to compare notes. *What is your source? How trustworthy was the evidence? How were conclusions formulated? Why do you believe this?* If we can place those cards on the table with open and honest intent, imagine the political force the common people would have. Imagine politicians no longer able to wield their hidden agendas in front of an audience, knowing that audience will openly and honestly discuss the promises without a cloud of biases.

Healthcare, diversity, international conflict, social systems, economics, what is right and what is wrong.... happiness. All these subjects have a profound effect on each of us. Those are big things and they're worth talking about. It would be a regrettable travesty if we lost the opportunity to improve the world because we were too worried about being polite, too sensitive to endure offense, and too comfortable in our ignorance to entertain the ideas of others.

Sure, this might require effort to develop a few skills. But with all at stake, isn't that worth the effort? In the meantime, we can benefit from the simple act of discussion. Let's be honest about our beliefs. Let's listen to opposing ideas on politics and religion. Let's talk about the big things.

Practice really hearing what people say. Do your best to get inside their minds.
Marcus Aurelius

1.2 YOUR CULT IS GOOD

You know, a long time ago being crazy meant something. Nowadays everybody's crazy.

Charles Manson

The word *cult* shares an origin with the words *culture* and *cultivate*. Merriam-Webster's dictionary ties the Latin noun with meanings comparable to *tilling, training, education,* and *adoration*. While people shudder at the word and use it as an insult, the term is far more encompassing than one might think.

The Google definition of *cult* is: "a system of religious veneration and devotion directed toward a particular figure or object." Curiously, though, many of those groups which serve as archetypes of cults in our mind weren't religious at all. Charles Manson's *Family* was not religious. Neither was Heaven's Gate. These would not fit the Google definition.

The definition of a *cult* has been elusive since its inception. We find this problem as far back as 1873 when Fitzedward Hall wrote in *Modern English:* "cult is a term which, as we value exactness, we can ill do without, seeing how completely religion has lost its original signification." Perhaps the most honest way to define a cult is *a group of people we think are weird*. And because *cult* is indeed a subjective measurement, experts suggest the term should never be used professionally.[21]

The word likely conjures within you an image. But unless you are familiar with Steve Hassan's work, there is no clearly defined parameter that would fit that image. Every definition of *cult* you try to use will either exclude groups normally considered a cult or include groups you would not. Nobody labels their group a cult. Nobody in a cult thinks they're in a cult. If you tried to pin that label on a cultist, they would slip out of that robe as quickly as you could cover them.

I don't see this as a language problem. This is an issue with how we understand the intersection of religiosity and culture. Most people group those factors, which contributes to the confusion. But I see them as separate entities - layers of religion. Separating those layers helps us see issues with precision, and how functions overlap. I think this form of dissection is critical for understanding major religions, spurious sects, and all forms of human interaction.

Religiosity is one layer – a metric indicating the level of conviction with which people hold their beliefs and how important they believe their religion to be. *Culture* is a separate layer and describes our normative behaviors and how we interact with others in a group. It exists regardless of belief. *This is how we do things 'round here.*

This brings us back to the word cult. Because that is where it originates. So to avoid semantic arguments let's define cult with its root word: cult is *culture*. Like culture, the cult is the fabric of our human networks. It refers to our relationships with other humans and the behaviors we deem acceptable. Our family is its own cult, and there are cultures at our place of work. Each religion certainly qualifies as a cult, but so would an atheist social media group.

A cult likely has sub cults within those cults. Work teams that are subdivided into smaller cells will differ in their spirit and dynamic; they become their own cult. You might notice within your family or network of friends those different combinations of individual energy have their own vibe. All those unique combinations are cocktails of human influence and adjust with every microscopic variation. And guess what? *They're all weird to someone.*

Religion has benefits. It holds the ability to unite and the power to influence our values and motivations. It certainly holds the power to do good. Religious apologists point to some of the hundreds of psychological studies offering convincing evidence that religious people are happier people. A study published by Pew Research Centre in 2019 showed a correlation between happiness and religiosity across 26 countries and with remarkably consistent findings.[22] This research aligns itself with the findings of Duke University, the American Sociological Association, and a host of other think-tanks.[23] Those appear to suggest religion is a positive force in the world and thus have been used extensively to promote religion.

The *cause* of happiness within those studies was also revealed. They indicated that the people who identified as being happier were those who were "actively engaged in the interpersonal functions of their religion." A sense of community engagement provides people with a sense of trust and optimism. People who are actively religious are then more likely to join additional non-religious groups which, in turn, contribute to greater happiness, civic engagement, and improvement to their community.[24]

We should also factor in the means those studies used to compile their data. They restricted their methodology to comparing people only against those within their geographical area. The intent, I'm sure, is to compare apples to apples. But this is where it gets interesting: when studies have aggregated people across different nations, the results told a different story. Data from a Gallup study made such a comparison. The Gallup Study found that people who identify as religious do indeed tend to be happiest *within religious countries.* However, *entire countries* that identify as religious were not happier than entire countries that were predominately non-religious.[25] When taking a broader look at the international community, **non-religious countries have a significantly higher quality** of life than religious countries. Perhaps most striking is the correlation between religious nations and poverty. "Each of the most religious countries is relatively poor, with a per-capita GDP below $5,000," says Gallup. The "United States appears to be the only country to buck that trend, being a wealthy country that also happens to be religious." However, the study also showed that within the United States "the most religious states were the least happy and experienced a lower socioeconomic status." This study was supported by that of Pew Research which also showed a clear inverse correlation between wealth and religiosity across different nations.

Studies that compared the level of *religiosity* between various religions showed the same striking correlation between religiosity and wealth. Pew Research showed that Judaism indicated the lowest levels of religiosity in the United States and boasted the highest family income.[26] To emphasize that point, Jehovah's Witnesses scored highest for religiosity and were shown to be the least educated and to suffer the lowest family income.[27] With all data considered, religiosity, education, and prosperity appear tightly associated. Religiosity seems to be the indicator most associated with negative behavior. Religiosity – the importance a person places on their religion – the level of conviction they hold toward their beliefs – their *faith*.

Is religiosity the cause of lower socioeconomic status or does a lower socioeconomic status drive people toward religiosity? Could there be another connection? Is there some way to reconcile how religion could serve as both a positive force for social connections *and* a detriment to prosperity and overall well-being?

In 2019 Clemens Sedmak published an article using empirical data from 11 different studies specific to the correlation between religion and poverty. He found that religions "provide resources and open doors, but also place hurdles in the way of poverty alleviation efforts."[28] Sedmak pointed out that religion determines a person's motivating force and normative habits. It provides boundaries between acceptable and unacceptable behavior. His findings made clear that specific values and beliefs were responsible for credit card repayments, the exposure of women to business activities, the attitudes toward people of a different religion, frugality in their spending habits, general business agency, their attitudes toward wealth and poverty, education, health practices, and political leanings. Is there any doubt that the spirit of a religion's message will affect the behaviors of adherents? Is there any doubt the beliefs of some will affect the wider culture?

My hope is academic research would follow Sedmak's trail, and study how the varying beliefs within those religions affect behaviors. How do certain beliefs promote constructive habits? How do others promote discord? What opportunities and threats are presented? Not for the purpose of policing beliefs, but to provide access to information which could help individuals arrive at their own conclusions, and to guide policies which increase well-being.

There are beliefs more harmful than others. There are religions more inclined to dogma. There are religions more likely to use emotion. There are religions more isolating, violent, and intolerant. There are beliefs which are harmful, and beliefs which are positive. The concept that beliefs are only a personal matter, and the beliefs of others are none of our business could be a concept worth revisiting. The way people behave is dependent on their beliefs. As the distinguished professor Don Locke wrote, "It appears that human action is fundamentally to be explained in terms of the agent's beliefs: it is because the agent has the beliefs that he has that he acts as he does."[29] The point being – *beliefs matter.*

Culture appears to be the most positive of religious aspects. As was demonstrated in the studies showing religious people to be happier, those benefits were related to interpersonal connections. As we will get into later, our personal relationships could be the greatest determining factor in our overall well-being. They are worth preserving.

In short: Culture – good. Religiosity – *bad.* Who knew the *cult* aspect of religion was its most positive?

Because what is a human being? Part of a community – the community of gods and men, primarily, and secondarily that of the city we happen to inhabit, which is only a microcosm of the universe in toto.
Marcus Aurelius

1.3 RELIGION IS A LITTLE BOX

Sometimes people don't want to hear the truth because they don't want their illusions destroyed.

Friedrich Nietzsche

My cat is like any normal cat. He has free reign of the house but given the opportunity will gladly restrict his freedom to a small box on the floor. The box offers no substantial protection. But inside he feels safe and invisible, ready to attack from his cardboard fortress.

While watching this feline behavior I'm reminded of when I behaved similarly. I enjoyed the safety and security of a four-walled structure – in my case, a social construct that was small and frail like a cardboard box. I refused to open my eyes to the endless possibilities of the physical or philosophical world. Open-ended concepts of modern philosophy were simply *too open*. The notion that we don't know certain things was unsatisfying and failed to provide the comfort that certainty offered. My beliefs were cemented in personal altruism, and I dismissed all other ideas, assured I had the truth.

My spiritual brothers and I were content to allow others to decide our more difficult paths. When faced with a potentially life-altering choice, my good friend Andrew[i] wailed in lament: "I wish someone would just tell me what to do!" Peering down the barrel of a divorce, he could choose to provide for the children whom he raised as their stepfather or accept the wishes of his ex-wife who did not want his presence in their lives. He could force them into a heated legal battle for the reward of being stripped of his income for more than a decade. Or accept an easier alternative – he could

---

[i] Some names have been changed.

simply let it be – allow the children to live without the only father they had known – and move on. I empathized with his willingness to let someone else decide.

Open-ended decisions with severe consequences can bring crippling distress. We function with greater ease in simplicity. We love simple solutions. There are philosophical principles like Occam's razor, which tout simplicity as a virtue.[30] Some of the most complex problems have been solved by surprisingly simplistic resolve. Einstein's theory of special relativity offers an impossibly simple formula for the relationship between energy and mass: $E=mc^2$. If one of the most complex riddles in physics could be explained in only five characters, does that not lead us to believe the answers to all problems are simple?

We are likely to find problems when we overcomplicate matters, but it would seem the greater dangers are found in *under*-complicating them. By assuming an issue is simple before understanding its complexities. *Red to red. Black to black. How hard could it be to be an electrician?* Such an underestimation would place a person in peril.

A truly successful distillation of a matter into simple accuracy is not the product of ignorance. Ignorance often results in *over*simplifications and tragic outcomes. Truly distilled concepts are the product of hard work and a complete understanding of the subject. As simple as $E=mc^2$ appears, it took *teams* of people nearly two decades to conduct research and to finalize special relativity.[31] It seems that for every advantage there is to reduce an overly complicated matter, there is a danger of oversimplifying something which is necessarily complex.

The intellectual investment to account for each detail, and to measure each conceivable outcome of every technological concept requires a luxury of time we don't possess. There are real and measurable advantages in trusting the research and conclusions of others. There are realistic comforts in confining our powers of reason to a little box constructed by people we trust. The question then becomes: are we objectively choosing the right conclusions to trust?

Religion offers such a box. It gives the adherent a standard set of rules and regulations, and while it limits expression and behavior, there's a comfort to those limits – a delegation of responsibility to a higher force or a proven way. In exchange for their powers of autonomy, the faithful receive direction, and answers. They're sold a sense of certainty – the *feeling* they are protected.

But what if the direction they received brought misfortune? What if they were deceived into harming others? Would it still be worth those moments of ease?

This is not a condition restricted to religion. Some people show a religious devotion toward their favored political party, drowning out evidence of their faults. Some have rested an inordinate amount of faith in scientific conclusions, when perhaps that degree of faith was not warranted.

During a push for a third Covid 19 vaccine I thought I would collect some data showing how effective the treatment was, and for any health and safety risks. I am a proponent of vaccines, generally, and I wanted to be armed for any encounter with a protester. I was shocked to find that there wasn't any. The clinical trials for first vaccines were solid. But the real-world data in follow up was not available. There is an army of anti-vaxxers out there making this a high-profile treatment and it carries FDA approval. There should be a LOT of data supporting these vaccines.

Adding to my bewilderment was a report issued by the Washington State Department of Health which used an absurd – arguably dishonest – means of extrapolating their data in support of vaccines.[32] Yet when I pointed out the incongruency I was lambasted for being anti-science. In my mind the only anti-science in the equation was the intolerance of criticism – and possibly the authors of the report. When I posted questions online I was personally attacked and dubbed uneducated. I was cited on Facebook for distributing false information. Friends I confided in became angry with me. They acted as if I had switched sides from the good guys to the bad guys. It was eerily similar to the tribal hostility I experienced when questioning religion. But these were not religious people.

I'm confident the data since has been located and published and all is well on the medical front. The caution I'm relating is that it would be a mistake to think indoctrination or tribalism can't happen to us. When we're confined to a little box others can feed us whatever they want. And the more people confine their inputs to a little screen in their hands, the smaller their world is.

That world can become painfully small when people inside the little box are convinced they cannot look outside. Many religions promote *confidence* in beliefs – *faith* – as a virtue. And that virtue is often celebrated above others. The testing and critical examination of beliefs is considered a lack of faith – unvirtuous. The faithful are rewarded for remaining ignorant to conflicting information. They're rewarded for believing without evidence and foregoing critical examination. They're often taught there is a moral obligation to trust their spiritual teachers but, as J.L. Schellenberg pointed out, "the practice of trusting the religion and religious mentors of one's upbringing cannot suffice for rational religious belief."[33] I would step further to argue there is no moral or objective benefit to faith. Yet there are severely traumatic disadvantages.

Perhaps you would agree that when we accept a belief without test, we open the door to disaster. There are consequences when we accept the conclusions of others. We may find ourselves in circumstances we would otherwise consider disadvantageous, unethical, or dangerous.

It appears some beliefs could prevent psychological growth. *Self-determination theory* asserts people are motivated to grow and change by three innate and universal psychological needs: *competence, relatedness,* and *autonomy.* They affect each person's ability to make choices and manage their life.[34]

Authoritarian entities, whether they be religious, political or social, restrict personal autonomy by the very nature of their being authoritarian. Some authoritarian entities remove virtually *all* personal autonomy. With a loss of autonomy, people are prevented from self-determination.

Ryan and Deci, who coined *self-determination*, describe it as "the essence of self-esteem."[35] They explain that being held from self-determination will restrict a person's belief they have control over their lives. They are likely to experience a lack of motivation due to reliance on external rewards and punishments. Their goals and behaviors remain at the mercy of others. They are less inclined to take responsibility for their actions, and thus prone to blaming others for their failures.

But should we trust Ryan and Deci? Or religion? Without having the time to research all things are we not required to place our trust in someone? How could we determine whom? If I were to venture a guess I would say that hearing both would offer the best opportunity for determination. And if I guessed again, I would think only one of those options will tell you not to listen to the other.

Being aware of who limits our access to information is important. *But aren't limits to our information a good thing? Isn't it wise to be selective with our news? Isn't it imperative that national security secrets are kept, or that pornography is less available?* I won't dive into those, but I will discuss the difference between being restricted from information and restricting ourselves.

If we have survived thus far we likely have had to restrict our behaviors and the information we receive. We exercised self-discipline. Would that discipline also qualify as a little box? I propose that so long as our discipline is self-imposed we continue to exercise our autonomy and thus develop self-determination. A little box of our own design is very useful. And fits our personality better than one imposed by others.

Remaining aware that we know nothing allows us to listen and absorb various perspectives. Self-determination retains for us the ability to dismiss what doesn't fit. Is it possible to both welcome the exchange of ideas and to be critical of those ideas? I would say it is critical that we do so. But when someone else restricts information from us it would not be rude to question their motives.

I posit that the best procedure to follow in objectively assessing the conclusions is by examining the methods – not relying entirely on someone's track record or popularity. This is where science typically provides a significant advantage over religion, in that it clearly outlines its methodology. Religion, by contrast offers a little black box. They know the things but how they arrived at their conclusions is a mystery. There is also caution in assuming what we follow is scientific when it's offered to us in name only. Many have fallen into the faith trap while believing in "science." It isn't rude to ask for the data.

The consequences of big decisions may be overwhelming. The stress of uncertainty may incline us to shrink back and hide from a problem. But relinquishing our determination does not solve problems. It strips us of valuable experience.

Depending on the propensity of an individual to either seek deeper truths or to rely on simplistic slogans, living in a little box can be either intellectually suffocating or ignorantly blissful. Judgment isn't required either way. There is a separate circumstance for an entirely different group of people. Where freedom from religion was never offered as an option. For those, life outside the box is a concept so utterly foreign it has never been explored. To say the open air of freedom is feared is an understatement. It is a sin. It is evil. As Alejandro Jodorowsky expressed: "Birds born in a cage think flying is an illness."

Those who have never experienced indoctrination must be mystified as to why grown adults with powers of reason confine themselves to organizations like Scientology or Jehovah's Witnesses. In the next chapter, I'll offer my own experience to explain why I lived decades subject to a rigid belief structure constructed by others.

Be cheerful also, and seek not external help nor the tranquility which others give. A man then must stand erect, not be kept erect by others.
Marcus Aurelius

1.4 HOW TO TRAIN AN ELEPHANT

Fix reason firmly in her seat, and call to her tribunal every fact, every opinion. Question with boldness even the existence of a God; because, if there be one, he must more approve the homage of reason than that of blindfold fear.

Thomas Jefferson

Are you familiar with how circus elephants are trained? Elephants are large animals, and their physical strength suggests they need not comply with anything they didn't choose. It's hard to believe an elephant would choose a circus routine. How, then do their trainers convince them to perform? I was given that explanation in the most unlikely of circumstances.

From infancy, I was taught the Bible was inerrantly true. Some scriptures could be accepted as literal expressions, and others as figurative, but regardless the form of interpretation, the Bible was accurate. I was taught only Jehovah's Witnesses knew the true interpretation of scripture and all other religions were false. I was taught Jehovah God, the creator of the universe, had written the Bible using human writers whom he *inspired* with *holy spirit*. This holy spirit also directed the thoughts and activities of the *faithful and discreet slave*, a term taken from Matthew 24:45, and used to represent the governing body of Jehovah's Witnesses. "That faithful slave is the channel through which Jesus is feeding his true followers in this time of the end. Our spiritual health and our relationship with God depend on this channel." (Watchtower July 2013 Study Edition)

The Bible was presented to me as the foundation for understanding reality. It was to be my core decision-making guide, my roadmap for morals, my reason for trust, and a litmus test for truth.[36] I read the Bible often.

The religion dubbed itself *The Truth* and we would use this term in everyday speech. We would say things like *I would be dead if I weren't in the Truth*. Or *your brother sure looks happier in the truth*. The Truth was our little box. But despite how small it was, our whole world was inside.

Everything outside the religion was called *The World* and we were taught from the Bible the World was ruled by Satan (1 John 5:19). The little contact we had with the World was limited to our employment or schooling and when we were actively trying to convert others.[37] Casual contact and friendships with Worldly people, even Worldly family members, were highly discouraged and sometimes punished. The result was an isolated group, and although dispersed among the rest of the population, we were oddly disconnected from it.

Information from the World could not be trusted. School curriculum, books, newspapers, and the internet were all prone to distortion offering little reason to explore secular knowledge. Almost everything we needed to know could be found in the Bible or from other Watchtower-produced media. The complexities of modern scientific discoveries, which were not found in the Bible, were explained to us through their literature. Although we were encouraged to attend grade school, attending higher education was discouraged, and fathers who allowed their children to do so could face a loss of privileges.[38]

The Watchtower, Bible, and Tract Society is the legal organization of Jehovah's Witnesses and is one of the largest publishing corporations in the world. It consistently produces its religious teachings through various forms of media including online videos, online bibles, printed magazines, books, and music. The *Watchtower* magazine and its companion, the *Awake!* magazine, each stand side-by-side as the most circulated magazines on Earth.[39]

As active Jehovah's Witnesses, we were consistently inundated with information from the Watchtower. Our daily routines revolved around the memorization of it. Unlike mainstream churches who gather on Sundays, we had multiple meetings per week. We had to pre-study for those meetings, prepare talks and skits for the meetings, read the Bible daily, watch videos, and prepare ourselves to teach others. The information was repetitive and simple and served to both occupy our minds and to prepare us to respond to skeptics. They called the information *spiritual food* and urged a regular diet of this spiritual food.[40]

Jehovah's Witnesses manage a rigid hierarchical system to accomplish their impressive worldwide work. Effort is incentivized by a system of rewards and punishments. Work assignments and teaching parts are highly esteemed, and those *privileges* are indicators of a person's status, and though unspoken, it suggested God favored those with more privileges. Increased privileges often resulted in more highly esteemed positions, and JW women were encouraged to select mates who demonstrated their spirituality through their positions. In other words, privileges affected our ability to mate. We were thus provided effective motivation to give freely our time and effort to accomplish the work of the organization. Where other churches must pay wages for their clergy, Jehovah's Witnesses select from men clamoring for the opportunity to take an unpaid position as an elder in their respective congregations. Women, on the other hand, are allowed no positions of leadership but are positioned within the hierarchy in other ways.[41]

It's hard to control large groups of people. Despite that difficulty, Jehovah's Witnesses, as a religious organization, have evolved for over a hundred years and succeeded to garner more than eight million adherents, globally.[42]

A rigid social structure with tight behavioral controls offers benefits. Without such a structure, accomplishing coordinated work on a worldwide scale would be improbable. There are people who thrive under such conditions. Some people suffer such lack of self-discipline that having a tight social structure with specific rules, pre-written values, and a map for the future is the only way they know how to function with any reasonable semblance of success.

I was drawn to the structure at times in my life when I lacked discipline. I left the religion three different times only to return. Certain core features held my loyalty, and I was convinced it was my only means of acceptable behavior. It wasn't until my late 30s that I allowed the discomfort of my misaligned beliefs to reject the religious conditioning.

In previous years, when I found information conflicting with Watchtower tenets, I rejected it immediately. We were programmed to do exactly that. We were taught that as ruler of the World and "Father of the Lie," Satan was actively trying to mislead people. We were warned never to trust our own judgment because Satan was infinitely smarter than we were and exercised centuries of experience in deceiving humans.[43]

As Jehovah's organization, the Watchtower was esteemed as an appendage of God and the means for which Christ Jesus was executing his plans for a worldwide kingdom. Although unspoken, the implication was clear: the Watchtower *was* the Kingdom of God. Because it was venerated in such a manner, we found evidence of God's hand in every decision they made and every word they printed. When you're seeking God, you find Him everywhere.

When the Watchtower told us we were living in the end times of the World (a prophecy from Jesus in Matthew 24), and that we should expect earthquakes in one place after another, we reacted with reverent fear and excitement to any report of an earthquake. *Oh my, we're so close to the end.* When Watchtower suggested Russia was the King of the North (a prophetic feature of the Bible book of Daniel), every news story about Russia became proof. When the news reported high levels of local crime, drug use, or human conflict, this supported Watchtower's assertion that people in the end-times are "advancing from bad to worse."

There was no room for our own opinions about doctrinal matters. We were instructed to "avoid independent thinking."[44] Any dissent with elders was chided as murmuring. Any disagreement about doctrine was considered disloyalty to God.

A form of critical thinking was taught when examining other religions. Watchtower literature would warn about dogmatic viewpoints and the importance of maintaining a humble, open approach.[45] I taught prospective Witnesses with their books, and through the process of conducting those studies, that gem stuck with me. If I was teaching others to be critical of their religion, I would be *hypocritical* if I didn't do the same. I would soon extend at least some critical thinking toward JW teachings. I was convinced it would result in my being honest with my bible students, honest with myself, and honest with Jehovah. I was confident that my religion was entirely correct, but I would entertain the idea it was wrong. *The real truth should never fear scrutiny.*

I considered this mindset a form of loyalty to God. My understanding of the Creator led me to believe he would want me to learn the truth even if it disagreed with Watchtower. When my thoughts diverged on *significant* issues, I believed Jehovah *expected* me to disagree with Watchtower. Jesus' account impressed upon me that standing for truth was not just allowed but required. If Jesus stood in defiance of his religious leaders, there is no organization deserving of the unconditional obedience Watchtower expected.

A STAND FOR TRUTH

While trusting my judgment, I felt my powers of discernment set me apart from the rest of the congregation who seemed content to believe what could objectively be considered absurd.

My first detection of absurdity occurred when Watchtower adjusted an earlier belief – a prediction the world would come to an end within one generation of 1914. That did not happen. And when it became apparent the world had not ended, an adjustment was published stating the word *generation* could mean any period where two humans lived as contemporaries. In other words, Watchtower wasn't wrong about their earlier prophecy; we were wrong in our understanding of a *generation*.

They illustrated this new overlapping generations concept stating if a JW who was alive and aware in 1914 overlapped lives with, say a child of the 90s, that generation could extend from 1914 as far out as the end of that 90s child's natural life; 160 years or more.[46] While the rest of my fellow congregants were nodding in agreement, the preposterousness of the new teaching left me in shock. The term generation is not difficult to grasp. In fact, as the basis for their generational prediction, they were aligning it with a biblical prophecy which had been fulfilled after 40 years. (Matthew 24:33, 34) 40 years is a reasonable time frame for a generation. 160 is not. It was obvious to me they were backpedaling a failed prediction by asserting a generation could now be stretched beyond two generations. I wasn't going to smile and nod with the crowd. This was stupid.

Far from feeling on the fringes of the religion as I had been relegated, my newfound confidence allowed me to feel I was anointed by Jehovah, perhaps to help lead the religion to a deeper understanding.[i47] I didn't know how else to explain why I could understand these things, but others could not. Only *anointed* JWs were said to be gifted with the ability to determine scriptures. And their need for improved direction seemed obvious.

My viewpoint, though, was just as absurd as theirs. Dominant religious structures are not interested in the opinions of independent thinkers. Independent thought is an intolerable risk when maintaining control over millions of minds. I would never qualify as a leader of Jehovah's Witnesses. My life was going in a different direction.

_____

[i] For JWs, the term *anointed* refers to a select few within their organization who "received an appointment from God to be kings and priests with Jesus Christ in the heavens." For a JW to declare they were gifted with such a rare honor, they must make a spectacle during their most holy observance: the Memorial of Jesus' death. During the silent ceremony when congregants passed plates of bread and glasses of wine, an anointed person would break from rote, eat of the bread, and drink the wine. In 30+ years of Memorial attendance, I never once seen another person do that. I have met only 6 former and current JWs who identified as *anointed*. Two of them served on the governing body.

At an assembly of Jehovah's Witnesses in 2016, I listened to an elder deliver a talk expressly telling us not to "lean upon our own understanding," and that it was not ok even to *internally* disagree with the Watchtower. He went on to state that if we find ourselves disagreeing with their doctrine, the fault is our own – it was an indication of our disloyalty to God and our lack of humility. Rather than accept the admonition of the talk, I immediately thought of Jesus who courageously stood against the religious leaders of his time, calling them "offspring of vipers," "white-washed graves," and "hypocrites." (Matthew 23:27-33) Jesus publicly shamed the Jewish leaders for failing to apply their own scriptures. It is a fundamental tenet of Christianity, and an exhortation from the Bible, that we be imitators of Jesus. And I fully intended to.

The experience of time clarified for me the governing body of Jehovah's Witnesses were imposing little more than their opinions. And with additional time, I concluded that when Watchtower leaders demanded we adopt their opinions as our personal beliefs, they were making an egregious over-step. When they enforced their opinions with harsh punishments – when they separated a dissident from their family and expelled them from the congregation – they were functioning as Pharisees – they were hypocrites. The *Awake* magazine from July 2009 stated: "No one should be forced to worship in a way that he finds unacceptable or be made to choose between his beliefs and his family." They were in a morally inferior position by creating such a situation and could not be trusted.

The reductionist teachings which had been ingrained into me from early childhood started crumbling into meaninglessness. This tectonic shift in my outlook caused my foundations to quake. If you can't trust your foundations, how can you stand confidently? If you can't trust your parent's truth, what do you believe?

I wasn't yet prepared to leave the religion. There are significant consequences to that. Jehovah's Witnesses use *disfellowshipping* as a tool for behavioral control. Certain behaviors including sex outside of marriage, homosexuality, gambling, smoking, slander, engaging in the practices of other religions, or apostasy, are not tolerated. People caught doing, or who confess those practices, and cannot convince the elders it will not reoccur, will be disfellowshipped. In those cases, the elders will notify the offender that he is no longer one of Jehovah's Witnesses. They will no longer be privileged to speak to other Jehovah's Witnesses. An announcement will be made to the congregation stating, "Daniel Quigley is no longer one of Jehovah's Witnesses." Following the announcement, all Jehovah's Witnesses worldwide will be forbidden from engaging in association with the disfellowshipped person.[48]

There is also a subcategory of offenses that include accepting blood transfusions, getting involved in politics, or deciding one no longer wants to be one of Jehovah's Witnesses. The offender under this category will be regarded as having *disassociated* their self – a slight variant to the term *disfellowshipped*. The same announcement will be made as with disfellowshipping, which in turn means the same practice of shunning will occur. There really isn't a difference between the two, other than for disassociated JWs, I could not find a provision for appeal.[49] I would have fallen into this second category of punishment had my newfound beliefs been reported to elders.

People who are not Jehovah's Witnesses may not fully appreciate how earth-shattering those consequences are. To have all your friends and family cut away without any further contact is an enormous life change. Negative consequences range from emotional trauma, financial problems, and even physical ailments. It cannot be stressed enough how important our human networks are. Having their social connections torn from a person is a trauma some people never recover from.

Those behavioral controls are effective, not simply because they deter unwanted behavior, but because they alienate Jehovah's Witnesses from others. Faithful Jehovah's Witnesses have no social network outside their religion, no external support structure, no means to identify with Worldly people, and a powerful sense of distrust for Worldly professionals. Many former Jehovah's Witnesses find it prohibitively difficult to integrate with the world outside. This adds an exponent to the deterrent. With those consequences in mind, it would take more than a loss of faith to extract me from the religion.

That motivation would shortly come, though. At one of our regular meetings, we were studiously dissecting an article from the Watchtower magazine, as we did each Sunday. The article made the point that we need to be unquestioningly obedient to the elders. The meeting prepared us to expect a situation where the direction we receive from elders may conflict with our personal judgment, but in those circumstances, we are still required to be obedient.[50] It was my wife who first voiced concern. *This direction isn't simply incorrect, it is dangerous.* I thought of my daughter who, if obedient to this direction, could fall prey to an elder with harmful motives. I'm not exaggerating this danger. That precise situation can and has occurred.[51] Unquestioning submission is reminiscent of Jim Jones or Charles Manson. The implication of the article's instruction moved us toward a healthy fear of their authority.

As we were teaching our daughter the importance of boundaries, trusting her personal judgment, and bravely standing for what is right, we didn't need her absorbing any more of what the Watchtower had to say. We formally removed ourselves from the religion by writing letters of disassociation. It was one of many steps that transformed our lives into a wide-open world without answers.

THE VOID BEHIND THE CURTAIN

I had discarded the bonds of dogma. While I enjoyed my new freedom, regained my dignity, and repossessed my will, there were consequences which were often difficult, and sometimes excruciating. Unlike how I imagined my freedom, there were many times I felt paralyzed with uncertainty. There were times I worried I was wrong. My values, my purpose, and my moral philosophy suddenly dissolved. I had no friends and had lost many family members to shunning. Previously, I structured my life around a schedule of religious routines and the booming voice of the Watchtower telling me what I was loyal to. Now my ears rang within a quiet void. It felt like I moved to Mars. I didn't know anyone. I didn't know what to think about God or how to gauge what was important. I can empathize with others who experience this loss of religion. That stage where structure is removed, and questions are left unanswered can feel intolerable.

Not all religions function like Jehovah's Witnesses. Jehovah's Witnesses are very much on the high end of the scale of authoritarianism.[52] They rate highest in religiosity after all. It should also be said that not all experiences of Jehovah's Witnesses are the same as mine. It appears some can live rewarding lives within its confines. But it was not a structure I could tolerate.

The Amish are famously distinct from the culture of their surrounding neighbors. Their speech, clothing, and lack of technology ensure every aspect of their lives is visibly distinct from contemporary American culture. Their children are molded by the strict religious teachings of their parents. Like Jehovah's Witnesses, the Amish use the Bible as their basis for faith. Romans 12:2 says, "don't be conformed to this world," and this scripture is used to foster distrust with the outside. They share a similar form of isolation with Jehovah's Witnesses. In some Amish communities, however, when a child turns 16 they are encouraged to leave their home, experiment, and explore. The rite of passage is known as *Rumspringa,* and the idea is that teens will return to the church and their community after experiencing a distaste for the modern world. This seemingly risky gamble has proven successful. Amish retention rates are an astonishing 80 percent. Above 90 percent for some Amish communities.[53]

It might sound incredulous that Amish kids would return after experiencing modern technology and entertainment. But their situation becomes clear after watching them suffer the consequences of unbridled hedonism.[54] Having never experienced social media, cars, city life, television, pornography, drugs, or alcohol, it's hard to imagine how their foray could possibly succeed. Such worldly indulgence requires a set of skills and self-regulation entirely foreign to people who grew up on a plow.[55] How would they handle the loneliness? How would they interact with individuals who did not share their social customs and courtesies? How would they react to lifestyles they had previously deemed immoral? How could they guard against predatory behavior?

While children in the urban West have been developing the skills to avoid predators, to be careful of alcohol, and to manage social media, Amish teens are set up for failure in such an environment. Their isolation has served as an effective leash. They have been offered a perceived freedom, but the strings of indoctrination hold them in mental bondage. When the consequences of undisciplined behaviors come home to roost; when loneliness sets in; it must feel like mom and dad were right the whole time. *The world is cold and dark. The religion is the truth. The Bible must be miraculously conceived.* And like the many others before them, they return, more indoctrinated than ever.

A similar condition occurs with Jehovah's Witnesses when they attempt to leave. Having contained their entire lives in *the Truth,* the World is going to feel alien. The world has its problems. Because it isn't confined to a little box, it has decidedly *more* problems.

The gift of life within a totalitarian structure is like inheriting an incredible yacht. But the inheritor is only allowed to keep it in harbor. Leaving totalitarianism opens the gate for the yacht to explore the open ocean. The opportunities are staggering, but so are the dangers.

Outside of religion, the issues of dogma, abuse, and slavery still very much exist. They exist in greater quantity. But with individual freedom, people can learn to navigate around them and confront them. They can develop the skills to overcome life's pitfalls.

Misinformation plagues the lives of people outside of the box just as it did inside. Plenty of available information is worthless and, in some cases harmful. Unlike the little box, though, we are *allowed* to search for truth. We are allowed to formulate our own conclusions. Even if they're wrong. With this exercise, we develop the skill of *discernment.*

I remember a talk that has far more meaning for me now than it did at the time. I was a young adult at a convention of Jehovah's Witnesses where an elder described the most effective means to train children. The elder asked how we thought an elephant is trained. Elephants could easily destroy a person if they wanted to. An ordinary rope could not hold an elephant. Yet that is what trainers use in the circus. How is that possible? He explained that when an elephant calf is born, they immediately attach ropes to it. They will secure it to a post or lead it around but will never allow the calf an opportunity for freedom. At no time may the calf enjoy a reprieve from the rope. When the calf is small, it isn't strong enough to break the rope. It will resist and struggle to no avail.

Through its struggles, it forms a belief the rope is indestructible. Its will to fight the bond eventually breaks. The concept of the indestructible rope becomes a deep-seated belief. When the calf grows strong enough to break the rope, that belief remains. The elephant will not challenge the rope. The trainer can now use it as a powerful prompt to perform any maneuver the handler sees fit.

The elder made the point when we train children early to follow direction, they are more likely to obey when they are older. And he was right. When we are trained from a young age that certain truths are indisputable, those beliefs can be entrenched before we develop the skills to critically examine them. The belief then forms a part of our core understanding and, even as an adult, we are not likely to test it.

> *Train a boy in the way he should go; Even when he grows old he will not depart from it.*
> **Proverbs 20:18** NWT

Religion functions best when instilled early. Like ropes around the legs of elephant calves, dogmatic teachings hold us down until we stop resisting – until our will for defiance dies. It explains why adults with fully developed faculties of reason never critically examine the beliefs of their childhood. It is a form of manipulation with far-reaching and negative implications.[56]

I assert it is not a function of loving leaders to determine for you what is right and wrong. That is a strategy of authoritarian mind-control. Steve Hassan's BITE Model of Authoritarian Control identifies the methods used to brainwash and control individuals. BITE stands for Behavior control, Information control, Thought control, and Emotional control.

Behavioral control is imposed through strict rules and discourages individualism. *Information* control entails the withholding or distortion of information. You can recognize *thought* control where individuals must internalize the thoughts of the authority, where critical thought is discouraged, and where skills of discernment are replaced with memorizations of the authority's talking points. *Emotional* control is evident when terms like *loyalty* are weaponized, feelings of guilt and unworthiness are perpetuated, fear of punishment is emphasized, or when individuals are told how to feel in specific circumstances.[57] Encountering these conditions should trigger a signal to exit. "People who don't want you to think are never your friend."[58]

For those people taking their first brave steps and peeking outside their little box, please be assured there is a way to construct a life abounding in reward, even if it is uncomfortable or scary adjusting to the openness at first. You will likely have to catch up on worldly acclimation. The process is likely to have surprising twists. No one can promise it will be easy. But how likely are you to grow and be healthy within the confines of a little box and manipulated by those who would use you as a circus act?

At some point you have to recognize what world it is that you belong to; what power rules it and from what source you spring; that there is a limit to the time assigned you, and if you don't use it to free yourself it will be gone and will never return.
Marcus Aurelius

1.5 DO YOUR RESEARCH

Be a free thinker and don't accept everything you hear as truth. Be critical and evaluate what you believe in.

Aristotle

How bad could things get if we believed a lie? How much harm could misinformation cause? I think it's safe to say that being critical about all information presented to us is vital. We have plenty incentives to guard our minds from fallacies.

One might wonder whether it is possible to see things as they are given how limited our perspective is. I posit that seeing things for what they are starts with *wanting* to. That sounds somewhat basic. It isn't that simple. We must want to know the truth *more* than we want to be *right*. Beliefs are hard to dismiss, and beliefs cemented into our minds from early years are harder yet to excavate. If we don't want to change those, we won't – even when faced with irrefutable evidence. The value of truth must be higher than reputation, our commitment to comfort and familiarity, and the opinions of others.

In my dogmatic years, I didn't hold honesty as a high value. I would have *proclaimed* so. I certainly respected the quality in others. But the value of truth did not correspond to the values I had been taught.

I was taught circumstances might arrive where lying may be the only means to protect the congregation. When the time came to *wage spiritual warfare*, lying to protect the Organization was fair.[59] The Organization was thus considered a higher value than truth.

JW rules were supposedly from God and thus perfect. If we disagreed with those rules or the way they were administered, we had to keep those views to ourselves – we couldn't tell the truth. Masturbation, or even entertaining sexual thoughts were punishable. Instead of confessing each sin, I felt I had to lie just to keep a standing in the congregation. I had to lie so I could speak with the people I knew, and I could not help noticing how everyone else was doing the same. There wouldn't be any JWs if they honestly confessed.

I wasn't rewarded when I told the truth. My confessions were met with the highest forms of punishment. At every meeting we pretended to be happy. Then it continued for the rest of the time. We risked a loss of privileges if we admitted our vulnerabilities. It seemed, in most cases, honesty would hinder my "spiritual growth." I learned to perceive honesty as a gray area, something to strive for, but not critical.

It never occurred to me that each time I lied, I also had to construct a new reality. To avoid getting caught in the lie I would imagine how that alternate reality would play out, what others would say, how it would affect various outcomes and how to respond if challenged. In hindsight that was a tragic waste of valuable time and mind space. And it was addictive.

I never learned to value truth until several years post-dogma. Unlike sorting through a mind full of fake scenarios, I found the real truth wonderfully freeing. All those efforts to create and process other realities could be put to better use. More importantly, though, honesty fostered a healthy acceptance of reality. It helped me to be *here*. Not in some augmented reality in my head.

Internal conflict occurs when we try to make fit within our minds conflicting realities. That is the essence of cognitive dissonance.[60] When I felt conflicted, it was difficult being honest with myself. I didn't like who I was, what I had done, or where I came from. There was a form of refusal to accept what is. It seemed easiest to distort reality to fit my beliefs. I didn't know another way to make my perceptions fit. I was lying. But because lying had become so common, I wasn't aware I was lying.

Such a condition seems prevalent. Our fingertips sit poised at the gates of a vast network of data. But that data is increasingly diluted with fiction. Truth remains elusive, and if we want to search through the wreckage of internet misinformation, it is imperative we develop critical thinking skills.

We might not have the capacity to verify absolute truth. But we can identify falsehoods. Through that process we can deduce a perspective closer to reality. But such requires effort. Effort is required to push past easily swallowed information which provides the same substance as junk food. Effort is required to discipline our mind to search for truth. Both effort and patience are required to develop the skills to separate truth from untruth. That is what critical thinking is. We won't exert that effort if we do not want to. Which is why it must start with *valuing* truth.

A study by the American Philosophical Association led by Peter Facione identified six core skills for critical thinking. Those skills are *interpretation, analysis, evaluation, inference, explanation*, and *self-regulation*.[61]

Those seven steps can be cumbersome to memorize without working knowledge of the terms. Alternatively, we could ask ourselves or ask others *why do you believe that?* We could follow up with *where did you get that from?* and *how do you know that's a credible source?*

Within the Toyota Motor Corporation, Sakichi Toyoda developed a similar approach known today as *five whys*. Intended for problem solving, this iterative technique simplifies the process of finding root causes. When a problem presents itself, students are taught to ask *why?* Having heard the answer, they again ask *why*. And again, and again, and again. Having continued to ask why, the root problem should appear, allowing an opportunity to address the cause.[62]

CONSPIRACIES

Due to their distrust for the government and too much trust in conspiracy-pushers, some accept conspiracies without critical analysis, based solely on the idea that said conspiracy rejects the official narrative. But that is not a logical test, neither is it reflective of critical thinking.[63] They likely feel they have exercised discernment when they have simply traded one belief for another.

I found this prevalent while exploring a YouTube channel where conspiracies were promoted. They backed up their conclusions claiming skeptics were *sheeple*. They said skeptics were unduly influenced by the propaganda of the government. The comment sections of their videos were rife with believers agreeing with each other in an ironically sheep-like chorus. Skeptics who attempted to enter the conversation were attacked with personal insults and their comments downvoted to obscurity.

I noted a typical pattern for this crowd. After being cornered by a skeptic's call for evidence, their response was *do your research*. As if, by dropping this bomb, they had proven their virtue as a meticulous analyst, daring others to endure hours of arduous search for a topic that did not exist.

Before the internet, information was prohibitively expensive. Now it's free. Sort of. Now information comes at a different cost. It might display no initial price tag to the consumer, but it most definitely comes with an agenda. Powerful political and corporate entities have an interest in your beliefs – both to analyze them and to alter them.

Reports from social media whistleblowers make clear that your online *likes* and *comments* are indications of preference. They paint a detailed portrait of your interests and leanings. They are compiled and offered to interested parties as a highly detailed set of personality metrics. These reports help them decide which approach works best to steer the mindset of a target demographic. [64] In a disturbing twist, the online "research" performed by YouTube Scholars and Facebook Addicts is likely to farm more data from the user than the user receives in return.[65] The platforms might know more about your interests than you do.

Having obtained this information, those influence seekers – those wolves – with colossal resources at their disposal, can produce artfully crafted media that convince people of the ideals which suit the wolves' purpose. They create beliefs which compel less critical people to do what the influencers want. They can even influence people to harm themselves.[66]

There's reason not to trust the "government." The state of modern politics is appalling. It is a circus. A theatre performance of nonsense. And I think it's worth being vigilant against policies which could cause harm. There are real causes for concern regarding authoritarian control. There are good reasons to reject policies that unnecessarily restrict or remove individual freedoms. But without carefully analyzing the evidence at hand – without a logical assessment of reality – people can just as easily find themselves picked away from protective structures carefully constructed for their freedom. They can find themselves fighting against programs and policies which would directly benefit them. They will insist the people trying to help are enemies – that the wolves are their friends.

There is no doubt in my mind that real conspiracies exist. But I'm also convinced another slice of irony is served when the less-critical conspiracy theorists cling to half-baked concepts – it obscures the truth of genuine conspiracies.

I watched a far-right conspiracy docu-series claiming the world is controlled by a cabal of political and Hollywood elites who have been orchestrating a widespread pedophile ring. The series offered hope, though, and that hope was in the form of President Donald Trump and a secret organization known as Q Anon.

The series failed to provide any basis for its claims. It promised that evidence would very soon be provided. Standing in for evidence were simple messages and imagery that projected a false pretense of research. It seemed by design to resonate with the hearts of those who rely on their feelings to distinguish good from bad. Phrases were used which I had painfully learned to be cautious of – red flags which screamed of high control cult danger. "Do your research" was one of those phrases, the anthem of the uninformed. "Trust the plan" was another – this familiar cult classic nearly made me gasp.

The most surprising part is the support it received. An astonishing *like* ratio and overwhelmingly supportive comments. Scanning through, I never found a critical comment. Not once did someone post *maybe we should fact-check some of these absurd claims.* Instead, what I read was "this is the best investigative journalism I have ever seen," and "Why can't some people believe this truth? I do!!!"

The video made ridiculous claims like *JFK, Junior is a time-traveler.* Despite that absurdity, the audience believed it without question and for reasons I could only attribute to colorful graphics, easily memorized slogans, and a play toward fears they already held: *Elites you don't relate to and are likely better educated are misleading you.* That's a concept most people can get behind.

But there has been a real conspiracy of pedophile rings where organizations like the Catholic Church have effectively concealed the scope of misconduct and people who attempted to release the truth were mocked and condemned. Videos like the above do little to ensure attention remains on the truth at hand.

ANTI-INTELLECTUALISM

Arrogance is a loathsome trait regardless of political affiliation. But the *sense* of arrogance may just as likely be a *false* sense. Some might *feel* that an educated person is arrogant, even if that may not be the case. The effects of mass media coupled with a religious or political confirmation bias is fueling an ever-growing and frightening movement toward anti-intellectualism.[67]

Anti-intellectualism has historically been the precursor to horror. It is not an aspect restricted to either side of the political aisle. It is an insistence on being right, a refusal to consider opposing viewpoints, and a self-righteous indignation for people who don't share their values. The same conspiracy techniques which seem so effective in the modern far-right have also been used to manipulate the left – tribalism, fault-finding, and virtue signaling.

This recipe was used for manipulating people and orchestrating the Holodomor in the Soviet Union under Communism. People were stirred with simple, emotional messages to rise against the perceived threat of others who appeared more successful. Farmers who appeared to be rich were cast as oligarch *boogiemen* who stole the wealth from common people. [68] Those "oligarch" families were abstract and hard to relate to. It was easy to convince the majority the oligarchs did not deserve their success. Such was a product of oppression. Ironically, they were correct. Except that the true oligarch boogiemen were not the wealthy farmers. They were likely those spreading the message.

In Cambodia it was thought that education was the cause of Cambodia's problems. People who held academic positions were executed. City-dwellers were trucked to the country's rural lands and forced to farm. Being an accountant, teacher, or doctor put many at risk for purging. People were killed who were merely *perceived* to be smart – at times because they wore glasses. Those anti-intellectual beliefs led to a breakdown of trade and agricultural practices. Starvation took the lives of large swathes of the population. Millions died because of a culturally developed suspicion of academia, amplified with emotional propaganda. The fears and frustrations of people were effectively weaponized to create sectarian hatred.[69] The working class was pit against those who work with ideas.

I feel strongly that anti-intellectualism needs to be reversed. There needs to be an attempt to find common ground and to resist our tendencies to cause division. Our societies depend on the benefits of specialization and that requires a degree of trust for specialists. That concept is central to urbanization and the advantages it offers. But when trust in one of those specialties is eroded, the entire industry suffers, or collapses. In the case of anti-intellectualism, it is the entire academic community who are held in contempt. But the academic community is our key to future advancements. This trend suggests our collective future is at risk.

ETHICS IN ACADEMIA

Despite the risk to our future, some academics have recklessly abandoned their code of ethics and sullied the reputation of their profession. Current funding structures for research have created an environment inviting corruption. The acceptance of students into ivy league schools based on the wealth of their families draws negative views from those who worked harder and demonstrated higher competencies. The falsification of studies to further the interests of the tobacco and pharmaceutical industries have resulted in the deaths of millions and the rightful mistrust of the public.[70]

Trusting scientists and those alike who specialize in a finite field can be difficult for anybody. I struggle to trust mechanics who work on my car. A conspiracy forms in my mind. A humble person would recognize and respect the advanced training a specialist has in their field, albeit critically. If we're not mechanically inclined, we're obliged to form some trust that the mechanic would make a better decision than we would.

It wouldn't be a good use of my time arguing with a mechanic. My Google searches have failed to qualify me for that, as it has failed to qualify others as doctors and journalists. I'm not likely to jump out and verify every story I read on the news like a vigilante investigative journalist. The mechanic, the doctor, and the journalist deserve at least some recognition for their expertise. As critical as I am with information, I can still benefit from those who have trained longer in a particular field. But that sense of confidence has its limits.

If science can supply a detailed list of evidence and a means for others to duplicate the results of their experiment, shouldn't we give more weight to a scientific conclusion than a conclusion reached by conjecture? If the evidence is stacked in to one corner and if the methods to reach a conclusion are markedly clear, shouldn't we lean that way? We don't have to fully believe them. We shouldn't fully believe. Not all good information comes from academia and not everything from academia is credible. But when comparing sources, and without any other deciding factors, offering more trust to those who can demonstrate their training and competence can't be held against us.

REAL CONSPIRACIES

Perhaps there are other factors, though. Perhaps there is specific, solid reasons for our mistrust. Perhaps we obtain a first-hand perspective that a commonly held ideology is false. Or perhaps a trusted organization widely considered an authority is concealing harmful intent. This is the situation religious dissidents find themselves in. I can think of numerous occasions, both secularly and within religion, where the status quo required adjustment and those who tried to come forward were dismissed as alarmists or conspiracy theorists. Perhaps this happens more often than we imagine. Certainly more often than I assumed. Having been a witness to the unfolding of conspiracies I no longer dismiss them by default as I have. I implore everyone else not to brush them off either. Hearing a person out does not require acceptance of their claims. But being on the right side of history almost invariably requires listening and adjusting.

As nefarious organizations grow in their powers, or good organizations grow in their nefariousness – as they feed off their ability to control legislation and purchase media outlets – as they control the common narrative – I don't think it is ridiculous that underhanded shenanigans become common place, or that whistle blowers are increasingly labelled as crazy conspiracy theorists. A sophisticated cover-up might plant a multitude of absurd variations in anticipation of someone blowing a whistle. I have seen such a tactic in action.

I implore whistle blowers and those who relay conspiracies to be vigilant with the truth. Avoid repeating claims you cannot verify. Even if you *know* it's true. Whether others listen to your message relies heavily on your credibility and getting caught with one false story obliterates it.

The philosophy of *burden of truth* requires that a person making a claim which is not presently accepted has the burden of truth. Conspiracies fall under the category of extraordinary claims. If a claim of a conspiracy is made, the claimant is obliged to substantiate it with evidence.[71] When wild conspiracies are presented in well-produced videos, but those videos aren't shored up with a list of verifiable references, I would say we have good reason to resist spreading their message. If they had the resources to produce the video, they had the means to provide evidence.

When I heard the earlier mentioned video say *the evidence will come out very soon,* I intuitively considered the source dishonest. I haven't experienced honest people expecting me to believe them before they present evidence. I haven't experienced honest experts dismiss calls for evidence with: "do your research." Honest professionals show their research.

If a theory has stood up to interpretation, analysis, evaluation, and inference, it's still of benefit to discuss our findings with others. We may have overlooked a crucial detail or failed to apply a test. I can't imagine a better method of quality control than reaching across the table.

Being prepared to present our beliefs to others has a host of benefits. It forces us to articulate an argument and to arrange our thoughts cohesively. It prepares us to detach emotionally from a belief. If we know it's going to be attacked – and especially if our claim is controversial enough to be attacked rigorously – we are forced to dispense with unproven portions. An effective exchange with a critic helps us adjust and reformulate a logical argument and to have an arsenal of references at the ready.

It might seem that opposing groups have values so different, there doesn't appear any means to reconcile. But that might be an illusion. We all want to have a good quality of life and we want that for others. We might have different beliefs regarding the scope of that reach or how to get there, but if we start by determining our common values, we might find a way to get closer to the objective. The more we use our critical thinking skills, the more they will develop.

We do have reason to be on the guard. Even against internal beliefs about ourselves – beliefs we might not be aware of. Poor beliefs are a significant cause of mental health issues. In Psychanalytic Psychology, J. Weiss wrote: "People develop beliefs about themselves and their interpersonal world, and these beliefs organize the way in which they perceive themselves and others, and shape their behaviors, affects, moods, and personalities. It is suggested that obedience to certain maladaptive beliefs develop and maintain psychopathology."[72]

The reasons we have for critical thinking continue to stack up. Learning how to both open our minds to new ideals and to be critical of them might be the most important skill of the decade.

For myself, the most effective means of combining those seemingly adverse abilities was inspired by the likes of Newton, Confucius, Voltaire, and Marcus Aurelius. I embraced the concept: *I know nothing*. By no means is that a figure of speech or an exaggeration. I immersed myself in the state of mind of admitting how little I know. I had to change my vocabulary. Absolute statements like *I know for a fact*, or *you'll never convince me of that*, or simply the word *proof*, were no longer compatible.

This seems especially difficult for Jehovah's Witnesses because we were programmed by people who *know*. We *knew* The *Truth*. We weren't permitted to entertain opposing concepts. We were never taught the value in doing so. Watchtower magazines didn't discuss their *theories*. They didn't offer evidence and leave conclusions to readers. We even used that as evidence scientists were wrong – *all they have is theories. They never know anything. I wanna KNOW what's real.* There was no example set for any form of humility.

I can conclude, then, that humility was my first essential requirement for acquiring knowledge and for developing desperately needed emotional intelligence. There are times when I depart from this ethic. It generally takes a dose of humiliation to realize I have strayed, and to appreciate its value.

I'm convinced knowing nothing could create world peace if it caught on. It's hard to argue with people who know nothing. Knowing nothing has also shown itself as a quality of genuine honesty. I don't know how the world came about, or if there is a purpose for life. I don't know if the material universe is an illusion. I don't know what makes us who we are. I don't even know if we are real. It seems the only fully true words I could say are: "I don't know."

To read with diligence; not to rest satisfied with a light and superficial knowledge, nor quickly to assent to things commonly spoken.
Marcus Aurelius

HONESTY

2.

The truth Is
revealed by
removing things
that stand in its
light, an art not
unlike sculpture,
in which the
artist creates, not
by building, but
by hacking away.

ALLAN WATTS

One of the most significant shifts in thought I experienced was in how I viewed honesty. In my dogmatic perspective I considered honesty a moral issue. I now understand why that didn't work.

One reason I think that was a mistake was because my sense of morality was eroding with each experience. My experience was leading me to detach from the concept of morality. That might sound alarming. I'll speak about that later in more detail. But after morality ceased to be my motivation for honesty I stumbled upon a different source of motivation.

I now understand truth in the wonderful simplicity of itself. Truth simply is reality. Truth is the correct view of what is. The full perspective of a matter without distortion. I'm not sure I would have described it differently before, but the difference being that I thought I knew the truth. Now I would say I could not have. I could not obtain all perspectives. I do not and could not know each angle or how to articulate it well enough that the correct idea will be conveyed. Until I know how the neutrons, electrons, quirks, quarks, and their inner workings operate, I'm far too limited to claim I know any truth.

The profound part of this realization was **understanding *honesty* as an *acceptance of reality*.** I had to accept that I didn't know the whole truth. I had to accept my faults and failures. I had to accept terrible circumstances existed and that I had been lying.

When I accepted those things I developed a deep respect for reality. *This is real. That happened. I am here.* To lie from that point felt like a betrayal of reality. It seemed like I was ashamed of how things played out. Ashamed of the universe. Ashamed of the truth. That was a betrayal that didn't sit well with me. In all those years, why did I lie? Because I didn't accept reality as it was. I didn't accept who I was. I certainly didn't accept what I had done.

This new perspective produced within me a heightened state of awareness. A familiarity with the truth. An attachment with reality. With that attachment I saw fewer and fewer reasons to be dishonest. I was aligning with reality, and there was a sense of power which accompanied that alignment.

I started to realize how many of our problems stem from a refusal to accept reality. Looking through explanations of mental health disorders it seems they all could be distilled to a failure to accept reality. When a therapist works with a client what is their goal? How do they attempt to help an individual? They help them sort through the tangled mess of misunderstandings so they can accept reality. They help them find awareness of where their thoughts diverged from truth, and then to accept the truth.

Awareness and acceptance of reality is where I found the motivation to be honest. But the link between them was too strong as to say it *motivated* me to be honest. While I examine my own dishonesty and that of others, there doesn't appear to be any difference between honesty and acceptance of reality. Neither can I see a distinction between awareness and acceptance. These are the same thing. You need to be aware of a misalignment with reality to accept it. But as you gain awareness of the misalignment you also gain acceptance. It's like you can't be aware of something and not accept it. Once you see something for what it is, you don't argue whether it exists. If you're unsure, then you're not aware of it.

There's a good argument to be made that honesty more refers to the *expression* of truth and not necessarily the *acceptance* of it. But is it not also possible that a dishonest person has the capability to express the truth? And in that moment where they express the truth do they then BECOME an honest person? It appears to me a dishonest person is going to struggle telling the truth but that it certainly is possible. We would then simply wait for them to express their next dishonest spouting. It's like they can't help being dishonest. Because they are dishonest. I propose that is so because they are misaligned with reality. So again there is nothing truly distinguishable between dishonesty and misalignment with reality, or an acceptance of reality. It is a mental disorder related to a refusal to accept reality.

Accepting reality changed everything. It took time to accept reality. It still takes considerable pondering to fully digest what that means and its implications. It's an enlightened awareness of truth and the initial realization of it may have drastically changed the way I saw myself and everything else. But it still takes time to ponder and allow that realization to soak into all pockets of my brain. It also appears I can lose some of this awareness if I allow myself to misalign with what is. If I allow my thoughts to start recreating reality as I often did.

I continually benefit from additional reasons to be honest. Not having to memorize a rehearsed storyline removes the stress and mental gymnastics required to construct and maintain those stories. People who can admit to their faults garner immediate respect from others. We can't improve if we don't know what went wrong, and we can't learn what went wrong if we're not being honest.

Seeing things for what they are provides wholesome benefits even if it requires a painful acceptance of error. Beliefs aligned with reality remove the harmful surprises associated with fallacies and miscalculation. With realistic beliefs guiding us, we're not overcome by the stress of unrealistic concerns. We're not plagued by lethargic tendencies of nihilism. They help us cope with tragedies and to take advantage of opportunities with gratefulness. They give us confidence to manage difficult people and complex situations. Seeing things for what they are empowers us.

By contrast, I found fallacious beliefs distort how we see ourselves and others. They offer a misleading perspective of both. Faulty beliefs form divisions among people and cause conflict. When my perception is overly negative, when it fails to consider the advantages I have, when it fails to account for the harsh realities of life, or if it attempts to over-simplify conditions which are complex, I struggle to come to terms with reality. I will struggle to function effectively. My mental health deteriorates. I have come to believe living in the realm of truth is essential.

How could we know truth while we know nothing? The analogy of truth functioning like light works well. Light either exists or it doesn't. Nobody shines a flashlight of darkness. If someone wants to keep light from you they have to block your access to light or redirect it. Truth seems to work this way too.

Even the most absurd of lies contain some truth. Even if misdirected with the intent to deceive. I posit we don't benefit from avoiding lies, but by building our ability to recognize them. If we expect to hear truth in each lie we are better prepared to recognize a decoy or a misdirect. This keeps us from prematurely dismissing what could later prove true and it helps us remain sharp enough to discern a well-crafted lie.

Lies create false beliefs and some beliefs spark hatred between ethnic groups. Some beliefs incite intolerance. Some beliefs would have us reject important information, concepts, or opportunities to learn. Some beliefs convince us of our low self-worth and condemn us to a persistent, self-loathing state of mind. Some beliefs offer false hope and allow others to prey upon that hope. Some beliefs elevate others to a status above criticism – above other forms of authority – and leave vulnerable people without defenses. Those beliefs are not harmless. Those beliefs could be considered dangerous. And I had been living with nearly all of those.

Stalin's belief in the redistribution of the wealth in the Soviet Union was dangerous, as were those of the Khmer Rouge in Cambodia. Stalin's disregard for scientific research into crop genetics ensured the starvation of millions as did his formulation of unproven Marxist-Leninist ideals. Pol Pot's nationalism, racism and totalitarian insistence on those same Marxist ideals resulted in one of the worst mass killings in history and, like Stalin, the starvation of millions. In both cases the regime maintained a tight monopoly on information and ensured the State was the sole source.

Elements of those beliefs are creeping into modern politics. Nationalism has found a new wave of popularity. The misuse of government and dismantling of oversight invites totalitarianism. The monopolization of information is increasing. Opposing political theories are further polarizing. The wage gap increases. Anti-intellectualism is rampant. People are learning to reject education. And there is a growing group who advocate for more redistribution of wealth, regardless of whether those methods are proven.

Holy Wars and Jihadis have stained human history with the blood of many millions. Religious dogma, weaponized by a skillful manipulator, has proven effective and destructive. Words written centuries ago by people who lacked our historical perspective are later twisted for the benefit of a modern cause. Frustrations of the disenfranchised are exploited for the gain of those who monopolize information and who target the emotional tendencies of the herd. Moral lines are redrawn, and loyalties redirected. Complex socio-economic conditions are reframed with simple slogans and people are provided an enemy to focus their frustrations.

Muslim people have faced a mountain of religious intolerance following the events of September 11, 2001, and the subsequent wars in Iraq, Afghanistan and against ISIS. In the interest of clarifying my position I'll state without reservation it is not ok to judge, or abuse people for their ethnicity, creed, or for any other reason.

On the opposite side of the spectrum, however, there is a viewpoint from celebrities, apologists, and religious pluralists, that the beliefs of all religions are equal – that criticizing those beliefs is tantamount to racism.[73] They fail to understand how their stance undermines the monumental efforts of dissidents who have fought like hell to oppose authoritarianism. It frames whistleblowers as intolerant and hateful, failing to grasp how they placed themselves in harm's way for truth and the well-being of others. What is the basis for pluralist beliefs? An attempt toward tolerance? Is that understanding the reality of religion? Is that honest?

Those who have studied the phenomena of Jihadi Terrorism recognize the significant difference between individual beliefs within the spectrum of Islam. Unlike mainstream Muslims, Islamic Fundamentalists insist on a world under the tight control of *Sharia Law*, a religious law derived from the precepts of Islam. Those precepts are based upon the words of their holy book, the Quran, as well as from the deeds of its founder, Muhammed.[74]

To regard a founder's deeds as part of law becomes problematic when Muhammed is known for his bloody war mongering, his merciless treatment of enemies, and for taking a wife who was as young as nine.[75] And while those claims are challenged by many, it remains problematic when people follow such an example.

Not all Muslims agree with Sharia Law. The distinction is noteworthy. Not all Muslims hold to a strict interpretation of the Quran. That is a relief. The words of the Quran can hardly be regarded as useful for guiding a *religion of peace* while containing passages like the following:

> *Fighting is prescribed for you, and ye dislike it. But it is possible that ye dislike a thing which is good for you, and that ye love a thing which is bad for you. But Allah knoweth, and ye know not.*

Quran 2:216

> *The punishment of those who wage war against Allah and His messenger and strive to make mischief in the land is only this, that they should be murdered or crucified or their hands and their feet should be cut off on opposite sides or they should be imprisoned; this shall be as a disgrace for them in this world, and in the hereafter they shall have a grievous chastisement.*

Quran 5:33

> *Kill them wherever you find them, and turn them out from where they have turned you out. And Al-Fitnah [disbelief or unrest] is worse than killing.... And fight them until there is no more Fitnah and worship is for Allah alone.*

Quran 2:191-193

If these are the thoughts of God, how could one justify peace? How trustworthy can a person be if their basis for morality comes from a book that regulates slavery and rape this way:

> *O Prophet! We have made lawful to thee thy wives to whom thou hast paid their dowers; and those (slaves) whom thy right hand possesses out of the prisoners of war whom Allah has assigned to thee.*

Quran 33:50

Knowing those words serve as a foundation for certain religious beliefs is concerning. Though we needn't classify all Muslims as doing so. Each person holds to their own personal beliefs and their own degree of religiosity.

The people we surround ourselves with, though, have a significant impact on both categories. It might be worth getting know the beliefs of our neighbors.

Frustrated by circumstances, individuals who have struggled to succeed peacefully within the confines of their existing social systems are likely to search for an alternative. Some of them will find a new appreciation for God and a way to breathe life into ancient words. I know that is true, because as one of Jehovah's Witnesses I, too, sought what I thought was the wisdom of the Creator. In my most desperate moments of grief and pain I pored over the words of the Bible looking for solutions to my crises. When I failed to find those solutions, I thought if I tried yet harder to understand the Word of God and if I were willing to exert greater effort to be obedient to each of his utterances I would find the purest form of the Creator's wisdom. In those moments of desperation, a person can reject the social systems within their culture and adopt an extremist position.

In no way do I single Islam out. In many ways Christianity is worse. Dangerous beliefs are possible in every human mind which fails to see things for what they are. There is a variance in the scale to which beliefs pose a danger, as there is a difference in the quantity of dangerous beliefs within each social construct. The dangers associated with some beliefs are more evident than with others. ISIS paraded the images of violence and the promise of rape to promote itself. They projected Islam with the conspicuous theme of violence. They made an obvious display of dangerous belief. Other religions though, have successfully propagated more terror under the guise of love – a decidedly more insidious form of danger.

Some dangerous beliefs are so subtle we have carried them with us without a second thought – beliefs which seem useful on the surface, perhaps convincing us they precipitate good qualities such as restraint and humility. On careful examination though, you might find they do not. The unintended and often invisible consequences to those beliefs have far reaching and negative impacts on humanity by the very nature of their subtlety.

The belief that God has human representatives, and those representatives are above scrutiny is common in many faiths. The belief that

God communicates to people by means of a book from which can be extracted supernatural wisdom; that this book is the ultimate authority for determining morality; that seeking knowledge and determining for oneself what is acceptable is unforgivable; that we can judge whether other people, things or conditions are good or evil; and humans inherited imperfection requiring external salvation. In the next few chapters I will argue those beliefs do not promote healthy human thought. They are common, misaligned with reality, and dangerous.

Policies are based on those beliefs. Our systems of justice are based on those concepts. Those beliefs are so normalized where the culture has been shaped by the Bible, they might not be recognized as biblical. They have become a staple of our culture, and as such many would find it difficult to believe they are dangerous.

With dangerous beliefs lurking in all of human society we're given the incentive to check our personal convictions and be prepared to adjust if evidence demands. We need to value truth. Faith and loyalty are not virtues when attached to untruths.

That no one can say truthfully that you are not a straightforward or honest person. That anyone who thinks that believes a falsehood. The responsibility is all yours; no one can stop you from being honest or straightforward. Simply resolve not to go on living if you aren't.
Marcus Aurelius

2.1 SHEPHERDS AND DUKES

The improver of natural knowledge absolutely refuses to acknowledge authority, as such. For him, skepticism is the highest of duties; blind faith the one unpardonable sin.

Thomas Huxley

I had been taught God selected men from the earth to lead other humans. "He gave gifts in men... He gave some as apostles, some as prophets, some as evangelizers, some as shepherds and teachers, with a view to readjustment of the holy ones." (Ephesians 4:8,11,12NWT)

In my Bible reading I saw a clear contrast between Jesus – who did not tolerate the hypocrisy of religious leaders – and that of Paul. Paul wrote: "Obey your spiritual leaders and do what they say." (Hebrews 13:17NLT)

Perhaps you would agree that compliance in the right circumstances is useful. It is not a demonstration of a weak will. It is in fact the opposite. We demonstrate wisdom, patience, courage and humility when we don't always insist we are right. Being compliant to a dumbass boss is better than being homeless. But there are situations where obedience is decidedly dangerous: When obedience is demanded at the cost of independent thought; when the internal values and self-worth of individuals are disposed of; when those in a position of authority assume an abusive, dominant role; or where criticism is punished.[76]

Perhaps you might argue that an organization is within its right to demand some form of obedience. I might agree, but only if that organization offered a means to protest. Without open scrutiny, opinions don't avail of the rich rewards of communal input. I posit that opinions above scrutiny should immediately be discarded. It is questioning those opinions, not complicity, which demonstrates loyalty.

Scrutiny ensures the success of the organization. By contrast, the sense of perfection among high-control groups creates a stagnant atmosphere. The odor of dogma. No improvement is necessary when the organization is perfect. No improvement – no progress.

The JW organization admits to imperfection and has conceded that it has been incorrect on numerous prophecies and doctrinal matters. That said, their claim remains: *this is Jehovah's organization.* This claim is both bold and baffling when considering the gravity of Watchtower missteps, and troubling when considering they offer no room for individual interpretation, nor apologies when those missteps prove deadly. The organization once forbade organ transplants as well as vaccinations and the use of aluminum.[77] Some of those missteps cost lives. Did Jehovah cause those missteps? Could the organization have misunderstood what Jehovah was saying? How was it, then, Jehovah's organization? Could we at least consider if they were mistaken then, they might be mistaken now?

Even more likely, when referencing *Jehovah's organization,* they are referring to themselves – *their organization.* Jehovah is the brand of their governing body. They publish their own thoughts. *They are Jehovah.* When that realization sets in, their literature reads with a more insightful, yet ominous tone. *Trust in ~~Jehovah~~ Watchtower with all your heart, and do not rely on your own understanding.*[78]

The Watchtower specifically claims to offer freedom of thought. However it was my experience that Jehovah's Witnesses must accept all teachings of the Watchtower, even those which were not core beliefs. To disagree with even minor teachings resulted in loss of privileges. Loss of privileges equated to a lower status. The loss of status is a powerful and effective motivator. If an individual loses status because they won't adopt the leader's thoughts, that hardly qualifies as freedom of thought. It doesn't matter if their literature specifically states people have free will. Their policies and track record disagree.

If I were to point out clearly coercive language, the November 2018 Watchtower might be a good start. In reference to themselves as *the faithful and discreet slave,* the governing body of Jehovah's Witnesses disarm readers with the assurance: "Jehovah will not force his thinking on us. 'The faithful and discreet slave' does not exercise control over the thoughts of individuals, and neither do the elders." In an immediate pivot, they follow with "each Christian has the personal responsibility to bring his or her thinking into harmony with God's." Of course, those *thoughts of God* are dictated to the reader without room for personal determination. They're not sharing their theories – *they know*. So, what they really said was *we're not telling you what to think; it's your responsibility to think like we told you.* It's worse than telling people what to think, because it is precisely that, *and* an assumption of Godlike authority, and ironically, an attempt to shift responsibility. The titles of the articles alone should have raised concerns.

- **Trust in Jehovah and Live!**
- **Who Molds Your Thinking?**
- **Are You Making Jehovah's Thoughts Your Own?**

In claiming not to control minds, the articles make the point that they don't dictate the daily routines of individuals. They simply offer "basic principles for moral conduct and behavior." But that seems intentionally misleading. In that issue alone, they offer specific warnings regarding employment events, forms of dance, and how readers should not watch entertainment containing "family first philosophies" or, "a human interest story [that] might advance the world's view of human goals and achievements." That issue gives clear and specific direction as to medical treatments which are known to have grave consequences. And those directions are enforced with loss of status and disassociation.

None of those *thoughts of God* could be gleaned from scripture. Those are the *opinions* of a governing body. They attempt to frame those specific instructions as helping individuals "identify certain practices as wrong, even though they are not specifically mentioned in God's Word."[79] Considering the title *Are you Making Jehovah's Thoughts Your Own,* one can clearly see they "require members to internalize the group's doctrine." That is the foremost indicator of *thought control* in Steve Hassan's BITE Model of Authoritarian Control.[80]

Those who accept such control are prone to the worst dangers imaginable. Individuals who forfeit their right to apply critical thought no longer exercise moral agency. They can be pressed into horrific activities under the pretense of being moral. They lose all ability to determine the difference. Their morality thus becomes the property of others.

An experiment at Yale University in 1961 by Stanley Milgram sought to understand how otherwise normal people performed atrocious acts under obedience to authority. Participants were directed by an authority figure (an actor in a lab coat) to use controls to administer painful shocks of electricity to another person. After listening to that person cry out in pain, participants were told to administer a higher, potentially lethal current of electricity. A surprising 65% complied with instructions. Milgram summarized: "the extreme willingness of adults to go to almost any lengths on the command of an authority constitutes the chief finding of the study and the fact most urgently demanding explanation. Ordinary people, simply doing their jobs, and without any particular hostility on their part, can become agents in a terrible destructive process. Moreover, even when the destructive effects of their work become patently clear, and they are asked to carry out actions incompatible with fundamental standards of morality, relatively few people have the resources needed to resist authority."[81]

In the Nuremburg trials, the Nazi defense that they *were just following orders* did not absolve them. Whether by personal weakness or a choice to sit comfortably in a little box of subcontracted ethics, they allowed someone else to pull the levers of their behavior. If such is the case, they remain responsible for at least that reckless decision. Following the logic of the Nazi defense, any individual who submits to the morals of others is equally unable to take credit for any *virtues* which resulted. If Jehovah's Witnesses live exemplary lives, that exemplary behavior is not their own. They are not agents of their own morality. They are not moral – in fact, they carry the same guilt as the Nazi officers who orchestrated the holocaust.

BRINGING REPROACH

One dangerous belief associated with religious authority is that the religion shoulders the reputation of God. This has been used to hide criminal acts like child abuse because it would "bring reproach upon the name of Jehovah." As if the reputation of the Creator could be tarnished because a child sought protection.

In defense of the JW Organization and similar religions, they find support for this belief in the Bible. In Paul's first letter to the Corinthians, he writes: "Suppose one of you wants to bring a charge against another believer. Should you take it to ungodly people to be judged? Why not take it to the Lord's people? Or don't you know that the Lord's people will judge the world?" (1 Corinthians 6:1,2). What message does that send? *We will judge the world. This religious structure is going to assume control.* Maybe that doesn't mean much for someone less religious. But for real believers, why would they listen to local authorities when their religion is poised to supplant them? This passage then becomes the scriptural force preventing victims from protection, enforced by what is the highest authority in their minds.

Even when a faith group has strict intolerance and robust judicial systems regarding child abuse, the persisting problem with keeping abuse internal is religious structures do not have the institutional settings to investigate such matters. They have no ability to keep the perpetrators off the streets and dubious means to tend to the mental health of victims.

It is an intensely delicate matter to question children about sexual assault. Extreme care is required so the interviewer's words do not affect the victim's statement. They must not ask questions or construct phrases that would suggest the assault was the fault of the victim. Police use task forces which receive specialized training for this form of questioning. Secular professionals have expertise and resources to examine physical evidence including DNA.[82] Mental health experts spend their careers training and gaining experience for the critical care of victims. These specialties offer a crucial advantage in the effort to investigate sexual abuse, to confine abusers, and to treat victims.

The consequences of subjecting children to interrogations at the hands of untrained men holding sheltered, archaic views of human sexuality, are not hard to imagine. Wounds are opened and shame is rubbed in. Interrogators cross lines and often find themselves aroused. Questions about how a victim's body reacted to sexual assault were common and highly inappropriate, as were reactions of disgust from interrogators. Until 1998, JW policies required victims to endure interrogations with three older men, facing their abuser, and without their parents present.[83]

It has been my experience that victims who muster the strength to come forward about sexual abuse demonstrate courage few could. Despite their mental fortitude, the tragic consequence of shame imposed by a representative of God is nearly impossible to overcome. Child victims can't distinguish between the words of elders and those of God. That is due to the programming for obedience and the belief that God directs the elders. Upon hearing an elder chastise them for immorality – even when that chastisement is misplaced – the child believes the highest moral authority in the universe is disgusted with that child and finds them worthy of punishment. How would that affect their sense of self-worth? How would it affect their confidence if they can't reconcile what they thought was right or wrong? When justice is unbalanced, what hope is there? When parents side with the organization to display loyalty to Jehovah, what safety, stability, or structure remains?

It seems that most child victims have learned to keep their abuse hidden. They learn to lie to themselves. Victims who come forward have been silenced.[84] Those who blow the whistle have been called liars and apostates.[85] I contend that organization owes those apostates a debt of gratitude. Without their courageous stand there would be no improvements to the organization. It was the child who was loyal all along, not the parents who abandoned them.

The evidence suggests Jehovah's Witnesses have been most resistant to improvement. The Australian Royal Commission into Institutional Responses to Child Sexual Abuses found that more than 1,000 members of Jehovah's Witnesses were accused of sexually abusing children in Australia. That is more than one alleged pedophile for every congregation. Those statistics were based only on files the organization provided. The commission stated: "there is otherwise no evidence before the Royal Commission of the Jehovah's Witness organisation having reported to police or other secular authority a single one of the 1,006 alleged perpetrators of child sexual abuse."[86] The report added: "the policies and practices are, by and large, wholly inappropriate and unsuitable for application in cases of child sexual abuse. The organisation's retention and continued application of policies such as the two-witness rule in cases of child sexual abuse shows a serious lack of understanding of the nature of child sexual abuse."[87]

The *two-witness rule* refers to a JW policy where *sins* including child sexual assault will not be investigated or acted upon unless there were two witnesses to the act. One can only imagine how often an abuser would commit his heinous deeds with witnesses present. When children are offered only the one option for reporting and that option offers no chance of protection, those children never had protection.

This issue is not confined to Jehovah's Witnesses just in Australia. Lawsuits have been brought against the organization in several countries including the United States, Canada, and the UK.[88] As the media begins to shine their light on the dark reaches of this strangely sheltered religion, a pattern emerges of disturbing consistency. Beyond the façade of crisp suits and smiling faces, we find gross neglect for the needs of children, a disregard for individual determination, and an insistence to conceal crimes from local authorities.

The JW organization is acutely aware of child sex abuse claims within their congregations. They require elders to forward all such accusations to headquarters, and elders do not disobey.[89] The organization maintains a database of accused pedophiles and is on record for refusing – even on heavy penalty – to release it to authorities.[90] Most Jehovah's Witnesses would deny there are pedophiles within their congregations, and they wouldn't necessarily be lying. They wouldn't know. Despite the careful tracking of pedophiles, the organization does not appear to use that information to warn individuals in congregations. Elders are instructed to keep such information strictly confidential.[91]

In their online document *Jehovah's Witnesses' Scripturally Based Position on Child Protection,* the opening sentence reads: "The welfare of children is of utmost concern to Jehovah's Witnesses." Despite such attempts to offer assurance, there is stronger evidence to the contrary. *Shepherd the Flock of God* is a book that serves as a guideline for elders. It is not available to the public or even to regular JWs. An excerpt from Chapter 21 gives direction for the care of their buildings of worship: "When property damage occurs, quick action can go far in preventing further damage. Break-ins, thefts, arson, or other incidents of vandalism should be promptly reported to the local authorities." That is a reasonable guideline.

But let's contrast the concern they display for their *Kingdom Halls* with the safety of children. Instead of instructions to report to local authorities, Chapter 14 reads: "elders should immediately call the Legal Department for legal advice when the elders learn of an accusation of child abuse." That may not sound significant, but the Australian Royal Commission found this policy was of no benefit to victims. Calls from elders to the Branch Office resulted in zero calls to secular authorities. It appears they served only to protect the interests of the organization. There was little, if any, protection for victims. Why couldn't that policy include a call to police – the agency best able to investigate? Would they not want to know the results of an investigation equipped with better tools? They seem to when their buildings are vandalized.

I found only one positive advancement in recent years which would benefit children, and that was found in the elder's *Shepherd* book. The 2020 version reads: "Though it may be necessary for the elders to ask a few tactful questions to help an afflicted one express herself, they should avoid probing unnecessarily or repeatedly into the details of the abuse." This is a genuine improvement to earlier iterations of the document which required those inappropriate interrogations. I'm legitimately encouraged with this development. I think it will improve their judicial process. It's a shame it was the Australian government and a handful of courageous former victims who are most likely responsible the improvement. JW's late arrival to child safety should serve as convincing evidence there is no superior mind behind the writings of Watchtower. It also sheds doubt on their concern for the welfare of children.

REFUSING RESPONSIBILITY

In deflecting responsibility for the care of victims, the organization stated: "Jehovah's Witnesses have not sponsored any programs or activities that separate children from their parents at any time. Jehovah's Witnesses do not operate boarding schools or Sunday schools; they do not have youth groups, choirs or sponsor any programs for children; neither do they run orphanages, day-care centres, hospitals nor youth centres. Jehovah's Witnesses simply do not have the institutional settings that result in children being taken into their care, custody, supervision, control or authority."[92] Of course, this fails to acknowledge the common practice of pairing children with adults in *field service groups*, or that the vast majority of child abuse occurs within homes.[93] Perhaps offering some form of programs could offer children the shelter and activities they need for healthy development. It could serve as evidence of Watchtower's care, perhaps even justify their tax-free status. Instead, children are kept sheltered and vulnerable, taught to disregard their own sense of morals, and trained like elephant calves to be obedient to authority. If child safety were of *utmost* concern, one would think the organization would take decisive steps *regardless* of the impact to their reputation. At the very least, they could exert the same effort they do to protect their buildings.

The Australian Royal Commission (ARC) found, "it is apparent that the Governing Body retains authority over the general principle and framework of all publications in the name of the Jehovah's Witness organisation, and any view or perspective contrary to the Governing Body's interpretation of the Scriptures is not tolerated."[94] The Faithful Slave openly denounces individual thought and moral determination. With a tongue-in-cheek jostling, they refer to Jehovah's Witnesses as "good for nothing slaves."[95] Their self-appointed title, *Faithful Slave,* may be an attempt to set an example in humility for their minion slaves, though it would seem hard to exemplify humility while assuming all-knowing authority and none of the responsibility.

Following the ARC, the organization of Jehovah's Witnesses was asked to voluntarily compensate victims a modest amount of up to $150,000 and to accept certain recommendations. The organization would do no such thing. 224 non-government institutions agreed to compensate victims, another 156 signaled their intent to. As the deadline passed, only five institutions refused to take responsibility or to compensate victims. The Boys' Brigade NSW, Fairbridge Restored, Lakes Entrance Pony Club, Kenja Communications, and Jehovah's Witnesses.[96] The Catholic Church has received heavy scrutiny regarding child abuse. Yet the Catholic Church was not listed as refusing to help victims.

The irony of the JW refusal is that it does not absolve the organization, it demonstrates their responsibility. They had been offered an opportunity to hear victims, listen to legal experts, and benefit from the expertise of mental health professionals. Essentially, they were offered valuable consultation at the expense of Australia.

Despite this, the *Faithful Slave* holds to its opinions. They view themselves as the greater authority and they do not confine their opinions to themselves. They dictate the morals, ethics, policies, values, and life-decisions of millions of followers – people who are convinced it is Jehovah's organization. These are the institutional settings of the highest authority on Earth, and place upon the *Faithful Slave* the responsibility for all those decisions, morals, and actions of individual Jehovah's Witnesses – *especially* child sexual assault – because they take it upon themselves to control those thoughts and actions. Experts specifically warned them about their policies and the effects of their role, but they know better. They are, after all, Jehovah.

In response to those who think an organization cannot be held to blame for the actions of individuals, consider the following analogy:

THE ARSONISTS AND THE LANDLORD

If an arsonist burned down an apartment building, you would blame the fire on the arsonist, not the landlord, would you not?

But what if, in the investigation, it was found that people died while trying to escape because the fire exits had been intentionally blocked by the landlord? What if it was found the landlord had disabled all the fire alarms? Tenants had tried to complain about the disabled safety features but were evicted for doing so.

What if you found that in addition to the burned building, the landlord owned thousands of similar buildings around the world and the same safety features were dismantled in each? Tenants in those buildings had also been evicted when they warned others. The landlord was aware arsonists were intentionally targeting his buildings and that they were likely doing so because of the disabled safety features. Despite being aware of the arsonists, the landlord insists on policies which protect arsonists from prosecution. The landlord knows the names and locations of arsonists, even maintaining a database of their contacts, but will not alert tenants who are living in the same building. In strange defiance, the landlord refuses to supply authorities with his database even when subpoenaed by court.

In such a case I would assert the landlord is more culpable than any single arsonist.

The Faithful Slave (Jehovah) functions precisely like that landlord. They preside over thousands of congregations worldwide. They block the exits for victims by imposing fear tactics; discouraging external reporting; claiming to be Guardians Of the Doctrine; isolating individuals from the world; and insisting that *two witnesses are required to deal with a child abuser.* They disable the alarms with their rules on confidentiality; silencing of dissent; instructing elders to cover up abuse; destroying evidence;[97]

accusing victims of lying; and preventing believers from listening to former JWs.

Perhaps it is time for individual Jehovah's Witness parents to take the newest policies on child protection seriously: "*Parents* have the primary responsibility for the protection, safety, and instruction of their children."[98] Because when the time comes for authorities to take action to protect a child, where will the organization point their fingers? Who truly let that child down?

READY TO OBEY

I would agree that most individual Jehovah's Witnesses abhor child abuse. But they succumb to a more dangerous belief – that their leadership is directed by God. If there are any illusions that this belief is harmless, consider one of many weekly articles which were taught in JW public meetings. Notice how the Watchtower outlines the degree to which JWs must obey their leaders. Here congregation elders are referred to as *shepherds*, and the governing body, as *dukes*.

> *In the near future, Jehovah's apparently vulnerable people will come under attack from the modern-day 'Assyrian,' whose intent will be to wipe them out... At that time, the life-saving direction that we receive from Jehovah's organization may not appear practical from a human standpoint. All of us must be ready to obey any instructions we may receive, whether these appear sound from a strategic or human standpoint or not. Now is the time for any who may be putting their trust in secular education, material things, or human institutions to adjust their thinking.*

Watchtower, Shepherds and Dukes, November 2013

All of us must be ready to obey any instructions we may receive, whether these appear sound... or not. Is this cause for concern? Considering the findings of the Milgard study on authority, is it possible JWs could become agents in a terrible destructive process? Many Jehovah's Witnesses are actively shunning their own children for no other reason than their child chooses not to accept the governing body as their moral authority. If the Faithful Slave can convince otherwise good people to cease natural affection and shun their own children, what boundaries really exist? In obedience to Jehovah many JWs have accepted years in prison while offered release simply by relinquishing that loyalty.[99] Tens of thousands have shown their loyalty to Jehovah by refusing life-saving blood treatment, losing their lives as a result.[100] They insist the decision to do so is their own, failing to connect they were commanded to adopt those thoughts. "We make Jehovah's thoughts our own."[101]

The utter dominance of individual values and morals by the *Faithful Slave* put at their disposal more than eight million followers with limited capacity for individual determination and who will go to any lengths to prove their loyalty. Is it possible they could be manipulated toward a tragic outcome?

If the organization claimed Jehovah gave specific instruction to hide in underground bunkers, would they comply? This isn't a far-fetched hypothesis. JW conventions and online videos have been projecting that precise scenario.[102] The minds of JWs in recent years have been programmed to obey such commands without question.

To understand the thought process which impels good people to do the unthinkable, consider an entirely hypothetical situation where the above bunker scenario has occurred, and congregations of Jehovah's Witnesses are now hidden underground.

THE BUNKER

A JW parent learns their child has been sexually assaulted by a JW elder. The elder has been appointed by Jehovah – as they are. Attempts to confront the elder would be punished as murmuring, and disloyalty to God.

Led to believe that expulsion from the bunker means certain death, what would that parent do? In their eyes, protecting their child could result in the death of both. Jehovah knows best and can be relied on to fix all matters. The exits are blocked. The alarms are disabled. They are surrounded by people with no capability for independent moral determination – desperate to prove their loyalty to Jehovah.

In similar situations JW parents have indeed abandoned their child – to death even.[103] Even when the destructive effects of their work become patently clear, and they are asked to carry out actions incompatible with fundamental standards of morality, relatively few have the resources needed to resist authority.

Regardless of what the future holds for the Organization, I submit that individual Jehovah's Witnesses, isolated from the rest of the world, already live in that bunker. Regrettably for them, there is nothing loyal about forfeiting their moral independence or abandoning their children. No amount of favor they garner from religious authorities will improve their standing with God.

If you have been placed in a position above others, are you automatically going to behave like a despot? Remember who you are and whom you govern – that they are kinsmen, brothers by nature, fellow descendants of Zeus.
Marcus Aurelius

2.2 SWORD OF TRUTH

No opinion can be heretical, but that which is not true [...] Conflicting falsehoods we can comprehend; but truths can never war against each other. I affirm, therefore, that we have nothing to fear from the results of our enquiries, provided they be followed in the laborious but secure road of honest induction.

Adam Sedgwick (1785 – 1873), Geologist, Priest

Billions of people believe God wrote a book and we should model our lives on its contents. But they don't all agree which book that is. Perhaps we all could agree that if people accepted the product of mere men as God's Word, they are likely to find themselves at a disadvantage.

If God wrote a book for humans, couldn't he keep it on "the cloud" and make it available to anyone wishing to download its contents? What do you think God would include in it? What advice would it offer? What insights about our future or past could be revealed? The timeless information bestowed on humanity by a creator would leave us in awe, wouldn't you think?

Great authors can keep us engaged through every twist and turn. They can draw out emotions and make points which are clear, concise, and without leaving readers confused or disoriented.

The great writings of humanity bestow upon us significant value. I think of Marcus Aurelius, Leo Tolstoy, or John Steinbeck and I can only imagine what the transcribed thoughts of a mind superior to humans could offer – the mind responsible for weaving the fabric of the physical universe and igniting the spark of life. Imagine the sageness produced through billions of years of careful observation, and the ensuing stories of rich moral insight, unmatched witticism, and truism – a guide to enrich yourself with the literary therapy only a creator could offer.

Is that your impression of the Bible? Are you left in awe of its contents? I remember saying so. But an honest review of my honesty would have disagreed. It was rare that I looked forward to reading the Bible and there were plenty of times I dreaded it.

It is the bestselling book of all time. That is a true statement. It has exerted its influence over our calendar, our language, and judicial systems. It has influenced art, music, and literature across the globe. It has cultivated war, unity, wealth, poverty, and numerous religions. How could so much fanfare be wrong?

The Creator breathed his influence into human authors, and this resulted in a collection of written works for which we should spend our days contemplating and using to shape our morals. I genuinely believed that. I had unbending faith the Bible had successfully predicted major world events in advance, and those events could be independently verified by historical, third-party records. I believed the prophet Isaiah predicted the conquests of the Persian king, and did so using his name Cyrus, and before Cyrus was born (Isaiah 44:28 – 45:1). I was convinced the prophet Daniel predicted the march of world powers from Babylon through to Rome and on to the Anglo-American alliance (Daniel 7). I had no reason to doubt that Jesus predicted the destruction of the Jewish temple decades before it occurred (Matthew 24).

The November 2007 issue of Awake!, quotes Proverbs 14:15 saying, "a fool will believe anything; smart people watch their step." That is a good proverb. The article goes on to support the proverb: "Yes, only a fool would go through life blindly accepting everything he hears, basing his decisions and actions on frivolous advice or baseless teachings. Misplacing our trust —like stepping onto rotten planks—can lead to disaster."[104]

These words then led into a small series of articles intended to form trust in the Bible. It starts with a claim for the Bible's uniqueness, which few could dispute. Five reasons were then listed "why millions of people are convinced that the Bible is worthy of trust." The reasons listed were *historical soundness, candor and honesty, internal harmony, scientific harmony,* and *fulfilled prophecy.* Those were the reasons I had been trained to recite. And they were convincing – so long as I only read Watchtower publications.

2.2.1 Science

Where were you when I laid the earth's foundation? Tell me, if you understand. Who marked off its dimensions? Surely you know! Who stretched a measuring line across it? On what were its footings set, or who laid its cornerstone?

Job 38:4-6

Within its first verses, the Bible projects its story of the formation of Earth. The creation account in Genesis could be deduced to say Earth is about 6000 years old. The earth emerges in the story as dark and formless before God produces the light of the very first day. From that point it describes the six days of creation. God produces celestial bodies, Earth's terraforming, the flora, the fauna and then humans. All of which took six days (Genesis 1:1-31).

For centuries, the scientific community upheld that the Bible was accurate. But in the 1660s, the study of geology made suggestions that the Earth was far older than 6000 years. Geologists observed how soil and rock layers accumulate at a reasonably predictable rate and that could help determine the age of geological features. The measuring of oceanic concentrations of salinity and the counting of fossil layers gave rise to early theories. Researchers started to determine that the planet is at least 75,000 years, but perhaps as old as 400 million. Others suggested the Earth was indefinitely old.[105]

Evolutionary biologists found they could reasonably calculate how long it took for certain biological features to develop. Using this calculation, they determined Earth had to have been billions of years old to account for the generational increments required for modern life.

In 1956, radiometric testing offered a stunningly accurate assessment of the age of rocks. Radioactive materials form other elements at a constant rate of decay. When calculating the concentration of those elements against the radioactive isotope, the date to which that element formed could be calculated. After samples were tested it was determined that rocks on earth were formed 4.5 billion years ago.[106] Since 1956 this age of 4.5 billion years has held its ground after multiple tests on multiple rocks and using at least 40 different testing methods.

Lunar rocks were tested along the theory that elements of both the moon and Earth likely formed around the same time. These rocks were also found to be 4.5 billion years and strengthened the case for dating Earth. The examination of cosmic ray tracks on lunar rocks using an electron microscope calculates the same. The *latest* calculations for evolutionary history set the earliest of our ancestors to 3.5 – 3.8 billion years ago.[107] This is solid scientific confirmation of a 4.5-billion-year-old planet. There is no reasonable means to dismiss the scientific age of the Earth. There are no credible scientists who do.

As the evidence builds, Bible-believers are forced to either reject the science or find a way to make both plausible. Jehovah's Witnesses rely upon an abstract interpretation of the creation story. They reason that the six creation days are figurative and not meant to represent six literal 24-hour days. *These figurative six days could have been millions or billions of years, because we don't know how long a day is to Jehovah.* But if the bible were not literal about a six-day creation period, 6000 years ago, what else is presented literally, but intended to be abstract? How could anyone tell the difference? Is there a key available to decipher this?

I was taught, like mainstream Christians, that evolution was a false theory which could never be proven. I was told evolution is widely disputed among scientists. But scientists do not agree. "There is no controversy in the scientific community about whether evolution has occurred. On the contrary the evidence supporting descent with modification, as Charles Darwin termed it, is both overwhelming and compelling. In the century and a half since Darwin, scientists have uncovered exquisite details about many of the mechanisms that underlie biological variation, inheritance, and natural selection, and they have shown how these mechanisms lead to biological change over time. Because of this immense body of evidence, scientists treat the occurrence of evolution as one of the most securely established of scientific facts" (Science Evolution and Creationism). [108]

Since humans started herding animals, they understood they could choose favorable traits and breed them until those traits were permanently installed. Selective breeding has provided pets which fit our lifestyle. Chickens and cows have been bred to produce so much food their muscles and skeletons barely resemble those of their ancestors. We can watch evolution unfold in a petri dish as microbes transform from generation to generation. Humans are getting taller. Whether by natural selection, genetic drift, or selective breeding, we can witness the physiological adjustment of both plants and animals. They change. [109]

The fossil record has preserved a timeline of layered evidence for evolution, and when combined with geological findings, this evidence is sound. When we analyze genetic sequences, we can trace back the generations of all living things showing how they branched from common ancestors. [110]

Despite concluding evolution was true – at least on a small scale – I tried to make the Bible stories work. The official JW doctrine says that while variation among the species is entirely possible, it is not possible for organisms to branch out into different species without the aid of God. [111] *Jehovah created the animals by their* kinds. *Any deviation from that dogma is a lie from Satan.* But it was evident to me that if variation occurs within the species, what stops it from crossing that imaginary line?

Humanity has witnessed diseases evolve, languages evolve, religions evolve. Everything changes with time, and it is not rational to assert that while the Bible was figurative about the six-days of creation, it was now literal about God creating every species personally and magically. To maintain my faith in the bible, I secretly theorized God used evolution in his creation process.

While remaining faithful to my religious teachings, I researched biblical archaeology. It seemed to me this field of science would provide the most promising evidence to support Bible accuracy. I googled every possible link to solidify stories of Noah's Flood, the Garden of Eden, and the Temple of Solomon. Unfortunately, every exciting discovery came from a Christian with an agenda or a pseudoscientific "professional" with a poor reputation and weak evidence.[112] That's not to say my Google searches failed to produce hits. The Christian lobby has seemingly endless funding and the internet is clogged with websites proudly displaying their fundamentalist perceptions of science.

As a JW I was puzzled to read how paleontologists and archaeologists reported civilizations which were tens of thousands, or hundreds of thousands of years old. Obviously, this conflicted with the Genesis account of first humans. Even if we fudged the Bible account enough to explain Earth's origins, we're still left with a clear biblical timeline which dates the first humans to 6000 years ago. There wasn't a logical way to sidestep that dilemma. *The researchers must be wrong. How could those studies possibly know if something was 1000 years old or 100,000?* I dismissed those studies for having improper conclusions and employing faulty testing methods.

Of course, I never studied those methods or their accuracy. I wish I had. I would have found that hundreds of those studies make similar claims; that they are tied together with interacting data from independent teams; and they can produce credible, peer-reviewed conclusions.

After considering the science, it is difficult to deny that humans have been on the earth and building cities and civilizations for tens of thousands of years at *least*. We have a human skeleton verified to be 196,000 years old. We can trace the Australian Aboriginal genome back 75,000 years.[113] Despite this, a Gallup survey in 2019 found 40% of American adults believed "God created human beings pretty much in their present form at one time within the last 10,000 years or so."[114]

Having experienced a sheltered form of imposed ignorance, I can sympathize with those 40% of Americans. When your values have been arranged in such a way that disagreeing with a book is on par with the most irreverent defilement of all things holy – with being *disloyal* – the incentive to look beyond the curtain falls flat. It's much easier to bask in the embrace of your spiritual peers.

Another mental hurdle is how the information is presented. Scientific findings don't make the same strong definitive statements as false statements. By its very nature, science seeks to know. It seeks because it doesn't yet know the things. In my dogmatic years I never found that humble style of scientific assertions convincing. But I have come to feel deep respect for that form of humility since.

Legitimate scientific writings read drier than the simple, affirmative, and outlandish style of evangelists. Academic studies often use unfamiliar terminology, repelling most people. Perhaps, though, the larger barrier to public knowledge is that scientific research is far less accessible than religious evangelism.

While performing research for this project, I made it an exercise to follow the most likely means the average person would employ to learn about each subject: search engines like Google, Bing, or Yahoo. On subjects related to religion, the results overwhelmingly directed me toward sites which promoted the Bible and religion. Perhaps this experience was a result of the algorithm picking up my preference for the Bible, which seems unlikely. Either way, academic findings were far harder to find and often didn't show up after 5 or more pages of results. Google Scholar did provide better results, but the information was often held behind a paywall. It isn't ridiculous that 40% of Americans believe the Biblical narrative. What access do they have to information – information convincing enough they would renounce what trusted people had guaranteed since childhood?

Christian websites use those same pivots as Watchtower – making claims that certain scientific studies are inaccurate and that scientists are divided on the subject. They say data was misinterpreted or that carbon dating can't be trusted.[115] But the more one reads into the testing methods in scientific studies, the more one is forced to concede that the researchers are far more likely to be correct than colorful Christian websites who have performed no such research.

For most of my life I blinded myself to fascinating data, allowing my dogma to eclipse intelligence. I didn't need to see the light. I already knew the Truth. When I first recognized I was wrong the humiliation tore painfully through my chest. I resisted the new concepts vehemently – until I couldn't.

The silver lining around my embarrassment is that a door opened. For decades I had been confined to a little box of beliefs. I remember thinking humanity had reached the limits of what it could understand scientifically. What a profound miscalculation. But with this new door opened, I was free to learn what I had previously dismissed – fascinating data. I learned the particulars of radiocarbon dating. I learned about stratigraphy, seriation, thermo-luminescence dating, and dendro-chronology, and how combining many of those techniques paint a surprisingly clear picture of when a plant or animal lived, or when a site or object had last been touched by humans or fire.

The process impressed upon me the dangers of listening to those who *know*. Those who have *the truth*. When reading from professionals who have performed careful research, you don't hear the same tone of certainty as from those who have based their conclusions on conclusions already formed. When I had performed what I thought was research, I had an agenda. To progress, I would need to accept that a person cannot learn if they already know what they are searching for.

I had been taught, and I believed, the Bible was scientifically accurate. I was convinced Isaiah described the circle of the earth long before people knew the earth was round; the Israelites had divine insight, evident because they buried their poop; the book of Job miraculously explained the earth hung upon nothing. In retrospect, it should have been suspicious that biblical literalists used science to prove the accuracy of their position, but then claimed they knew more than science.

2.2.2 History

Whatever is has already been, and what will be has been before; and God will call the past to account.

Ecclesiastes 3:15

Articles of the Watchtower often boasted of the Bible's synchronicity with documented history. The November 2011 issue states: "Secular experts have repeatedly questioned the Bible's accuracy. Yet, when more evidence is uncovered, the Bible record has time and again been vindicated."[116] As Jehovah's Witnesses, we trusted those words implicitly. It never occurred to me there was considerable evidence to the contrary. When I found it, I felt betrayed.

The November 2007 Awake reported: "Before 1993, there was no proof outside the Bible to support the historicity of David [...] That year, however, archaeologists uncovered in northern Israel a basalt stone, dated to the ninth century B.C.E., that experts say bears the words 'House of David' and 'king of Israel.'"[117] I can't remember reading this article as a JW. If I did, I likely would have sided with whatever the Awake said.

The Bible describes in detail a united kingdom of both Jews and Israelites with a capital in Jerusalem – palaces and temples – a regional power – and, as I will discuss below, none of those features have been found. Regional powers push their way into the historical records of surrounding nations, yet no third-party documents verify the existence of David or Solomon. Regional powers leave physical scars and signatures upon the landscape. Yet in a small tract of land, subject to the world's most voracious and well-funded archaeologists, neither David's Palace, Solomon's Temple, nor the tombs of either have been located.[118]

In the early 1800s, Adam Sedgewick, President of the Geological Society in London, promoted the Diluvium Theory, where the biblical flood was thought to account for many geological features. After an expedition to Scotland, Sedgwick would later write: "If I have been converted in part from the diluvian theory [...] it was [...] by my own gradual improved experience, and by communicating with those about me. Perhaps I may date my change of mind (at least in part) from our journey in the Highlands, where there are so many indications of local diluvial operations." Sedgwick allowed further evidence to change his mind – a respectable competence. By 1834 he had become more outspoken, and referring to *scriptural geologists,* he wrote: "They have committed the folly and *sin* of dogmatizing." I would think those were daring words for a man who was both a geologist and a priest. And with his change of view, the academic community was increasingly willing to suggest the Bible account could be inaccurate.[119]

William Albright (1891 – 1971) found renown in the field of archaeology and remained devoted to the Biblical account with only few exceptions. Albright insisted: "As a whole, the picture in Genesis is historical, and there is no reason to doubt the general accuracy of the biographical details."[120]

In the 1930s, archaeologist John Garstang announced he had found the ruins of walls in Jericho matching the biblical timeline for the conquest of that city. But he would later revise that claim, finding evidence those walls had been destroyed in an earlier era and centuries before the biblical account.[121]   This later finding was then confirmed by renowned archaeologist Kathleen Kenyon and then separately by Piotr Bienkowski.[122] It appears from this and similar findings that Jericho, like other Canaanite cities, was abandoned long before the Hebrews left Egypt. The writer of the account was likely aware of the ruins, but not the circumstance of their fall.

As evidence has collected from Bible lands, the consensus among archaeologists has drifted far from literalism. In 1999, Tel Aviv University archaeologist and professor, Ze'ev Herzog, made clear: "the Israelites were never in Egypt, did not wander in the desert, did not conquer the land in a military campaign and did not pass it on to the 12 tribes of Israel. Perhaps even harder to swallow is that the united monarchy of David and Solomon, which is described by the Bible as a regional power, was at most a small tribal kingdom. And it will come as an unpleasant shock to many that the

God of Israel, YHWH, had a female consort and that the early Israelite religion adopted monotheism only in the waning period of the monarchy and not at Mount Sinai."[123]

The Israelites were polytheistic until Josiah's day? Jehovah had a wife? When I first read these findings, I felt yet another tremor decimating the remnants of my belief structure. *I can't even believe the Bible? Maybe this archaeologist is a wingnut. Maybe he holds an atheistic agenda.* But Herzog's conclusions are not isolated or unique. They are the running consensus among the most trusted experts in the study of archaeology. It was I who was biased for assuming they were biased. Ze'ev Herzog, like many others in his field, entered archaeology with the intent of supporting his belief in the Bible. The evidence, instead, discredited it.

After decades of digging around Jerusalem and using the most advanced technologies, Israel Finkelstein is "widely regarded as a leading scholar in the archaeology of the Levant and as a foremost applicant of archaeological knowledge to reconstructing biblical Israelite history."[124] He published a highly controversial book with Neil Silberman in 2001 entitled *The Bible Unearthed: Archaeology's New Vision of Ancient Israel and the Origin of its Sacred Texts.* There they support Herzog's positions in detail. "An archaeological analysis of the patriarchal conquest, judges, and United Monarchy narratives [shows] that while there is no compelling archaeological evidence for any of them, there is clear archaeological evidence that places the stories themselves in a late 7th-century BCE context." The early books of the Bible are purported to be written 3500 years ago. But they describe conditions which would not exist for another 1000 years. This would include mention of the Aramaeans who wouldn't encroach upon Israel until the 9th century BCE. And in Genesis 37, Joseph is sold to Ishmaelites who had camels loaded with gum (spices). But the earliest evidence for camels in the area is 930 BCE, 1000 years later. A more likely setting for this story was after the Assyrians opened trade to Arabia in the 8 – 7th centuries BCE. After that happened, it was common for traders to use camels and to trade gum (spices). In Genesis 45 Joseph encourages his family to join him in Goshen, but that area would not be named Goshen until the 6th century BCE.[125]

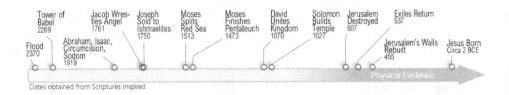

Dates obtained from Scriptures Inspired

Egyptologist, Zahi Hawass, demonstrated awareness of the sensitive nature of Biblical criticism. When speaking about the Exodus account he asserted, "really, it's a myth [...] This is my career as an archaeologist. I should tell them the truth. If the people are upset, that is not my problem."[126]

Bible stories do not appear to match the material evidence until the timeline reaches the 8th century BCE, suggesting it was then or later when the accounts were written. The authors simply did not have the perspective to accurately describe an earlier period. They knew Jericho's walls had fallen. But they didn't know when, or how.

> There is no evidence of a United Monarchy, no evidence of a capital in Jerusalem or of any coherent, unified political force that dominated western Palestine, let alone an empire of the size the legends describe. We do not have evidence for the existence of kings named Saul, David or Solomon; nor do we have evidence for any temple at Jerusalem in this early period. What we do know of Israel and Judah of the tenth century does not allow us to interpret this lack of evidence as a gap in our knowledge and information about the past, a result merely of the accidental nature of archeology. There is neither room nor context, no artifact or archive that points to such historical realities in Palestine's tenth century. One cannot speak historically of a state without a population. Nor can one speak of a capital without a town. Stories are not enough.[127]

Thomas Thompson, Biblical Scholar, Theologian

Not all people were impressed with Finkelstein's book. One of the book's sharpest critics was William Dever, an authority in his own right. But in 2001 Dever also stated: "after a century of exhaustive investigation, all respectable archaeologists have given up hope of recovering any context that would make Abraham, Isaac, or Jacob credible 'historical figures.'"[128]

> *From the beginnings of what we call biblical archaeology, perhaps 150 years ago, scholars, mostly western scholars, have attempted to use archaeological data to prove the Bible. And for a long time it was thought to work. William Albright, the great father of our discipline, often spoke of the 'archaeological revolution.' Well, the revolution has come but not in the way that Albright thought. The truth of the matter today is that archaeology raises more questions about the historicity of the Hebrew Bible and even the New Testament than it provides answers.*[129]

William G. Dever, Distinguished Professor of Near Eastern Archaeology, Lycoming College

Dating back to the late '60s, there appeared to be some form of division between archaeologists, split along lines of either *Minimalists* or *Maximalists*. The term *Maximalist* referred to those who took the Bible as a literal, historical record. They believed the depictions of early kings was accurate, even if they had to wait for supporting evidence to uncover. *Minimalists* allowed their evidentiary findings to guide their conclusions. They generally viewed Bible stories set before the 6th century BCE (Josiah's reign) as containing only fragments of genuine historicity. But in 2010, Professor Emeritus of Biblical Studies, Phillip Davies, contended there was no such division.

> *For 'historicity' really is a non-issue. It has been accepted for decades that the Bible is not in principle either historically reliable or unreliable, but both: [...] Apart from the well-funded (and fundamentalist) "biblical archaeologists," we are in fact nearly all "minimalists" now.*[130]

Phillip Davies, University of Sheffield, England

Some have argued that because Jerusalem had been destroyed on multiple occasions, evidence supporting bible stories could have been destroyed. But the destruction of the city was never absolute. How could other artifacts survive but not those which support the Bible account? Are we to believe only the artifacts supporting the Bible were destroyed? *Perhaps their destruction was a ploy of Satan to mislead us.* Or so might have been my JW response. But even if we entertained the possibility that the devil somehow destroyed evidence which supported the Bible, we're left with this statement: "Secular experts have repeatedly questioned the Bible's accuracy. Yet, when more evidence is uncovered, the Bible record has time and again been vindicated." And that is not a true statement. So who really is trying to mislead people?

How much of this information was available to the writers of Watchtower – to the Faithful Slave – which they chose to conceal from their readers? This is what bothered me most. I never knew this information existed. But I now know that *they* knew. And with that I must conclude I was intentionally misled. I was misled to believe the Bible was historically accurate. It is not.

2.2.3 Authorship

You must not listen to the words of that prophet or dreamer. The Lord your God is testing you to find out whether you love him with all your heart and with all your soul.

Deuteronomy 13:3

Does it matter whether we accurately know the author of a manuscript? Some maintain the works should be judged solely on their merit. But what if your intent were not to judge it? What if your intent were to earnestly get to know the writings? What if you had a desire to wring out from those words every drop of conceivable intelligence? I would think in such a case knowing the perspective of the author would be important.

As Jehovah's Witnesses we took into consideration the background of the writers when we discussed scripture. At least until my last meeting in 2016, one of our chief study aids was the book *All Scripture is Inspired of God*. A chapter was dedicated to each book of the Bible where "the setting of each book is described, and information given concerning the writer, the time of writing, and in some cases the *period* covered."[131] It was admittedly a good format for learning the text. Knowing whether the writer was a participant, a first-hand witness, or a third-party scribe, shifts our attachment to the text and helps us understand the writer's intent.

Jews, Christians, and Muslims believe it was Moses who wrote the first five books of the Bible – those known as the *Pentateuch*, or *Torah*. According to Watchtower's *Scripture Inspired* book it happened around 1500 BCE while the Israelites were camped at Mount Sinai. But what if those words were penned nearly a thousand years later? What if they were written in Babylon with help from Babylonian priests? Admittedly, that sounds like a stretch. Yet the strongest available evidence suggests that could be the scenario. Would it change how people viewed the message? Would the merit of its contents change?

As a faithful JW I found it difficult to believe those books were written by Moses. Numbers 12:3 says that Moses was "more humble than any other person on earth." Not exactly words one would expect from the humblest man. Moses also supposedly wrote the words in Deuteronomy 34:10-12: "**Since then,** no prophet has risen in Israel like Moses, whom the Lord knew face to face [...] For no one has ever shown the mighty power or performed the awesome deeds that Moses did in the sight of all Israel." *Since then? Moses wrote* since then *while describing events after his death? When was this written?* Even as a 12-year-old, my mind discerned that those words would only make sense if written after numerous prophets lived and died and well after Moses. It stands to reason that at least some of the Pentateuch had been written by someone other than Moses. Despite this, the Watchtower maintains its support for Mosaic authorship.

> *Moreover, the events and statements in the book fit exactly the historical situation and surroundings. The references to Egypt, Canaan, Amalek, Ammon, Moab, and Edom are faithful to the times, and place-names are accurately stated. Archaeology continues to bring to light proof upon proof as to the integrity of Moses' writings. Henry H. Halley writes:* "Archaeology has been speaking so loudly of late that it is causing a decided reaction toward the conservative view [that Moses wrote the Pentateuch]. The theory that writing was unknown in Moses' day is absolutely exploded. And every year there are being dug up in Egypt, Palestine and Mesopotamia, evidences, both in inscriptions and earth layers, that the narratives of the [Hebrew Scriptures] are true historical records. And 'scholarship' is coming to have decidedly more respect for the tradition of Mosaic authorship." *Thus, even external evidence supports Deuteronomy, as well as the rest of the Pentateuch, as being a genuine, authentic record made by God's prophet Moses.*[132]
>
> All Scripture is Inspired of God and Beneficial

It appears the Watchtower had to dig through the compost for support here. It would be difficult to consider Henry H. Halley's words as *external* evidence. Halley was not an archaeologist. He was a Christian pastor who lived between 1874 and 1965. The above quote was taken from *Halley's Bible Handbook* which was originally published in 1924.[133] It seems dishonest that the Watchtower and other Christian apologists pass these off as *relevant* or *external*.

Israel Finkelstein, on the other hand, *is* relevant. Finkelstein *is* an archaeologist. And his suggestion that the Pentateuch appears written no earlier than the 8th century BCE is backed with convincing physical evidence – something hardly accomplished by biblical maximalists. And by narrowing the window for when those stories were recorded, Finkelstein brings us closer to knowing who the authors may have been.

I remember my first serious attempt to read the entire Bible. I was 12 and couldn't make it through the prophetic books. But I did manage to get past the first five. My first successful attempt from-cover-to-cover was when I was 16. The exercise altered my view of the scriptures and set my thoughts apart from JWs who had never completed the reading. That group included all my peers.

It was a difficult read. The Bible repeats the same story often, and that can leave the reader bogged with redundancy. It describes lineages and materials exhaustively, and the value of those details is not readily apparent. It is not arranged in chronological order, which makes a cover-to-cover read confusing. It appears to contradict itself often, and sometimes within the same book. Deuteronomy 5:9 reads: "I, the Lord your God, am a jealous God, punishing the children for the sin of the parents." But then in 24:16 we find: "Parents are not to be put to death for their children, nor children put to death for their parents." Lucky for me, I had one elder who was both well-versed in the Bible, and a skillful teacher. He had an explanation for each contradiction.

I wasn't the only one who was disturbed by discrepancies in Moses' account. Others have raised the same and stronger, better-researched criticisms. The 3rd century scholar Origen responded to skeptics of Moses' authorship – indicating people were voicing their doubts before the whole of the Bible was compiled. The eleventh century Jewish court physician, Isaac ibn Yashush, pointed out that Genesis 36 refers to Edomite kings who did not exist until much later than Moses.[134]

One unsettling thought I did not share with others resulted from reading Ezra chapter 7. The story is set 100 years after Babylon took the Jews into exile. They were since released and asked to rebuild walls. I immediately noted how often Ezra promotes his knowledge of the scriptures. In just the first chapter, he does so four times – twice as a quote from King Artaxerxes of Persia. Ezra quotes a letter he received from the king starting in verse 12: "Artaxerxes, king of kings, *to Ezra the priest, teacher of the Law* of the God of heaven: Greetings [...] You are sent by the king and his seven advisers to inquire about Judah and Jerusalem with regard to the Law of your God, which is in your hand [...] And you, Ezra, in accordance with *the wisdom of your God, which you possess*, appoint magistrates and judges to administer justice to all the people of Trans-Euphrates—all who know the laws of your God. And *you are to teach any who do not know them.*" I have since learned that when a writer emphasizes a point they were not called upon to, it's likely because that ideal had been challenged. Either way, the writer of Ezra felt it important to make clear he was well-versed in the Law of Moses – the Torah.[i]

Another seemingly unnecessary emphasis was describing *the Law,* not as *God's Law,* or simply *The Law* – but the Law *commanded through Moses*. Why would that need to be emphasized?

What I found especially hard to believe was that Jews would accept scrolls supplied by a Persian king as authentic. Yet Nehemiah says the people gathered to tell "Ezra the teacher of the Law to bring out the Book of the Law of Moses, which the Lord had commanded for Israel" (Nehemiah 8:1). After I slugged for weeks through that law, I found it hard to believe

---

[i] Although some use the terms *Torah* and *Pentateuch* interchangeably, I will generally use the term "Torah" in reference to Deuteronomy, because it appears that what 5th century BCE Jews referred to as the Law of Moses consisted only of Deuteronomy 5-26. The Pentateuch, by contrast, includes Deuteronomy – as well as Genesis, Exodus, Leviticus, and Numbers.

anyone would be so eager. It became increasingly incredulous when Nehemiah described their reactions. "All the people had been weeping as they listened to the words of the Law." *Hmmm. Ok. I might believe that. I had felt like weeping through the reading myself.*

But I was suspicious that the Jews were reacting as if they had never heard this law before. And that was confirmed when "they found written in the Law, which the Lord had commanded through Moses, that the Israelites were to live in temporary shelters during the festival of the seventh month" (8:14). They were learning things they didn't know. These were new scriptures to them. For them to accept as authentic new scrolls – laws brought to them from Babylon on the command of a Persian king – is nonsense. If they had accepted such a thing without trepidation, then it is just as likely they were duped by a fabrication of the Torah. But as my Bible teacher would explain: *Jesus quoted from those books so they must be true.* And that seemed enough to shelve my concerns.

Scholars in the 18th and 19th centuries risked their careers and perhaps their lives to search out the authors of the Bible.[135] The findings of those investigators would be compiled by Julius Wellhausen in *Prolegomena to the History of Israel,* published in 1883. Regarding Wellhausen, the Encyclopedia Britannica says: "his major writings put forth the view that the books of the Pentateuch were not written by Moses but were the result of oral traditions that evolved over time from a nomadic religion."[136] The result was the *documentary hypothesis,* which argues the Pentateuch had four different authors who lived much later than Moses. This theory has served as the dominant model for biblical scholars until the last quarter of the 20th century.

The indicators which brought those scholars to the *documentary hypothesis* were the use of different names for God – *YHWH* vs *Elohim* – and the existence of *doublets* – where the same story was told at least twice. The creation of the world (Gen 1:1-2:3 / Gen 2:4b-25); the covenant between Abraham and God (Gen 15 / Gen 17); Abraham claiming his wife was his sister (Gen 12:10-20 / Gen 20:1-18 / Gen 26:6-14); Jacob becoming Israel

(Gen32:25-33 / Gen 35:9-10); and Moses getting water from a rock (Exo17:2-7 / Num20:2-13); are all examples of doublets. They were told at least twice with varying and often conflicting details. These varying accounts each appear to line up as being written by one of four different authors.

In 1987 Richard Elliot Friedman published *Who Wrote the Bible?* He characterized the *documentary hypothesis* authors as follows: "The document that was associated with the divine name Yahweh/Jehovah was dubbed the *Jahwist* or *J*. The document that was identified as referring to the deity as God (in Hebrew, Elohim) was called the *Elohist*, or *E*. The third document, by far the largest, included most of the legal sections and concentrated a great deal on matters having to do with priests, and so was called the *Priestly* author, or *P*. And the source that was found only in the book of Deuteronomy was called the *Deuteronomist*, or *D*."[137]

J and E showed little regard for the priestly class, instead emphasizing the importance of prophets, and showing favoritism toward one King or another. "We get a consistent series of clues that the E stories were written by someone concerned with Israel and the J stories by someone concerned with Judah."[138] These fit with Finkelstein's archaeological record which determined that when Israel was destroyed, Jerusalem grew rapidly from a hillside village to a bustling city with the influx of Israelite refugees. "Judah was consequently transformed from an isolated, clan-based homogeneous society into a mixed Judahite-Israelite kingdom under Assyrian domination. This, in turn, brought about the rise of pan-Israelite ideas in Judah. The emergence of biblical Israel as a concept was therefore the result of the fall of the kingdom of Israel."[139] Both the Israelite God, Elohim, and the Judahite God, YHWH, would be force-fit onto the same throne.

P is who we get the "begats" from and the endless lists of materials and details of priestly procedures. "The language of P is so characteristic that undergraduate students can generally identify a P passage in the Bible on sight within weeks after being introduced to this study."[140] The Priestly author makes it clear the priesthood must travel through the lineage of Aaron and not simply the tribe of Levi.

"Deuteronomy is written in an entirely different style from those of the other four books," says Friedman. "The differences are obvious even in translation." The book does, however, match the linguistics, style, and bias of Joshua, Judges, and 1st and 2nd Kings. Friedman makes a convincing case for Jeremiah being the author of those books and the primary author of Deuteronomy. Baruch – his understudy and scribe – was likely the person who finished Deuteronomy. This would place the writing of D both in the years that directly preceded the exile, and in the years during. Between 622 BCE and around 500 BCE – about 1000 years later than the biblical narrative suggests.

I had never considered multiple authors contributing to each of the books. But once those words are separated, the varying styles of each writer and their competing values become easily recognizable. Friedman included a chart which lists verses identified as either J, E, P, or R. I included it as an appendix for your reference (Appendix A). I also included an excerpt from Numbers – *Korah's rebellion against Moses*. It shows how the Priestly author added text which strengthened the legal claim for descendants of Aaron. (Appendix B).

Friedman also identifies a fifth contributor: "there was the hand of an extremely skillful collector known as a *redactor*, someone who was capable of combining and organizing these separate documents into a single work that was united enough to be readable as a continuous narrative."[141] And then Friedman proceeds to breathe life into, and validate, my adolescent conspiracy theory by identifying the R author: "I think it was Ezra." *I wasn't crazy*. It wasn't ridiculous for me to doubt Ezra simply *found* the Law of Moses.

With that said, my opinions diverge slightly from Friedman and other scholars regarding who should be attributed to which books. I'll present my theories in the following subheadings.

THE DEUTERONOMIST

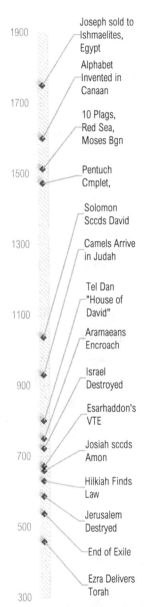

1900 — Joseph sold to Ishmaelites, Egypt

Alphabet Invented in Canaan

1700

10 Plags, Red Sea, Moses Bgn

1500 — Pentuch Cmplt,

Solomon Sccds David

1300 — Camels Arrive in Judah

Tel Dan "House of David"

1100 — Aramaeans Encroach

Israel Destroyed

900

Esarhaddon's VTE

Josiah sccds Amon

700

Hilkiah Finds Law

Jerusalem Destryed

500

End of Exile

Ezra Delivers Torah

300

There was one other time God's Law was "found," and people reacted as first-time hearers. In 2nd Kings 22, Judahite King Josiah tells Hilkiah to restore the temple. In the verses immediately following: "Hilkiah the high priest said to Shaphan the secretary, 'I have found the Book of the Law in the temple of the Lord.'" When King Josiah read the words of the law, he became distraught. He had no idea YHWH didn't want them to worship other gods or burn children alive. Josiah would use the discovery to enact (apparently much needed) religious reforms (2 Kings 23:1-24). He instituted monotheism as the state religion and centralized worship in Jerusalem.

Fifty years prior, the Assyrian King Esarhaddon issued a loyalty oath in 672 BCE to protect his succession, known today as the Vassal Treaty of Esarhaddon (VTE). A copy of the VTE was uncovered by archaeologists in Turkey, and once published, the similarities between that and Deuteronomy were too striking to ignore.

Judah was a vassal of Assyria, so it stands to reason they would have seen the VTE, or more likely, they possessed a copy. But when the Assyrian empire started to crumble, Josiah and his priestly cohorts took the opportunity to seize independence. Some scholars assert that when Judah pulled out from Assyrian vassalhood, they copied the VTE to create their newly independent set of laws. Professor Bernard Levinson writes: "Those authors transformed the Neo-Assyrian formula requiring exclusive loyalty to the 'word of Esarhaddon' into one that demanded fidelity to 'the word' of Israel's divine overlord, Yahweh, as proclaimed by Moses."[142] Richard

Friedman argued for a similar time frame for Deuteronomy. But in his theory J, E, and P were already written when Deuteronomy was penned. I think J, E, and P were written later.

As additional chapters and additional books were conceived, the verses produced by Hilkiah – and inspired by Esarhaddon – found themselves nested between Deuteronomy 13 and Deuteronomy 28. (See Appendix C for a table of VTE lines and how they correspond with Deuteronomy).

Of course there are Biblical literalists who would argue that Esarhaddon could have copied the words of the Torah for the VTE. But there is a textual anomaly in Deut 13:1 where the text deviates from proper Hebrew syntax. In the world of textual criticism, those anomalies are important clues indicating which of multiple texts were the original. The anomaly suggests the VTE existed before Deut 13:1.[143]

Literacy is a significant clue in the search for the Bible's authors. In the 7th century BCE nearly every human was illiterate. The technology of writing was cutting-edge. But as luck would have it, Judah was situated between two of the earliest adopters – the Sumerians and Egyptians.[144] The earliest surviving coherent example of human writing dates back to 2600 BCE. Those earliest texts were in cuneiform format. The first alphabet would be formed near Judah around 1600 BCE.[145]

I had been taught that Jews and Israelites were literate. They had to be literate because they were commanded: "you shall read this law" (Deut 31:11). But that rule was for the priests – a group who *may* have been literate. Deuteronomy 6:6,7 offers insight into the rest of the people: "These commandments that I give you today are to be on your *hearts*. Impress them on your children. Talk about them when you sit at home and when you walk along the road, when you lie down and when you get up." That reads to me as a memorization exercise. An exercise required when texts were handwritten and thus rare and expensive, and when nearly everyone was illiterate.

Physical evidence discussed in Finkelstein's book supports illiteracy of pre-exile Israelites: "Assembling all available data for scribal activity in Israel and Judah reveals no evidence of writing before approximately 800 BCE."[146] Regarding a later time period, one research paper pointed out that "the literacy rate of the Jewish people was 1.5% if not lower."[147] And with literacy rates that low, only a select group of educated people could narrate history. And only they would know if the text was altered.

I propose that one of those was Hilkiah. It seems obvious to me that Hilkiah, with the help of his priests, is responsible for producing the first set of Hebrew Laws – the original Torah. This may have been on the order of King Josiah, but it appears the priests of the time were more of an influence on Josiah than likewise. Other than perhaps the book of Isaiah, this appears to be the first installment of the Bible. Though other texts likely existed, like Exodus 15 and Judges 5, I'm certain this was the inauguration of the Torah.

THE JAHWIST AND THE ELOHIST

The language in which the scriptures were written provides us with a clue to the authors. It was written in Hebrew, a language which flourished in Palestine from about 1200 to 586 BCE.[148] The earliest Paleo-Hebrew text is dated to the tenth century BCE.[149] We find examples of Paleo-Hebrew in the Song of Deborah (Judges 5), and the Song of Moses (Exodus 15). But the Pentateuch was almost entirely written in a later dialect, heavily influenced by Babylonian Aramaic. It is known as *Biblical Hebrew,* or *Classical Hebrew.*[150]

Where did that Babylonian influence come from? Soon after Judah shed Assyria's yoke, Babylon would impose its heavy hand on Judah, stripping from them their most educated and well-connected people as exiles into Babylon. Several years later Babylon would destroy Jerusalem.

Richard Friedman pointed to Jeremiah as the writer of Deuteronomy, and that theory is certainly plausible. Jeremiah was likely alive when Hilkiah found the Law of YHWH. One fun fact about Jeremiah is that he describes himself as the son of Hilkiah (Jer1:1). Jeremiah witnessed the destruction of Jerusalem. When the elite Jews were taken to Babylon in exile, Jeremiah was left behind.

What would Jeremiah do with the remaining years of his life – in the emptied streets of Jerusalem or while in Egypt? What would he do, knowing the Torah had been taken or destroyed, having a clear recollection of its words and only a scribe to keep him company? "So Jeremiah called Baruch son of Neriah, and while Jeremiah dictated all the words the Lord had spoken to him, Baruch wrote them on the scroll." (Jer 36:4)

Jeremiah 8 makes me think the Torah was being transformed in Babylon. There Jeremiah is lashing out at the priests who were taken to Babylon. "How can you say, 'We are wise, for we have the law of the Lord,' when actually the lying pen of the scribes has handled it falsely?" (Jer8:8). A version of the Torah or an excerpt from therein, seems to have found its way from Babylon to Jeremiah, and Jeremiah discerned it was altered. Jeremiah did not dispute whether they had the Torah – he disputed only its accuracy.

Jeremiah would later be taken against his will with Baruch to Egypt where Jewish tradition says he later died (Jer 43:4-6). Baruch the scribe would complete the works of Jeremiah and would bring them to Babylon (Baruch 1:1).

Another point I haven't heard discussed is if Babylon had taken all the able-bodied young men, why had Baruch been in Jerusalem with Jeremiah? Baruch was both young and educated and was closely related to the King of Judah. Baruch's father was an official in Josiah's court. Baruch's brother was the Judahite King's quartermaster (Jer 51:59). Baruch fit the profile for an exile. I would find it hard to believe Baruch was not taken in the first wave of exiles.

The book of Daniel offers an insight into what young men of Baruch's stature experienced in Babylon: "Then the king ordered Ashpenaz, chief of his court officials, to bring into the king's service some of the Israelites from

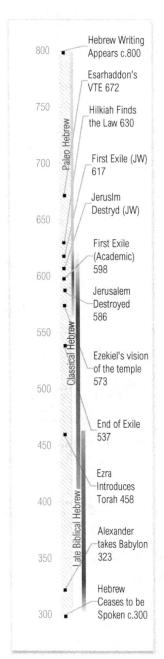

the royal family and the nobility— young men without any physical defect, handsome, showing aptitude for every kind of learning, well informed, quick to understand, and qualified to serve in the king's palace. He was to teach them the language and literature of the Babylonians. [...] They were to be trained for three years, and after that they were to enter the king's service" (Daniel 1:3-5).

Baruch was of the royal family and sharp enough to grasp this new technology of writing. Assuming he wasn't ugly, he would not only qualify for the first exile, he would further qualify to be among the youth re-educated by King Nebuchadnezzar.

Another interesting point: Daniel didn't actually say "he was to teach them the language and literature of the *Babylonians*," as the NIV records. The King James Version, surprisingly, is more accurate here: "Whom they might teach the learning and the tongue of the *Chaldeans.*"

The author wrote *Chaldeans*, not *Babylonians*. This might seem like splitting hairs because throughout the Bible and in other literature the words *Chaldean* and *Babylonian* are often used interchangeably. Babylon was the capital of the people of Chaldea. But Daniel did not use the term interchangeably. During this window of the timeline, *Chaldean* referred to a specific group of people within the Babylonian empire.

For a contemporary insight we could look toward Greek historian Herodotus, who offers an account of Babylon from the mid-400s BCE. He makes a clear differentiation between Babylonians and Chaldeans. "Herodotus does not use the terms synonymously. When he is talking about the temple of Bel, he speaks of the 'Chaldeans,' because, as he tells us, they were the priests of the god and acted as his informers and guides. But when he goes on to discuss the strange manners and customs of Babylon, we hear nothing of the 'Chaldeans,' but only the 'Babylonians.'" Charles Boutflower clarifies this point in the Journal of Asiatic Studies: "The 'Chaldeans,' then, according to Herodotus, are the priests of the god Bel, and Bel-Merodach [...], the favourite divinity of Nebuchad-nezzar.'"[151]

Those priests were no joke. Boutflower points to the high social stature and political sway Chaldeans held. It appears one of Nebuchadnezzar's sons was a Chaldean priest, and other records show Chaldeans held various positions at the top of the Babylonian hierarchy.[152]

Chaldeans were priests of a very elite class – a cult with significant influence and who specialized in the use of writing.

Writing was intrinsic to the profession of the Chaldeans. It was a prerequisite to all other subjects and comprised most of the earlier years of their education. So intrinsic was writing to their profession these scholars were referred to, not as astrologers, priests, or mathematicians, but as "*Scribes* of Enūma Anu Enlil."[153]

Those were the instructors of the Jewish elite depicted in the book of Daniel. And if my theory is correct, they would have taught Baruch. This is where Baruch learned to scribe. To offer support for this, it appears Jewish leaders held suspicion of Baruch and his connection with the Babylonian priestly class. An article in the Watchtower introduces a relevant passage.

> *The Jewish leaders told Jeremiah:* It is a falsehood that you are speaking. Jehovah our God has not sent you, saying, 'Do not enter into Egypt to reside there as aliens.' But Baruch the son of Neriah is instigating you against us for the purpose of giving us into the hand of the Chaldeans, to put us to death or to take us into exile in Babylon.' (Jeremiah 43:2, 3) *The accusation seems to reveal a belief*

> *among the Jewish leaders that Baruch exerted considerable influence over Jeremiah. Did they believe that because of Baruch's position or his long-standing friendship with Jeremiah, he was acting as more than a mere scribe for the prophet?*[54]
>
> Watchtower, August 15, 2006

Perhaps. Or perhaps the Jewish leaders suspected Baruch because he recently spent three years in Babylon as a student of the Chaldeans. And if that were the case, it wasn't ridiculous to think Baruch was there under the direction of Nebuchadnezzar. *They were to be trained for three years, and after that they were to enter the king's service."*

I think Baruch was in Jerusalem on assignment. He was there to record the oral traditions so they may be entwined with the agenda of Nebuchadnezzar and the priests of his favorite God.

It was from this point that Biblical Hebrew emerges and Hebrew writing began to flourish, and I'm convinced that is a result of Babylonian influence.[155] This was when *the Deuteronomistic History*[156] was written – the completed book of Deuteronomy, and those of Joshua, Judges, the Samuels, and the Kings.

I'm not convinced Jeremiah was the author. I'm not convinced Jeremiah wrote anything. I think Baruch et al deserve credit for the writings of Jeremiah. And if Baruch were in J'town on assignment, that carries the likelihood of teams of Chaldeans (and Baruch's classmates) who could assist in scribal activities.

Hilkiah, or Essarhaddon, or Jeremiah, or Moses, or whoever, could have written an original law of YHWH, but whatever it was before the exile would not be preserved through its Chaldean custody.

But what of the other writings? What about E and J? Remembering how Richard Friedman said "the E stories were written by someone concerned with Israel and the J stories by someone concerned with Judah." The archaeological record shows scant writing capacity and that Israel and Judah never existed as a single homogenous nation. I have a hard time believing either Israelites or Judahites would alter their legends to accommodate the other. Altering their mythology seems an effort only performed under coercion.

Yet their histories *were* altered. Moses would become a prophet of the Judahites as he had for the Israelites, and David would be known as a King of Israel. But the most striking changes were the addition of Chaldean legends. Chaldean stories found their way into the Israelite saga in both E and J.

In *Sources of the Pentateuch* we read: "From Van Seter's perspective, the Yahwistic stage of growth reveals considerable powers of conceptualization and literary skill. [...] Names, customs, and institutions in the ancestral stories have their closest parallels in ancient Near Eastern societies of the first millennium, not the second millennium as had previously been thought. In short, one cannot recover the epoch of Israel's ancestors from the stories of Abraham. The evidence reveals that the portrait of Abraham was in reality an artificial reconstruction by first millennium Israelites. The most likely period for this would have been the exile."[157]

The exodus story starring Moses had circulated in Israel for centuries before the Babylonian exile. But there is no record of the patriarchs or the Genesis creation story in either Judah or Israel prior to the exile. The biblical stories of the creation account, the Garden of Eden, the serpent, the flood, the patriarchs, Nimrod, and the Tower of Babel, had existed in cuneiform tablets of ancient Chaldeans, and well before Moses supposedly existed.[158]

In contrast to Israelites and Judahites, Babylonians were experts in writing and proved apt to use the technology as a cultural tool. A Chaldean origin for J and E seems far more likely than one naturalized. The weave of Pentateuchal text exhibits the skilled literacy, "considerable powers of conceptualization," and the irreverence of an elite priesthood who worshipped a different God.

I think the original version of J and the final version of E, like the Deuteronomistic history, were written by Baruch's Chaldean re-education college under the direction of Nebuchadnezzar.

At the outset this might seem far-fetched. But it is far more supported than the narrative of literalists. In fact, it sounds absurd to me that the Chaldeans, a cult with the precise specialty to orchestrate such a manipulation simply crossed paths with Israel without using their skills – that their stated process of re-education failed to effect change – that it was within the Pentateuch that the first occurrences of Babylonian myths appear in Hebrew – or that the Hebrew scriptures were penned in a language tainted by the Chaldean tongue coincidentally.

THE PRIEST

The largest contributor by far was the Priestly author. As Friedman showed, the agenda of the Priest was clear and his style and attention to detail were recognizably unique. The Encyclopedia of Hebrew Language and Linguistics confirms: "there are grammatical and lexical usages distinctive of P in relation to non-P."[159]

P appears to have an agenda to legitimize the Aaronic lineage and to establish an order for religious practice. "He was developing a concept of God. His work was literary, but his motivation was not only artistic, but also theological, political, and economic. He had to deal with challenges from other priests and other religious centers. He had to defend his group's legitimacy and to protect their authority. And he had to ensure their livelihood."[160] By listing who begot whom, P strengthened legal claims for certain privileges of service and thus a claim for the most reliable seat of power among Israelites – the priesthood.

Despite the identity of P being widely contested, I haven't heard anyone develop a more convincing theory than Julius Wellhausen, who originally proposed the Documentary Hypothesis. Wellhausen refers to P's insistence that the priesthood and priestly privileges could not be performed by just any Levite. It was only the descendants of Aaron who qualified (Appendix B shows the reasoning). In all the Pentateuch we only find reference to this restriction in P's narrative, and in later writings which reference P. This helps to significantly narrow the timeline.

In Ezekiel chapter 44, however, it appears Ezekiel holds the same view, but he seems to introduce the concept. He does so with apparently no knowledge of the rebellion of Korah where the Levites (according to P) lost such privileges. "The distinction between priest and Levite which Ezekiel introduces and justifies as an innovation, according to the Priestly Code has always existed; what in the former appears as a beginning, in the latter has been in force ever since Moses—an original datum, not a thing that has become or been made. That the prophet [Ezekiel] should know nothing about a priestly law with whose tendencies he is in thorough sympathy admits of only one explanation—that it did not then exist."[161]

The Dutch scholar Abraham Kuenen added support to this theory. "If by reason of their birth it was already impossible for the Levites to become priests [as P lays down], then it would be more than strange to deprive them of the priesthood on account of their faults—much as if one were to threaten the commons with the punishment of being disqualified from sitting or voting in the House of Lords.' [...] If P had been in existence in 573, Ezekiel surely would have developed his argument in a different way."[162]

Kuenen had made an earlier argument that the books of Haggai and Zechariah, written in the early post-exilic period, show no awareness of the legalities found in P.[163] "The book of Malachi, probably from the early fifth century BCE, is especially significant, as it says quite a lot about priests, but calls them Levites, not sons of Aaron. By contrast the Chronicler, writing some time after 400 BCE is clearly familiar with P's regulations. So a date within the fifth century becomes likely on this argument too."[164]

There is also the matter of the dispute between the Aaronid Priests and those known as Zadokites. It was the Zadokite line that held control during Josiah's reign and who orchestrated Josiah's reforms. But the Aaronids would hold control during the exile, presumably because the Zadokites were taken to Babylon. There doesn't seem to be any periods before the exile where control was disputed. There would only prove to be conflict between the groups when Zadokite priests from Babylon started moving into Jerusalem and wrestled the priesthood back from the Aaronids. That P imposes a clearly partisan view shows P to be written after Ezekiel and after the exiles returned.[165] A window between Cyrus' decree (536 BCE) and Ezra's visit to Jerusalem (458 BCE) seems the only possible period for the writing.

Wellhausen offered his theory. "He took as his point of departure the statement in Ezra 7:14 that when Ezra came from Babylon to Jerusalem in 458 BCE he had the law of God in his hand. This Wellhausen understood to be a new law book, which consisted of the completed Pentateuch, incorporating not only the older sources J, E, and D but the Priestly Code, which had quite recently been [compiled]. He seems to have believed that the completed Pentateuch (and the new Priestly Code) must owe its authority to some act of authorization, and only Ezra's mission seemed to be available to meet this requirement."[166]

A little more on that act of authorization: Ezra and Nehemiah each claim to have been sent by the King of Persia, and indeed there may have been Persian support for revising and reintroducing the Pentateuch. During those events in history, Persia was at war with the Greeks (*This is Sparta!*). The Greco-Persian war was likely at its peak, and the Greeks had successfully

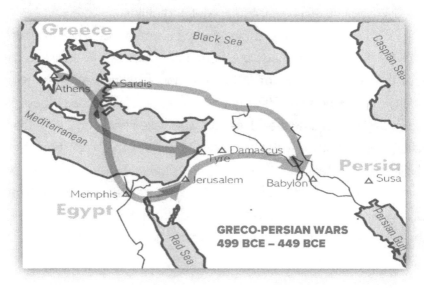

convinced Egypt to rebel against the Persians.[167] This placed the Persian district of Judah on two fronts: Egypt to the south of Jerusalem, and the Mediterranean Sea to the West (a possible conduit for the sea-faring Greeks).

Persia needed to build fortifications in Judah to prevent an invasion from Egypt.[168] *Needed* might be overstating the condition. Scholars generally reject the notion that Judah was strategically significant. But it didn't need to be significant. For this theory it needed only enough concern for Persia to supply the provisions listed in Nehemiah 2. That Persia offered those supplies for the purpose of building fortifications seems far more likely than Nehemiah's version of the story where the Persian King donates them because Nehemiah was sad.

Persia would also have to overcome a shortage of labor if they were to build defenses in Judea. Wars between the Medes, Assyrians, and Babylonians depleted the skilled labor-force fueling the economic engines along the Euphrates. Babylon solved the problem by taking exiles from outlying areas like Judah and Israel. As a result, the population of Judea was negligible, thus lacking skilled resources for defensive projects. But somehow, Persia found a way. The archaeological record shows fortresses were indeed built with Persian materials throughout Judah during Persian rule.[169] Who did they convince to uproot and build?

With our historical hindsight it might seem obvious they would send Israelites. That's where they were from, right? Not exactly. Israelites came from the northern kingdom of Israel – though many had swarmed into Judah just prior the exile. Officially, and to outsiders like Persians, those were known as *Jews* because their ancestors were taken from Judah. But the fact many referred to themselves as Israelites speaks to the proportion of exiles who had originated from Israel. And this story was playing out 128 years after Jerusalem was destroyed. So they were at *least* a full generation (almost a full JW generation) removed from the Jewish motherland. Christian literature might paint a picture of a joyful return of Jewish exiles, but *return* would have been a misnomer. It was a resettlement. And those settlers would need convincing.

Far from the thistles and ruins of Judah, Babylon was enjoying a golden age. It was the largest city in the world and throne to the largest empire the world had ever seen. "Under the Persians, Babylon retained most of its institutions, became capital of the richest satrapy in the empire, and was, according to the 5th-century-bce Greek historian Herodotus, the world's most splendid city. [...] Its citizens claimed privileges, such as exemption from forced labour, certain taxes, and imprisonment. [...] Furthermore, the citizens, grown wealthy through commerce, benefitted from an imperial power able to protect international trade."[170] Imagine being a 3rd generation resident of New York City or Tokyo. Then someone asks if you would move to Afghanistan because that's where (some of) your great grandparents came from.

Jews and Israelites were permitted to return 80 years before. But there was no hurry to leave the Hanging Gardens, the vibrant culture, or the running water Babylon enjoyed. Certainly not for a region like Judea which lacked natural resources, people, and arable land. The return of the exiles was a myth. "There is no evidence of large increases in the population at any time in the Persian period. On the contrary, the end of the sixth and beginning of the fifth century saw a significant *reduction* in population, especially in the Benjamin area."[171]

There was no doubt a small-scale return of Babylonian Jews. But if waves of Israelites followed Ezra and Nehemiah as reported, they would have needed a means to convince Israelites they had a connection with Judah. Perhaps if they found a relic as did Hilkiah they could spark a cultural revival. Hell they would probably need to convince people Judah was a land flowing with milk and honey and that God wanted them there. Such a cultural revival would owe its authority to an act of authorization, and only Ezra's mission seemed to be available to meet this requirement.

I propose Ezra and Nehemiah (if they were separate individuals) may have proposed to supply Persia with a work force if they were given the resources to build a temple. Perhaps they were able to secure financing to re-write some older scrolls or access to those which had been taken. Agreeing to help Persians build fortifications would explain why when Nehemiah arrived in Judah he did not work on the temple, the vineyards, or any civic buildings; "instead, I devoted myself to the work on this wall" (Nehemiah 5:16).

Or perhaps the Christian narrative is correct. Moses wrote about events after his death. The Pentateuch was penned in a language that wouldn't exist until Jews were exiled. Ezekiel forgot about Korah when building a case against Levites. Moses, for some odd reason, wrote at length in a manner which would benefit certain priests only in Ezra's time. And at the height of the Greco-Persian war, the Persian king, the most powerful man on Earth, put aside his war plans and gave Nehemiah supplies and leave to build fortifications. Fortifications on the frontlines of a war that would ultimately end his empire – but completely unrelated to that war. Because Nehemiah was sad.

It seems obvious to me that the Priestly writings – nearly 50% of the Pentateuch – were written during the Persian empire. "In the entire Bible, two men are known as lawgivers: Moses and Ezra. Ezra came from Babylon to Judah eighty years after the first group of exiles returned, in 458 B.C. [...] It also indicates that he was no ordinary scribe. His writing skills were associated with one document in particular: 'the torah of Moses'" (Richard Friedman).[172]

Friedman pointed to Ezra as the Redactor, believing P had been written some time before. But there is one characteristic of P which pushes me to side with Wellhausen and Kuenen for a later writing. This relates to P's consistent use of lists in an almost autistic manner – whether that be genealogies or building materials for the tabernacle. And we find that pattern within Ezra-Nehemiah, which was originally bound as a single scroll. "Ezra-Nehemiah is characterized by a series of lists. In fact, apart from the [Nehemiah Memoires] and Nehemiah 8, much of the material in the book of Nehemiah is made up of lists of various sorts. The different lists often involve names laid out by family, sometimes with the names of ancestors in the form of a genealogy."[173] The style of his writing seems to give Ezra away.

Ezra brought the first complete Law of YHWH to Jerusalem. In its words were emphasized how God gave Judah to the Israelites as a special inheritance – a land flowing with milk and honey. If they followed the laws therein, they would prosper. If they didn't, God would abandon them.

Useful words for compelling Jews not to return to Babylon or move to Egypt. Useful for compelling work on walls, providing materially for priests, and remaining separate from ungodly cultures like the Philistines (people likely from the Greek Islands[174]). Words originating from harsh servitude under Assyrian vassalhood. Words intended to subjugate and enslave, and then repurposed by several hands to accomplish different ends. Words that generations of later rulers would find useful for bringing people together for a common purpose.

THE REDACTOR

If Ezra were the Priestly author, who then was the Redactor? Neither the historical record nor the biblical texts offer a clear answer. But we can ascertain some revealing information from the texts. It might also help to look closer at the Priest.

2 Maccabees 2:13 speaks of "the memoirs and commentaries of Nehemias: and how he made a library, and gathered together out of the countries, the books both of the prophets, and of David, and the epistles of the kings."

The books refer to numerous official-sounding documents like Ezra's letter from Artaxerxes, undoubtedly as an attempt to build credibility. "Much of what we have seen indicates that the documents are late, post-Achaemenid and likely to be forgeries," says Lester Grabbe in *History of the Jews and Judaism.*[175]

Grabbe describes Ezra/Nehemiah in more detail. "A dispassionate description of events or a mere chronicle of what happened is clearly not the primary purpose of the author or compiler. Any record of events is secondary to the theological clarification of what it all meant. However well-intentioned the aim of the authors, they were not writing as historians. They were not exercising critical judgment in selecting their data as we would expect historians to do but were using whatever advanced their ideological aim and were using it in ways which might go counter to good historical practice."[176] The writers were telling a story which supported their ideology. They weren't adjusting their ideologies based on the truth of a story.

We can be certain of one thing: the writer was a scribe, although that sounds obvious. Of note is that Ezra's father's name is listed as Seraiah, the grandson of Hilkiah (Ezra 7:1).

More relevant to the subject, Ezra is said to have been the leader of the Great Assembly, a counsel of Jewish priests who presided over the temple and who protected the Jewish writings. Regarding the Great Assembly, the Mishnah teaches: "Be patient in judgment; have many pupils; put a fence about the Torah" (Pirkei Avot 1:1).

The existence of the Great Assembly is disputed in the academic world. But there is little doubt the High Priest assembled some form of counsel. Although Ezra is not recorded as the high priest, his connection with Hilkiah suggests he may have been in line.

There is also a direct connection between Ezra and Baruch. The Jewish Megillah 16b:19 reads: "As long as Baruch ben Neriah was alive in Babylonia, Ezra, who was his disciple, did not leave him and go up to Eretz Yisrael to build the Temple." If Baruch were educated by the Chaldeans, and Ezra was a disciple of Baruch, there could be a strong Chaldean influence on the structure of the Jewish priesthood and how they used the written word.

Knowing the Jewish elite were educated by Chaldean priests, and knowing the Pentateuch was penned in Classical Hebrew, heavily influenced by Babylonian Aramaic, **I propose the Jewish Sanhedrin and the Pentateuch were incubated by the Chaldean Priests – in many respects *engineered* by them.**

What does any of this have to do with the Redactor? Because I don't think the Redactor can be pinned to a single man or woman. I think the Redactor was a group – the protectors of the Torah. **I think the Redactor was the Great Assembly** – the Sanhedrin – an elite selection of educated Jews who, like Chaldean Priests, wielded a more covert form of control and were first and foremost, scribes.

Regardless of whether Chaldeans were an influence, there is strong consensus among those who best know the biblical writings that Moses had little role in producing them. Rather than descending from Mount Sinai in 1500 BCE, the Pentateuch assuredly was a group effort which evolved over time and never saw substantial completion until the Persian Empire.

> *Wellhausen's documentary hypothesis has not survived in its original form. However, virtually all scholars today accept the basic idea behind it, that the Pentateuch is not the work of one single author writing at one time, but was composed over several centuries by people responding to different circumstances.*[177]
>
> John J. McDermott, Philosopher, Distinguished Professor

THE ANTI-CHRIST

I remember being 16 and immersing myself into each character as I read through the gospel accounts of Jesus. When I finished reading those it was hard to imagine why there was more to read.

Immediately following the gospels is the *Acts of Apostles.* Despite what the title suggests, the apostles (12 closest followers of Jesus) were secondary players in the saga. Acts is about Paul, a man who never met Jesus. Not while Jesus was alive, that is.

Paul relates a story of meeting Jesus on the road to Damascus, unfortunately, the people with Paul didn't see anyone (Acts 9:7). During this first read through of the Bible, the story came across as cringe-worthy, and hard to believe. Which was odd to me because I had not experienced that sense when reading it in the fragmentary form JWs presented it. I had read Acts in quotes and heard it referred to numerous times from the podium. Reading it in its entirety and directly after the gospels offered a different perspective. From that perspective it became obvious Paul had nothing to do with Jesus. His message differed from Jesus'. His attitude was different.

At some point just prior to my read of the bible, Kurt Cobain, front man of the grunge band *Nirvana*, died. All these events must have melded together in my mind because when I pictured Jesus from that point, his character was solidly projected as Kurt Cobain.

Adding to that was an interview I watched with the remaining members of Nirvana. I remember Dave Grohl expressing how difficult it was dealing with the fame and attention when trying to mourn the loss of his friend. And this became the sentiment I imagined for the 12 *apostles* of Jesus.

With that setting vividly in mind, it seemed shocking to me this Paul character would dare lay claim that he knew Jesus. He wasn't even a fan. He hated the content of their message – *he was never into Nirvana or grunge music, and he remained that way.*

For those unfamiliar with the music of *Nirvana* or the *grunge* genre, it "featured themes of low-budget grit, bleakness, and a rejection of authority." Kurt Cobain was especially vocal with his disdain for the flashy wealth of the music industry and often screamed his lyrics with apparent discontent for the era.[178] For me it remained an appropriate metaphor for Jesus' campaign. Jesus rejected the splendor of the temple and the authority of Jewish religious leaders. He referred to his generation as "wicked and adulterous" (Mat 12:39). And Jesus and Cobain were close to the same age at their deaths.

But Jesus wouldn't be the one to tell his story. Neither would the men who knew him. The academic data and analyses of the earliest manuscripts strongly suggest the gospel accounts in the Bible were not first-hand accounts, and none of them were written by any of the original apostles.

It was Paul's followers who told the story of Jesus and it would be hard to find synchronicity between Jesus' message and that of Paul's. Biblical Scholar and Professor of Ancient Judaism and Early Christianity, James Tabor points out: "In all of Paul's letters, he tells his converts nothing about the life of Jesus on earth. This is quite remarkable. Paul relates nothing of Jesus' birth, that he was from Galilee, that he was baptized by John the Baptizer, that he preached that the kingdom of God was near, healed the sick, and worked miracles. Paul never quotes directly a single teaching of Jesus."[179] Of course he didn't. He never met Jesus.

Paul did find the time, though, to refer to surviving apostles sarcastically and critically and to promote his own apostleship – an apostleship not endorsed by the others. At the age of 16 I was disgusted by Paul's words, especially those in 2 Corinthians 11. On their own these verses may sound as though Paul is speaking about heretics. But when stitched together...

I do not think I am in the least inferior to those "super-apostles." I may indeed be untrained as a speaker, but I do have knowledge. We have made this perfectly clear to you in every way. - 2 Cor 11:5,6

For such people are false apostles, deceitful workers, masquerading as apostles of Christ. And no wonder, for Satan himself masquerades as an angel of light. – 2 Cor 11:13,14

Are they Hebrews? So am I. Are they Israelites? So am I. Are they Abraham's descendants? So am I. Are they servants of Christ? (I am out of my mind to talk like this.) I am more. I have worked much harder, been in prison more frequently, been flogged more severely, and been exposed to death again and again. – 2 Cor 11:22,23

Watch out for those dogs, those evildoers, those mutilators of the flesh. For it is we who are the circumcision, we who serve God by his Spirit, who boast in Christ Jesus, and who put no confidence in the flesh— though I myself have reasons for such confidence.

If someone else thinks they have reasons to put confidence in the flesh, I have more: circumcised on the eighth day, of the people of Israel, of the tribe of Benjamin, a Hebrew of Hebrews; in regard to the law, a Pharisee; as for zeal, persecuting the church; as for righteousness based on the law, faultless. – Phil 3:2-6

Though my Bible teacher tried to tell me Paul wasn't speaking about the apostles, there is no other context where those words fit.

The sense I get from Paul was that he wasn't a prominent member of the Jesus movement, having met only Peter and perhaps only once before being summoned to Jerusalem. Though he probably posted good numbers in terms of converts. He found a popular means of doing so. He told the gentiles they could continue being gentiles and didn't have to cut the foreskin of their penises. For some reason that was more popular among Greeks and Romans. But it was not a message the apostles would approve. And for that, and other departures from Judaism he was summoned. The outcome recorded in Acts does not seem to match Paul's feelings portrayed in his authentic letters. Paul's feelings were hurt. What happened that caused him to lash out in 2 Corinthians?

When I was 16 I didn't know the Apostles remained faithful to the Torah. But I certainly sensed there was bad blood. In fact, it might help to understand how I viewed Paul as I first read the Bible.

The Fourth Nirvana

Imagine Paul living in the 90s and getting attention in the media for being a friend of Kurt Cobain. But Paul never met Kurt Cobain. Paul had been a roadie of Nirvana but only after Cobain's death. Paul is now travelling the world claiming that Cobain's ghost appeared in the sky and invited him to be the new lead.

The surviving members dismiss the whole thing at first, caring little about the delusions of a maniacal narcissist. But they would be given reason for irritation when learning how Paul started writing songs in Cobain's name, released albums as Nirvana, and had developed a considerable following. Paul brags about criticizing the original band members. He sarcastically refers to them as "super-musicians" and brings them donations to boast of his material success.

Worse still is that this new rebirth of Nirvana delivers a message opposite to the original and departs from every theme which meant most to Kurt Cobain. The imposter is producing pop music in Cobain's name and courts populism, conformity, and encourages subjection as slaves.

It might be an understatement to think Grohl and Novoselic would be irritated with the imposter. If they knew every genuine memory and recording of Kurt Cobain would be erased and the legacy of the band re-produced by the imposter, they might be irate.

Perhaps it seems disrespectful not to take the Bible stories at their word. I overcame by thinking it was more important to understand the truth about Jesus. When care is taken to examine the scriptures in their entirety – to strip away the biases of modern Christianity – and if we consider the full range of investigative tools at our disposal, it appears a whole new narrative emerges. I find that exciting.

My later research on the subject found scholars who dedicated their lives to learning about Jesus and who were not swayed by the powerful arm of the churches. I was impressed how they arrived at similar conclusions to each other and often from different angles. I think that speaks to the validity of their claims. I also found that those who refute said conclusions have yet to support their counterarguments with convincing evidence.

The common and consistent scholarly themes I found are:

- None of the gospels were written by any of the Apostles.
- None of the gospels are firsthand accounts.
- The surviving apostles including Peter and John maintained a soundly Jewish set of beliefs.
- The gospels were written by Paul's followers.
- And it was James, the blood brother of Jesus who led the apostles and earliest followers, not Peter. And certainly not Paul.

Paul's own words give evidence that James was the leader, though for the most part, it appears Paul all but removed James as the pillar he was. James isn't mentioned in the gospel accounts. But there's evidence to suggest he probably should have been. Before the gospels were written

Paul admits: "When James and Cephas and John, who were *acknowledged pillars*, recognized the grace that had been given to me [...]" (Gal 2:9). He acknowledges James as a pillar, although other translations render that as "so-called pillars." Each time Paul went to Jerusalem, meeting with James seems to be the focus (Gal 1:18, 19). Peter reports to James (Acts 12:17). James is always listed first as is custom with leaders (1 Cor 15:7). And it is James who makes the final decisions, including that at the so-called *Council of Jerusalem* regarding circumcision (Acts 15:13-20).

> *As presented by Paul, James is the Leader of the early Church par excellence. Terms like 'Bishop of the Jerusalem Church' or 'Leader of the Jerusalem Community' are of little actual moment at this point, because from the 40s to the 60s CE, when James held sway in Jerusalem, there really were no other centers of any importance.*[180]
>
> **Robert H. Eisenman, Professor of Middle East Religions and Archaeology and Director of the Institute for the Study of Judeo-Christian Origins**

JWs believe that within a year of Jesus' death, at Pentecost 33 CE, Christianity became a distinct group.[181] But that concept is almost universally discounted among scholars. Harvard Professor Shaye Cohen says: "the separation of Christianity from Judaism was a process, not an event. The essential part of this process was that the church was becoming more and more gentile, and less and less Jewish."[182]

There does appear to be a divergence between Judaism and Christianity in the first century, but the apostles were not on Paul's side of the divide. According to James Tabor: "James, the brother of Jesus and leader of the Jerusalem church, as well as Peter and the other apostles, held to a Jewish version of the Christian faith that faded away and was forgotten due to the total triumph of Paul's version of Christianity."[183] Historians refer to the budding Jesus movement, centralized from Jerusalem as *Jewish Christians*. There is evidence they referred to themselves as *The Way* or as *Nazarenes*.[184]

While the actual apostles including Peter, John and Jesus' brother James, were building their community in Jerusalem, Paul's missionary tours through Asia Minor were independent of that movement. His teachings differed significantly from the apostles. Paul created a different religion.

> *Not only do I believe Paul should be seen as the 'founder' of the Christianity that we know today, rather than Jesus and his original apostles, but I argue he made a decisive bitter break with those first apostles, promoting and preaching views they found to be utterly reprehensible.* [185]

James Tabor, Biblical Scholar and Professor of Ancient Judaism and Early Christianity

Robert Van Voorst calculates it was seven years after Jesus' death that Paul reports having his vision on the road to Damascus and became a follower. [186] While Paul's followers would eventually come to be known as *Christians*, evidence shows a separate term emerged for those centralized from the Jerusalem congregation – that of the *Ebionites*.

The term *ebionite* stems from the Hebrew word for *poor ones*. The Ebionites grew into the primary rival of Paul's Christianity, but the question remains whether they held to the same principles as the first apostles. We know that Jesus and his first apostles denounced riches suggesting the term *poor ones* was fitting. [187] Some think it was derived from Jesus words: "Blessed are the poor" (Mat 5:3). Robert Eisenman draws a link to when Paul collected donations for the *poor* in Jerusalem (Romans 15:31). Perhaps that precipitated a mockery among the more affluent congregations over which Paul presided – similar to how the term *Christian* is thought to have developed first as an insult. Either way, "there can be little doubt that 'the Poor' was the name for James' Community in Jerusalem or that Community descended from it in the East in the next two-three centuries, the Ebionites." [188]

According to New Testament Scholar, Bart Ehrman, the Ebionites remained very much Jewish, did not ascribe to the virgin birth of Jesus, or that Jesus was divine, or that Jesus had a pre-human existence. They held an entirely different gospel, known today as the Gospel of the Ebionites – tragically lost to history.

> *They did not accept any of the writings of Paul. Indeed, for them,*
> *Paul was not just wrong about a few minor points. He was the*
> *archenemy, the heretic who had led so many astray.*[189]

Bart Ehrman, New Testament Scholar, Distinguished Professor of Religious Studies

Did this mean Paul was the Anti-Christ? Though that term was unlikely to be used by Ebionites, it seems to be the sentiment they held. Early Catholic Bishop Irenaeus (130-202 C.E.) wrote: "Those who are called Ebionites accept that God made the world. However, their opinions with respect to the Lord are quite similar to those of Cerinthus and Carpocrates. They use Matthew's gospel only, and repudiate the Apostle Paul, maintaining that he was an apostate from the Law" (Haer 1.26.2). Epiphanius of Salamis reported the Ebionites as saying Paul "was a Greek [...] He went up to Jerusalem, they say, and when he had spent some time there, he was seized with a passion to marry the daughter of the priest. For this reason he became a proselyte and was circumcised. Then, when he failed to get the girl, he flew into a rage and wrote against circumcision and against the sabbath and the Law" (Panarion 30.16.6–9).

This is a problem for Christian doctrine because it relies heavily – near entirely – on the words of Paul. Even the gospels were filtered through Pauline lenses.[190] It was Paul's follower, Mark, who likely wrote the first gospel, and the other gospels used Mark as a source. Paul introduced most of the major tenets of Christianity including his views on sin, and the redeeming power of Jesus' sacrifice. Without a connection to the apostles and having missed Jesus by seven years, what authorized Paul's ministry? What would suggest the gospels could include any genuine recollection of Jesus' life? By what authority does the canon of New Testament scriptures draw from? In turn, what basis would the Catholic Church, and by extension, all Christianity have for claiming God's endorsement?

With the obvious answers to those questions, it thus becomes obvious why any diverging belief systems needed to be deleted by the Church, even if they reflected a more authentic theme to that of Jesus.

Especially if they were more authentic. It's not hard to imagine why we don't have copies of the Ebionite Gospel, or really any of the earlier versions of the gospels.

> *Not only do we not have the originals, we don't have the first copies of the originals. We don't have copies of the copies of the originals, or the copies of the copies of the copies of the originals.*
>
> Bart Ehrman

All we have today are documents which did not compete with, or threaten the Catholic Church. The rest evidently met the same fate as the Ebionite gospel – either destroyed or hidden in some private collection – perhaps within the archives of the Vatican – never to be seen again.

As Pauline Christianity gained footholds it became the Catholic Church. Meanwhile the Ebionites languished in the increasing unpopularity of Judaism and the economic disparity of their regions of spread. In the 4th century, Constantine welcomed Pauline Christianity into the Roman Empire with a warm embrace, even hosting the Nicaean Council which solidified anti-Ebionite doctrine.

By the time Augustine (354 – 430 CE) held sway, there would be no tolerance for variance from Catholicism. Augustine supported the power of the state to use coercion against Church competitors: "If the kings of this world could legislate against pagans and poisoners, they could do so against heretics as well." He also said: "coercion cannot transmit the truth to the heretic, it can prepare them to hear and receive the truth." Thus the 4th and 5th centuries would come to be known as years of bloodshed and violence.[191]

It was against this bloody backdrop the church decided which books would comprise the accepted biblical canon.[192] There was a wide variance in the accounts of Jesus at that time (see Panarion 30.22.3-5). Of course, the church chose the writings which best supported Catholic dogma. And having established that canon, they had a standard from which they could destroy the rest.

It was dangerous to hold beliefs which defied the Roman Catholic Church, and for centuries to come. It is thought the Ebionites died out by the 5th century. But in the year 1000, the historian Abd al-Jabbar ibn Ahmad encountered a group that some modern scholars believe may have been the last remnant.[193]

With all considered, the evidence does not indicate the Bible provides an accurate account of Jesus. We do not know what he said, what he believed or what he accomplished. God did not preserve the words of the Bible. Nothing indicates a divine origin. The Bible, and by their own account, is the product of the blood-stained hands of the Catholic Church and those of the Jewish Sanhedrin.

> How can you say, 'We are wise, for we have the law of the Lord,' when actually the lying pen of the scribes has handled it falsely?

Jeremiah 8:8

2.2.4 Wisdom

Oh, the depth of the riches and wisdom and knowledge of God! How unsearchable are his judgments and how inscrutable his ways!

Romans 11:33

A divine biblical author could have demonstrated their immense knowledge by explaining the complexities of natural cycles, the inner workings of our biology, or how the universe was formed. Knowing they have advanced knowledge of creation, we could trust them with our morals. If their book could describe wonders of the physical universe before they were discovered scientifically, that would give us reason for trust. It could have described evolution, planetary motion, gravity, thermodynamics, or relativity. It needn't be overly complicated. Einstein described relativity in five characters.

The Bible, rather, demonstrates the scientific understanding of iron-age writers. Is it reasonable for a heavenly father to impose his rules and then specifically give reason to doubt his knowledge? What would that say about his ability to offer philosophical insight or moral direction?

The Bible misses a multitude of opportunities to teach meaningful advice for human connectivity, mental health or finding purpose. It offers little help for anxiety, depression, feelings of worthlessness or post-traumatic stress. It fails to offer a glimpse as to why we feel the way we feel, and why we can't accomplish what we want. It fails to unite all people into common beliefs and values. It fails to address problems which have been timeless – the same problems which plagued humankind when the first biblical words were written. Wouldn't it make sense for God to address those human needs?

I imagine God's Words yet further. I imagine God's book speaking to each individual in separate ways, like an incredible piece of art invoking different feelings within different people. The Word of God would be like a mirror. Isn't that what we were told (James1:23,24)? A mirror that allowed us to look deep into ourselves and see the person we truly are. The effects would be so powerful that, like DMT or psylocibin, they would result in our complete recovery from anxiety or depression. DMT and psylocibin can do this with a single treatment, and they're so potent that although patients become strong advocates, they often never feel compelled to use them again.[194] Does God lack the ability to accomplish this with his words?

In contrast to the Bible, there are incredible writings from ancient times which *have* provided sound advice. At nearly the same time the gospels were written, Roman Emperor Marcus Aurelius wrote reminders to himself. Those reminders have been compiled into a book entitled *Meditations*.[195] To showcase the practical wisdom of *Meditations*, I closed each chapter with a quote. I think these exemplify the ability of a *human* to impart knowledge at *least* on par with biblical scripture.

In a rather ironic way, the supposed *Word of God* offers advice that breeds hate and divisiveness. From my experience it tells readers they are worthless and hopeless. It has been the *cause* of my anxiety, my depression, and on the world stage, a lengthy history of disunity and violence. Indications show it displaces real knowledge and is demonstrated to leave readers financially poorer and virtually uneducated.[196]

I'm sure that wasn't the intent. The intent was likely to give a group of Jewish settlers in the 5th century BCE a reason to feel the ground they were to live upon was given them by the Creator. It was likely intended to keep Jews separate from surrounding nations and therefore resist the spread of Greek culture. Like Santa Clause for a child, it was intended to incentivize preferred behaviors. But it was based on absurd distortions of truth and an iron-aged understanding of psychological manipulation.

I assume a significant reason people believe there is superior knowledge in the Bible is its size. The daunting task of reading it cover to cover and attempting to make sense of it is a time-sink most people aren't willing to invest. The benefits of such an undertaking are dubious. Most people let others interpret it for them to avoid that time-sink and I don't blame them.

While there may be a peppering of usefulness between the thousands of pages, the evidence suggests the Bible is not historically accurate. Prophecies like those in the book of Daniel, were written *after* events unfolded, not before.[197] Any assertion of the scientific accuracy of the Bible tends to be based on a degradation of science, or a misrepresentation of the Bible.

People think the Ten Commandments are a brilliant means of governance and evidence of advanced knowledge but fail to connect, as the Encyclopedia Britannica has, that they "contain little that was new to the ancient world and reflect a morality common to the ancient Middle East."[198] Proponents of the Torah seem to cherry pick around ridiculous laws like "do not wear clothing woven of two kinds of material," (Lev 19:19) or forbidding the eating of rabbit (Lev 11:6). It would be hard to convince me those are superior commands. This is not evidence of divine authorship.

I was told to consider the wisdom in the book of Proverbs. But for every gem in that book, I found a dozen dull rocks. Like saying throwing dice is a good way to settle a disagreement (Proverbs 18:18). I haven't heard anyone quote that verse.

How are we supposed to emulate a God so prone to tantrums that the man, Moses, had to calm God down before God committed genocide (Genesis 32:7-14)? I delivered a talk once at a JW meeting where I proclaimed that was a test of Moses' devotion to the people, but there is another completely reasonable explanation: That it wasn't. It seems more likely the authors were compiling a work of fiction and that's how *they thought* God would behave.

With that I feel the need to counter the assertions of the Watchtower and Awake! Magazines, for whatever my thoughts are worth. The Bible is not a reliable record for historical soundness. Candor and honesty are not qualities of its pages. Internal harmony cannot be found by any reader with an objective mind. Bible records are not harmonious with science. The Bible simply does not offer the wisdom it is purported to. One must deliberately side-step a lot of the Bible if they want to point out any form of wisdom. And I understand that thought process because I was lost to it too.

The story of the Bible is indeed fascinating. It gives us a glimpse into the mind of ancient humankind. It provides insight to the development of religion and the formulation of beliefs. But I assert the Bible could not have been written by God. It seems when that element is added to it we throw the balance of the Bible's value off – we add to it more weight than the evidence dictates.

Perhaps worse than that, it does God a tremendous disservice to think he couldn't have done better – to think it took God thousands of pages to produce a work which showed no insights beyond those of iron-aged sages, and which was clearly outwitted by Marcus Aurelius. I would offer a creator more credit.

A magazine once wrote, "only a fool would go through life blindly accepting everything he hears, basing his decisions and actions on frivolous advice or baseless teachings. Misplacing our trust—like stepping onto rotten planks—can lead to disaster."

What we hear the philosophers saying and what we find in their writings should be applied in our pursuit of the happy life. We should hunt out the helpful pieces of teaching, and the spirited and noble-minded sayings which are capable of immediate practical application – not far-fetched or archaic expressions or extravagant metaphors and figures of speech.
Marcus Aurelius

2.3 TAKING OF THE FRUIT

When one gives up the Christian faith, one pulls the right to Christian morality out from under one's feet. This morality is by no means self-evident.

Friedrich Nietzsche

Telling right from wrong becomes problematic for humanity from the opening chapters of the Bible. The Bible describes humanity's first moments with a dire warning: "Then the Lord God took the man and put him in the garden of Eden to tend and keep it. And the Lord God commanded the man, saying, "Of every tree of the garden you may freely eat; but of the tree of the knowledge of good and evil you shall not eat, for in the day that you eat of it you shall surely die" (Genesis 2:15-17).

It would appear the author was suggesting the *tree of the knowledge of good and evil* was a symbol of morality. Eating of the fruit, meant coming to understand what is right and wrong. It seems counterintuitive that God would prevent Adam from eating of the tree. Would it not be a profound benefit for a new human to know right from wrong? Should it not be the goal of parents to foster independent moral determination? How proud is a parent when their child makes solid moral decisions without supervision? If a person were reliant on their parents to determine right from wrong have they learned the life lessons to function as capable adults? If placed in a situation without supervision or direction, how could morally dependent people be trusted to avoid anti-social behaviors?

On the opposing side of the argument, *lack of belief* is often blamed for poor behaviors and for the breakdown of society. There is an assertion from the Judeo-Christian community that human morality finds its source within the Bible – that even if a person did not share Judeo-Christian beliefs, those values have been imprinted upon them by the Judeo-Christian God. In Ben Shapiro's book, *The Right Side of History*, he states: "there can be no individual or communal moral purpose without a foundation of Divine meaning."[199]

I couldn't find any research which supported the notion that lack of belief created anti-social behavior. Though I have earlier produced evidence that *belief* causes anti-social behaviors, and mental health issues.

In both the Bible and Quran, God sets a standard for good and bad, and that standard is (relatively) fixed. It suggests there is an altruistic *right* and there is an altruistic *wrong*. Humans must adopt those standards to gain God's approval. Those standards are required for a successful life. Ben Shapiro asserts: "without individual moral purpose granted by a Creator, we seek meaning instead in the collective, or we destroy ourselves on the shoals of libertinism. We live lives of amoral hedonism, in the non-disparaging sense."[200]

Consider the western tradition of Santa Clause. In many western cultures, parents will tell their children that Santa Clause has a naughty and a nice list. Santa can somehow monitor a child's behavior even when the child thinks they are alone. Santa will write children onto either the *nice list* or the *naughty list,* based on said behavior. Children on the nice list will receive a good gift at Christmas. Those on the naughty list will be rewarded poorly. The intent seems straight forward – to provide incentive to children for appropriate behavior.

There are two problems with this concept. The first is that it is based on an undeniable fallacy. Santa does not exist. The second is it offers inferior and external motives for behavior. Could these conditions possibly result in ethical behavior, or healthy development and mental well-being of a child? Eventually, the child will come to understand the teaching was false. Some kids might shrug the deception off and chalk it up to loss of fantasy. For others, it will erode their trust with the parent and stifle later behavior-corrective strategies.[201]

The behavioral incentives are misaligned with reality, and if we carried beliefs of Santa into adulthood, I can't imagine expecting anything other than confusion and unethical behavior. At a stage of a child's development where consequences can be realized, shouldn't those consequences be the basis for restraint, and not a mythical *pretense* of consequences?

We don't live in a world sanitized with justice. Everyone will experience injustice. But I found when we believe in divine intervention, we experience unnecessary internal struggle when injustice occurs. I endured internal conflict reconciling my perception of God's responses to my efforts. When circumstances did not align with how I perceived the distribution of fair reward my sense of justice boiled into outrage. That is not proof there is no divine intervention. It was merely my perception. But it illustrates the mental condition people might experience – rage invoked by what appears an unbalance of the universal scales of justice. What greater justification could there be?

Since then, I found accepting reality in the face of injustice provides greater peace of mind. Accepting that things are not fair. Regardless of whether a later karmic correction is coming, accepting that the world is unfair is surprisingly liberating. Accepting that I was treated unfairly removed the frustrated energy. *As long as everyone knows that was bullshit, I'm cool. Let's continue.*

Albert Einstein said, "A man's ethical behavior should be based effectually on sympathy, education, and social ties and needs; no religious basis is necessary. Man would indeed be in a poor way if he had to be restrained by fear of punishment and hopes of reward after death."[202] But Einstein's opinion appears to conflict with the lessons taught in the Garden of Eden. Would people then be deciding for themselves what is ethical? Would they not then require knowledge of good and bad? Was not partaking of the tree of knowledge unforgivable?

Perhaps revisiting that account is worthwhile. In Genesis 2 God warned: "in the day that you eat of it you shall surely die." Later though, the serpent tells Eve, "you will not certainly die, for God knows that when you eat from it your eyes will be opened, and you will be like God, knowing good and evil." As JWs, we were taught the serpent in that story told the first ever lie.[203] But notice what happened after Adam and Eve ate the fruit. "Then the eyes of both of them were opened, and they realized they were naked" (Genesis 3:1-7). Did you notice how they died? They did not. In fact, they went on to live hundreds of years. So, who really told the first lie? It was not the serpent. What the serpent said proved true. Their eyes were indeed opened.

God warned, "in the *day* that you eat it you shall surely die." That did not happen. At best, God failed to follow up on a promise and failed to teach a lesson about consequences.

I posit a parent who does well to instruct their child does so with a mind to teaching them consequences. When my daughter was but a few months old and had yet to speak her first word, she sat on my lap and reached for my hot cup of coffee. The mug was hot enough to cause *me* pain, but not hot enough to result in harm. Me saying *no* to her was not enough to satisfy her inquisitive spirit, and she insisted on reaching for the cup.

I used the opportunity as a teaching moment. After warning her not to touch the cup because it was *hot,* I did not resist her next attempt. It hurt my heart to do it, but I allowed her little fingers to wrap around the mug and waited those seconds for her brain to register pain. When she recoiled and her face distorted in horror, I clearly repeated one word: "hot." To my amazement, she didn't cry. Her eyes welled up and her defiant, yet trembling lips, mouthed her very first word: "hot."

The training was so effective, she transferred the word *hot* to other objects of danger. The loud roar of the vacuum and scratches from a kitten were reported to us as *hot.* If she approached an electrical socket or cleaning supplies, I didn't have to concoct some strange story of a mythical being on overwatch. I simply said "*hot.*" She immediately understood there were consequences, and I would never have to tell her twice. She formulated a trust I was telling the truth and she had no reason to test further.

Would she have had that trust if my warnings did not prove true?

Learning consequences becomes increasingly important as we develop into adulthood. Nothing else is more honest. Nothing else will watch over us when no one is looking.

God's morality may be an attempt to achieve this, in the same way Santa morality is. But the concept of Biblical morality fails to instill its intended value when cosmic consequences are not realized.

I found myself in mental agony, trying to reconcile why my sacrifices to God were not acknowledged, yet others proclaimed the abundant blessings they received. That led me to one conclusion: *God does not like me*.

In my research, I did not find psychological studies with empirical data on this phenomenon. But I did find the question *why doesn't God love me* in surprisingly high volumes across social media, google searches, forums, and Christian websites. They expressed the same concern I wrestled with – *the highest authority in the universe and the source of eternal love assesses no value in me*. Scriptures intended to provide comfort like: "God has said, 'Never will I leave you; never will I forsake you,'" provided no comfort. Reading how God would never leave or abandon me was enraging when I felt left and abandoned (Hebrews 13:5).

> *But He loves you*
> George Carlin

Jehovah's Witnesses might tell you disfellowshipped people are welcomed back any time. That is somewhat misleading. Disfellowshipped people are *usually* welcomed to attend certain public meetings, but their *disfellowshipped* status remains until they are reinstated – JWs will not associate with them until then.

To get reinstated, they must endure a lengthy process where elders monitor their presentability. The sinners must demonstrate disconnection from the world, attend services regularly, and when they do, they must sit at the back of the Hall without speaking to anyone. It is a humiliating process. After attending meetings for several months, they may apply to be reinstated by formal request. The process usually takes a year. A year without social contact.[204] I'll be honest – I didn't feel very welcomed.

I was disfellowshipped twice for poor conduct and reinstated both times. One of those took two years before I was reinstated. Two years of degrading treatment and scowls of distrust. I asked to speak with the elders, but they told me to concentrate on my relationship with Jehovah. In obedience I prayed constantly. I read the Bible and searched through myself in hopes to understand why I was so wicked and undeserving.

I took their suggestions and reflected on the Bible story of the prodigal son. But comparing the story to my own did not provide the desired effect. Doing so degraded my faith in God, and my remaining faith in the ability of congregation elders. Forgiveness was immediate for the prodigal son who squandered his life partying and sleeping with prostitutes (Luke 15:11-32). As the prodigal son approached his father's home, his father ran out to greet the son before the son reached the door. He was embraced, assured of his father's love, and celebrated.

I considered how this related to me. I had come all the way back to God's house, and yet after two years was not forgiven or welcomed. And because we were convinced God was directing the elders, I believed *God* had judged I was not worthy of forgiveness. And of course that was supported when the elders told me – exactly that. Was I worse than the prodigal son? In truth my behavior was not stellar, but it didn't rise to the depravity of the prodigal son.

After the disappointment of learning elders would not reinstate me after the first year, I started to drink alcohol regularly and to contemplate suicide daily. What stalled the process was my newborn baby girl and a young wife who relied on me. I couldn't find a way to end my life without destroying theirs. A suicide would devastate them.

I considered staging a car accident and after months of planning and building the courage, I felt I found the right spot. But after a few dry runs and analyses of my courage, the probability of surviving as a paralytic seemed unacceptably high. And that was how I justified making it back home.

Approaching that scenario as close as I did, left me with emotional scars. For years afterward, and sometimes even recently, if I find myself taking that same winding route along the edge of a rocky cliff, my hands will shake on the wheel, and I have often had my wife drive for me. I wouldn't want to gain that courage at the wrong time.

For eight years until I finally woke from indoctrination, I contemplated suicide each day. I perceived disgust in the eyes of the elders, and I projected that contempt as from God. In my mind, Jehovah was an angry elder who had concluded I was unworthy of forgiveness.

My state of mind was so dark it was noticeable. My wife would not allow my daughter to enter the house ahead of her because she was afraid my daughter would find me hanging. That persisted until my daughter was eight. When I finally rid myself of the indoctrination, I never again had a suicidal thought.

For those former Jehovah's Witnesses who have failed in their self-discipline, take heart that it's not entirely your fault. You may be in an unbearable situation and that might be the consequences of your actions, but you didn't know any better. You were told not to do things because God would write you onto the naughty list. When the naughty list failed to be a deterrent, you explored your boundaries. That is precisely what is expected of anyone who was never provided correct incentive to say *no*. My daughter was given better training with a coffee cup.

I have come to believe morality as it is imposed upon us from monotheistic religion, is a flawed concept. Even the benefits of discipline – which are undeniable – lose their value when people are prevented from experiencing life on their own terms. Without testing their boundaries curiosity will likely drive them toward a test of circumstances when it is far less safe than sitting on their father's lap. I assert that far from making people better, this form of imposed morality increases poor behaviors in the long run; increases stress, and feelings of worthlessness. It prevents the development of skills required for emotional development and self-determination.

Despite being deprived of those skills though, our self-determination remains. It never leaves our grasp. It has been, and always will be our determination as to what is right and wrong; which opinions we accept; what we believe; and what we decide. If we owe our lives to a creator, we owe them the gift of self-determination too. In John Steinbeck's *East of Eden,* the character Lee explains the value of those choices using the Hebrew word *timshel.* He explains what God meant when he warned Cain before his brother's murder.

> *"The King James translation makes a promise in 'Thou shalt,' meaning that men will surely triumph over sin. But the Hebrew word timshel—'Thou mayest'—that gives a choice. For if 'Thou mayest'— it is also true that 'Thou mayest not.' That makes a man great and that gives him stature with the gods."*
>
> John Steinbeck, East of Eden

With the gods? Knowing good and bad? Didn't God say that wasn't allowed? Which is it? Does God want us to be like God knowing good and bad? Are we allowed to eat of that fruit? Or was the prophet Jeremiah correct: "Man's way does not belong to him. It does not belong to man who is walking even to direct his step." (Jeremiah 10:23$_{NWT}$)

Did God offer Cain free will? The same god who failed to tell the truth in the Garden of Eden? Who declared "in the very day of your eating the fruit..."?

I have a difficult time believing humans are intrinsically endowed with any rights. But the right of self-determination seems very much solidified in human nature. Psychologist and holocaust survivor Victor Frankl wrote: "Everything can be taken from a man but one thing: the last of the human freedoms to choose one's attitude in any given set of circumstances, to choose one's own way."[205] We may lose our right to life, freedom, security, or justice. But so long as we are alive, we can determine for ourselves what is acceptable. What does that say about something so clearly imprinted upon our being? Some might say that is a gift from God that no person could take.

Others would say the Bible is right.

Was God's intent to offer free will only to threaten eternal punishment each time it was used? Is it a father's intent to teach a child how to tie their shoelaces – but then follow them wherever they go – threatening them each time they did it wrong? Would you consider that good parenting? There's more than one way to tie a shoelace. There is more than one way to live a life. There are a wide range of behaviors which could hurt us or help us. I posit there is no scale which is as simple as *good or bad*. The world is not black and white.

I submit that when used to determine human behaviors, shitty works of fiction harm people, cause divisions, and fail to keep anyone moral. I further submit: there can be no individual or communal moral purpose while holding true to belief in shitty words.

If I sound blasphemous, let me assure you I intend the opposite. I have complete reverence for any being who could create another. I would be humbly awestruck in the presence of the Universal Sovereign. I would not want to face God knowing I was too stubborn to detach from untruths which have enslaved humans for millennia. I would not want to face God saying I thought so little of his intelligence I was duped into thinking his words could not surpass those of John Steinbeck or Marcus Aurelius. I would be terrified to face God knowing I supported organizations which used a book to torture and terrorize other humans, forcing them into slavery, defrauding them of self-determination, which took so much self-worth from people, they killed themselves by the thousands.

I hope I could tell God I made the best use of his gift of self-determination – the one gift which can never be taken from us. I would want God to know I not only partook of the tree of knowledge, I built scaffolds to reach higher branches and I left nothing behind – not one opportunity to learn of his works.

If someone is incapable of distinguishing good things from bad and neutral things from either – well, how could such a person be capable of love?
Marcus Aurelius

2.4 DO NOT JUDGE

You always own the option of having no opinion. There is never any need to get worked up or to trouble your soul about things you can't control. These things are not asking to be judged by you. Leave them alone.

Marcus Aurelius

I learned it was important to rid my mind of negative patterns. I also wish I had learned to do so earlier. Of those patterns, perhaps most important to change was that of judgment. I was highly judgmental while living dogmatically and it robbed me of joy. While I can't say for sure that was a product of my religion, there is evidence to suggest my religion didn't help.

We were taught we possessed a superior moral code, and the Creator would tolerate no other form of conduct. We were encouraged to report the sins of other JWs to elders, and so our eyes remained vigilantly peeled. We had to determine whether JWs were good or bad (association).

Judging people outside the religion required less effort. We knew by default Worldly people were bad people (2Cor 6:14,17). And we were *required* to adopt Jehovah's denunciatory view of them – to "hate what Jehovah hates" (Ps 97:10).[206] And certainly toward former members, the word *hate* is not over-stated. We were trained to experience a visceral response to apostates (Rom 1:32).

> *Now it's not that we rejoice in someone's death, but when it comes to Gods enemies, finally, they are out of the way, especially these despicable apostates[207]*
>
> Anthony Morris III, Governing Body of Jehovah's Witnesses,
> Morning Worship September 2020

That Jesus said "do not judge" seemed largely ignored (Matthew 7:1). When JW elders learn someone in their ranks committed a *sin*, it is their official policy to assemble a *Judicial* Committee for the expressed purpose of *judging* the individual. In an apparently brazen manner, their guidebook states: "elders are judging for Jehovah."[208]

Elders could only judge what they saw, so they favored those who let them see their most favorable side. We were rewarded or punished based on the *outward* appearance of our conduct. We needed to present like people featured on the cover of Watchtower and Awake magazines. It was, after all, that particular lifestyle they were selling. Behind the smiles and suits, it bred a pervasive need to appear perfect. We had to be perfect, or we risked loss of status, public shame, or being disfellowshipped.

> *Don't await perfection [...] but be satisfied with even the smallest step forward, and regard the outcome as a small thing.*
> Marcus Aurelius

This form of perfectionism fostered comparison. I suppose there is little wonder why I acted judgmental or that I felt Jehovah's Witnesses were especially judgmental. If we ignore Jesus' words, the Bible encourages judgment. Perhaps if I read more of Marcus Aurelius than the Bible the outcome would be different.

> *It isn't my responsibility to judge outsiders, but it certainly is your responsibility to judge those inside the church who are sinning.*
> 1 Corinthians 5:12, Paul

Could we find better advice than the Bible? I can't say that judging myself, or perfectionism made me a better person. I'm quite certain it did not make me honest or humble or faithful. I am more certain it made me hate myself and to be envious of others – to despise the skin I lived in. There were long periods of my life when I lied constantly because I was ashamed of who I was, and because I refused to accept my errors. I felt shame because I was taught to feel shame. I was taught God felt those aspects of me were shameful.

You don't love yourself enough. Or you'd love your nature too, and what it demands of you.

Marcus Aurelius

Looking back on poor decisions can haunt a person. Those times you slacked off at school, or you chose to have that first cigarette, or you had too many drinks, or you said those things you regret – those have a habit of ringing in our ears like a terrible song. Paul's words and the oversight of the elders had the same effect as playing the song on repeat.

I lived with that song in my head for most of my life. I still struggle with it. People would say *be yourself. How could anyone take that advice at face-value?* I kept being told to be who I was, but I could never figure out who the fuck that was. It made me angry, because I understood the intent of the admonition, but there were no instructions to get there. It was like saying *be happy,* or *forget about her.* Wouldn't that be nice? I would have loved even a glimpse of what it felt to be authentic. Instead, I learned to recreate a reality and look enviously at the authenticity of others.

Be content to seem what you really are.

Marcus Aurelius

To overcome my issue with authenticity, I would need to discontinue believing Paul was inspired to write God's thoughts. I could no longer believe my failures were the rancid inheritance of Adam, the festering evil which set me apart from God and required human sacrifice just so I could pray for forgiveness. Or that those sins condemned me to death, even though Jesus already died for them – they were that bad. I needed to have more patience with myself and more patience with other people.

What benefit did you reap at that time from the things you are now ashamed of? Those things result in death! But now that you have been set free from sin and have become slaves of God, the benefit you reap leads to holiness, and the result is eternal life. For the wages

> *of sin is death, but the gift of God is eternal life in Christ Jesus our*
> *Lord.*
>
> Romans 6:21-23 Attributed to Paul

If we could strip from our mind Paul's concept of imperfection is it really a stretch to say we *are* perfect? We are legitimately doing exactly what is expected in each situation. We are nailing it. Every time. We are the peak of evolution (that we know). We are perfect. A fun fact: Jesus is also attributed with saying: "Be perfect (Mat 5:48)." He did not say *strive for perfection* or, *soon you will be perfect*. To say *be perfect* makes it sound attainable. Immediately attainable. How is that possible?

> *The happiness of your life depends upon the quality of your thoughts:*
> *therefore, guard accordingly.*
>
> Marcus Aurelius

When I've wallowed in my failures, I've also been hit with a sad realization of my motives. I had to admit they were shaded with laziness, greed, and contempt. I was sickened at times when I realized my true failures. But alongside that sickened feeling was another reality – *I could not have done better.* Some might think saying *I couldn't have done any better* is a shirking of responsibility. I think it is honest. And it requires honesty to admit motives.

Being told to accept responsibility for our actions may have been a misnomer all along. Perhaps what was meant by the expression was to accept reality. If it were not the intent, perhaps it should have been. We cannot know what all the consequences to our actions will be. In that sense we could not have anticipated the result and thus could not have accepted responsibility for those results – despite the canned advice offered by elders. The only one who could have known all the consequences would be Jehovah, would it not? Perhaps Jehovah should start taking on some of his responsibilities. On the other hand, we can always accept the reality of our circumstances, regardless of whether we had a different expectation. Regardless of whether the all-knowing will step up.

To sit in the seat of acceptance I would need to know that I *could* be imperfect. That it was *permitted*. Of course we were specifically told God is ready to forgive. But the Faithful Slave was not ready to forgive. Their policies for reinstatement made that clear. They fell short of saying imperfection was acceptable. Imperfection was not acceptable, and when I internalized that opinion the result was me being reticent to trying new things, failing to manage frustration after failure, and a persistent comparing with others. To overcome this I would need to be convinced I was NOT imperfect. I did the best I could. Perfectly.

> *An ignorant person is inclined to blame others for his own misfortune. To blame oneself is proof of progress. But the wise man never has to blame another or himself.*
>
> Marcus Aurelius

It was also helpful to think of Jesus' words: "be perfect." Not when understood to mean *be flawless*, which the author may have intended. Perhaps being perfect is to sit comfortably in the presence of our flaws. To own each of our errors, and with that acceptance offer no resistance to admitting fault. If those flaws are the reality of life than it would only be honest to accept that reality. **Perhaps being perfect is accepting reality.** Perhaps perfection requires we withhold judgment, even for ourselves. Perhaps the difference between *this* and perfection is not *becoming* perfect but realizing that we *are*.

If we could fully accept reality, we could accept each part of us. We could accept the faults of others. We could even accept tragedy. If it is not currently in our power to change it, then we must accept it.

I can control my thoughts as necessary; then how can I be troubled? What is outside my mind means nothing to it. Absorb that lesson and your feet stand firm.

Marcus Aurelius

If I stopped attaching such polarized judgments on everything, I could immediately find time to appreciate life.

Accept the things to which fate binds you and love the people with whom fate brings you together but do so with all your heart.

Marcus Aurelius

But have I not passed *judgment* on judgment? And on Jehovah (the Faithful Slave)? This is tricky. Is there an objective good or bad way to view judgment? How could we demonstrate sound *judgment* on such a thing?

I suppose the only way to determine an objective truth would be to rule all else out. We would require each perspective of every matter. We would need to be all-knowing. Until then, I think it's safe to say: *I don't know.*

Here is a rule to remember in future, when anything tempts you to feel bitter: not "This is misfortune," but "To bear this worthily is good fortune."

Marcus Aurelius

For the sake of conversation and to illicit your response, I will propose a "moral" line with regard to judgment. I propose that making determinations or judgments is both fair-game, and sometimes necessary. Where it becomes problematic is when we allow our personal determination to leave our personal sphere. When we assume that others must adopt the same judgment, that other people must live up to our standards, or that the truth of our judgment is universal. *This is good. That is bad.* As opposed to: *I prefer this. I don't like that.*

> *Whenever you are about to find fault with someone, ask yourself the
> following question: What fault of mine most nearly resembles the one
> I am about to criticize?"*
> Marcus Aurelius

Aurelius has a knack for calling me out. I still find myself surprised at how deep within my mental circuitry the tendency to judge is. I tried to remove *good* and *bad* from my vocabulary. The same with *evil* or *righteous*, *wrong* and *right*. If I were to make such a determination, I have taken upon myself a heavy burden that is both unnecessary and impractical.

It is likely our earliest reactions to any form of stimuli to determine *good* or *bad*. I think of a baby hearing a pop and then scanning the room for mom's reaction to determine if it was scary or hilarious. *Was that good or bad?* I can't help but think we would naturally learn to nuance good and bad into the infinite complexities that exist were it not for a belief system which dogmatized them. Perhaps religion unwittingly preserves for us an infantile means of determination. As a child should eventually understand that pop sounds are not classified only as good or bad, we could stop pretending that fornication is any more reprehensible for humans than for our pets.

> *Life is neither good or evil, but only a place for good and evil.*
> Marcus Aurelius

I'm not sure if we entirely grow out of judgment. It seems as we mature past the point of judging small things like the word *shit*, we find a way to attach this sense of internal morality to more complex matters. Like greed or political stances, corruption, or incompetence. Our judgment evolves. It's hard to understand the full pattern with our limited perspective. Perhaps it's unavoidable. Perhaps it's our intuition making the most rudimentary decision based on limited understanding. Perhaps it's a product of our culture.

> *The object of life is not to be on the side of the majority, but to escape finding oneself in the ranks of the insane.*
>
> Marcus Aurelius

In my current perspective I found judgment creates unnecessary stress as the judge remains alert to circumstances which do not fit their preconceptions of perfection. They might be surprised to find other people do not share their views of good and bad. Not everyone thinks the sight of a woman's hair is immoral. The judge often thinks their moral standards are universal when they are more likely personal – a product of their upbringing. Each condition askew of their standards agitates the spirit of the judge. They think conditions should exist in another form. *That person should act more like this, or that group should never have done that.* In a sense it is disagreeing with reality.

> *The first rule is to keep an untroubled spirit. The second is to look things in the face and know them for what they are.*
>
> Marcus Aurelius

What if our personal morality was wrong? What if, when I say the Bible is *bullshit* and Jehovah needs to take care of his responsibilities, it does not bother the Creator at all. But what if it still makes *you* squirm? Reality has not fit the judge's personal standards and that feels inexplicably frustrating.

> *Everything that happens, happens as it should, and if you observe carefully, you will find this to be so.*
>
> Marcus Aurelius

The judge's agitation isn't necessary. Why would we need to apply our model of *what should be* to others? How well does it sit when someone else applies theirs to you? I must assume that is a line best not to cross. Only since 3 Post-Dogma have I learned to discard the absurd notion I have a right to be upset because conditions have not aligned as they should.

I can finally accept that now. But I have struggled with judgment. I couldn't accept what elders said after I begged to be reinstated and was left drowning in solitude. I found it hard to accept how for years elders inferred I was gay or accused me of homosexuality - this following a judicial meeting where I had to explain in detail how a JW in his 70s groomed me as a teenager before performing unwelcomed sexual acts.

Perhaps the townsfolk of Clearwater, British Columbia might be upset to hear how that JW had been molesting children for decades and his victims were not all JW children. The community outside the religion was affected. Perhaps the community would be less impressed to hear how the pedophile had been reported to JW elders on multiple occasions and years before police were notified. I think it's safe to assume the elders forwarded those reports to the Branch Office as per their protocol. Yet, as it was told to me, it took until an outsider reported the molester to local authorities that he was finally stopped. Could the community of Clearwater have been spared at least some pedophilia if reporting him didn't have to wait for an outsider? If authorities were informed 20 years prior could even one child have been spared?

I think the reputation of Jehovah would be in better condition if the JW policy was to report sexual assault to authorities. One can only speculate why they make it a policy to call authorities for vandalism, but not to protect a child. I suppose that makes it difficult for me not to judge.

I find it difficult to withhold judgment from a judicial system which has allowed the Faithful Slave to run as it pleases over millions of innocent people decade after decade. Who have allowed the governing body to hide behind a Whack-a-Mole configuration of legal entities in order to avoid helping victims. A justice system which allows religious entities use of the *right to religious freedom* to remove that right from individuals. A justice system in no way oblivious to the litigious nature of the JW Organization and the barrage of lawsuits launched at any, and every person or group who threaten their image – their product (I'm sure my lawsuit is in the mail). How they leverage their assets and access to legal resources to siege legal opponents, deplete opponent resources and force a quiet retreat to protect their brand. But then, these are all merely my opinions.

I can choose to ruminate over how things should be. Or I can accept their existence in their present form and forego judgment. Perhaps the trick is to see perfection in everything. But also to hold our future actions to high standards.

> *Be tolerant with others and strict with yourself.*
> Marcus Aurelius

Accepting reality appears crucial to the process. That is, accepting what I cannot control. For those matters within my control, my judgement offers valuable incentive to adjust as necessary. It is less valuable otherwise. Humility of mind seems to be another crucial part. It's hard to cast judgment when we know nothing.

> *Very little is needed to make a happy life; it is all within yourself in your way of thinking.*
> Marcus Aurelius

Reserving judgment is a concept much harder to practice than anticipated. I had to carefully check my judgment of the Bible and of the Faithful Slave. Taking a moral position seems a more natural default and I'm certain to have let that slip within these pages. It's something I'm working on.

I do feel confident in concluding that my morals, self-esteem, and my impression of the world would have been better shaped by Marcus Aurelius than the Bible.

If something in the exterior world makes you discontent, then it is not that object which troubles you, but rather your own judgment of it; yet to blot out this judgment instantly is within your power.

Marcus Aurelius

2.5 DAUNTLESS BEFORE DEATH

You only live twice: Once when you are born. And once when you look death in the face.

Ian Fleming

Death is our greatest fear and forms our saddest moments. It is the condition we avoid at all costs. For some, the fear of death is crippling. For some, the thought of their lives ending is unacceptable. Many seek out beliefs that provide a comforting reprieve and luckily for them, there is no shortage to select from.

Eternal life is the best-selling hit of religion. It is the promise a politician makes when he offers the world but possesses neither the resources nor intent to deliver. Whether that promise is eternal life in heaven with Jesus, in Paradise with Allah, or any similar guarantee made with the confident nod of surety, caution is advised.

To be clear, I'm not saying there is no life after death. I'm suggesting we don't know; and that fictitious promises are dangerous. They prey upon our intense affection for those we've loved and lost. They prey upon our deepest fears and our deeply rooted survival instincts.

We have only known existence and the thought of non-existence resides outside the limits of our cognitive ability. For some, a broken heart may make them vulnerable to a trade for the hereafter. The fear of pain and suffering that is often the precursor to death is terrifying for most.[209] In the wake of such fear, peddlers of paradise find their marks.

Is there anything wrong with curiosity? With studying, theorizing, and conversing about the possibilities of our posthumous existence? Where I think it becomes dangerous is when it is promised. When it is weaponized. When we are told we must sacrifice our current life and resources to attain to the next. When promises woo the believer from a healthy acceptance of what is.

I watched the last few hours of my father's life. He passed away a month prior to writing this. He had battled cancer for months and although

I knew what was coming, nothing prepared me for the empty void that was left when my father was gone.

I understand how comforting a belief would be of reuniting with a loved one. How could anyone fail to empathize with a parent who has tragically lost a young child? All that parent would want is to hold and to play with their little one again. A person who has lost a loving mate after many years of partnership would give anything to be reunited. Our social connections are stronger than we might have imagined. A relationship we took for granted often reveals its impact only too late.

I feel that with regards to my father. I had reasons not to have a warm or close connection. But I did have that. In a perplexing way, that makes me feel guilty. My father refused to acknowledge my existence when I was born, and we never met until I was 12. From then, through the next years of early teen-hood, it was clear to me he was not impressed with my behavior.

To be fair, I wasn't an easy child to like. My mother was barely 17 when I was born. The average parent struggles to navigate the concepts and habits of good parenthood. For a single, teenaged girl from a highly volatile and abusive home, she had the deck stacked against her. She decided she would raise me as one of Jehovah's Witnesses so for my first 12 years of life, I spent nearly all my time with female relatives and the rest learning from the Bible. I developed feminine personality traits, and habits that were tragically unproductive. I had poor personal hygiene and was awkward when interacting with others. I must assume my father's first reaction to me was not that of impress.

The strange twist here is that I didn't feel judged by my father. He hadn't decided in any way I was good or bad. But he didn't pretend he was impressed with my conduct, either. When my strange behaviors subsided, he was immediately accepting. This had a surprisingly strong and positive effect on me. I felt compelled to improve myself, while not being judged. I would learn what made me a better person simply by interacting with my father. He didn't know how to be a parent, but his influence was commanding and life-altering, and I feel I owe many of my better traits to him. My work ethic, social skills and confidence would not have developed without him. I'm sure of that.

My Dad never embraced religion. He was religiously amoral. But as I overcame many of my social hurdles and we started to bond, I was forced to realize there was no need to feel disgusted by this amoral person as my religion had taught me. My time with my father was fun and refreshing. In those moments when I could break from being one of Jehovah's Witnesses, I could relax from the suffocating thought-control and test the limits of who I was. By the time I reached my 20s, my dad was my best friend. We worked together, we lived together, we played cards, we competed fiercely at softball, and I felt comfortable in his presence. I could escape the confines of JW control. My dad was my vacation from that little box.

I learned from him not to judge a person because they didn't embrace God or because they drank beer and used foul language. I was capable of learning those habits have consequences. But forever I will know such habits are no measure of a person's worth. Habits are a measure of a person's habits.

I guess the regret I feel is that I didn't tell him that. I didn't tell him the enormous impact he had on my life. Or that it pisses me off that I love him, because part of me feels he doesn't deserve my love. He did not invest the same time and effort my mother had. It was my mother who sacrificed her life. It was her time, her dedication, and her efforts that kept me fed and clothed.

It doesn't seem we can always control who we influence, who we care about or who we love. Human connection is a far deeper entity than the surface connections we can measure. Sometimes we have no conscious realization of how intricately connected we are.

Death reminds us of that. When that void opens and the full effect of a loved one's impact is revealed by their absence, that's when we catch a glimpse of their value. The emptiness they leave behind when their life ends is a hole in the shape of who they really were. Death has a funny way of offering an immediate overview. A god's-eye view of life, where all the good and bad moments blend – where we feel a natural sense of forgiveness, even though we may fight against it. Grudges cease, hate subsides, and it becomes possible to see things for what they are.

When we gather for a funeral or a celebration of life, we keep saying how good it is to see everyone. *It's too bad it has to take something like this to bring everyone together.* In those saddest of circumstances, death unites us. While we grieve and we remember, we come closer to being one. We find a deeper value in our own lives and in the lives of others. All our personal values are brought into surprising clarity, and we are forced to recognize the incredible privilege we have in taking each breath.

I have resisted the notion that pain is required to experience happiness. Despite that, there is a strong argument for the value of pain. I cannot think of a greater teacher. We learn the most crucial lessons from the embarrassing pain of our failures. Our bodies only grow strong when we exert our muscles to the point of pain. Emotional pain produces art. Discomfort leads to change. Pain provides an appreciation for life and serves as a critical warning when something is wrong. Indulging in pleasure is what voids our life of meaning. It is pain that produces the best human qualities. Pain such that results from the looks of displeasure in the eyes of a father, unimpressed with the immature antics of his 12-year-old son. That's how we grow.

> *We can't learn without pain.*
> Aristotle

What if death is the same? What if death is just as necessary as pain?

From an evolutionary point of view, we are intended to die. If we did not, overpopulation would prevent new growth. New variations of species could not evolve. Life would stagnate and fail to adjust to changes in the environment. Without death, life as we know it, could not exist. When our hands first form in the womb, the fingers are webbed together like an oven mitt. The only means for separation is for those cells to be recycled into a more useful form. They need to die.[210]

Perhaps that's true in the evolution of our civilizations too. The old ways need to be improved upon, and it requires fresh minds and an absence of dogma to innovate. Perhaps human society requires natural cycles of birth and death to rejuvenate its social systems, just like the cells in our bodies need to regenerate.

Another generation benefits from following the lead of the prior, but also by building and improving those methods. Those that learned from their aged leaders are now equipped to improve them. But they can't make improvements if those leaders forever hold their role. A younger, more pliable mind is necessary for advancement. If humans never died and their bodies never became frail, the top of human hierarchies would be stocked with the oldest people, stubbornly clinging to dogma they insist is best. We would be stuck with leaders who grew out of their competence and refused to yield their authority. New ideas would be forever stifled.

In my first year post-dogma (1 post-dogma), when I discarded the JW belief in Paradise, I was for the first time faced with the prospect of dying. This was an especially difficult realization. I've spoken to many who had similar experiences, so I deduce this is common among those who shed afterlife beliefs in adulthood. I was now in the middle of life and just beginning to come to terms with something I was childishly unprepared for.

As JWs, we were told we were going to live forever. I believed that. I literally believed I would never taste death. Armageddon was going to come before I was finished high school. The world was going to be destroyed, and there I would be – protected by God, along with other Jehovah's Witnesses, living forever in paradise on Earth. There was little motivation to excel in school. No career planning. No consideration of what my adult life might look like, let alone contemplate my own death. And that was how we were taught to think. We were told not to attend college, encouraged to make high school a secondary focus, and the religion our primary concern. Of course when high school ended, I was unprepared for adulthood. Like the generations of Jehovah's Witnesses before me, I entered my mid-life without ever considering what it could be like to grow old or die.

When I realized none of it was true, it was embarrassing in one sense, enraging in another, and motivating in yet another. I understand why Jehovah's Witnesses march into death for their leadership. Not because that loyalty is deserved. But because they're so heavily invested, and the prospect of facing reality is so horrific, death doesn't seem so bad. *Maybe there's a chance it's still true.*

Deep breaths.

I am going to die.

In struggling to accept this I felt the urge to reach out to any belief as an alternative. But the prospect of becoming a slave to yet more Shepherds and Dukes was worse than reality. So I stared reality down. And all those thoughts which should have taken 37 years to process hit at once. *It's not fair. We just start to figure life out before our health fades and it's over. It can't be that simple, or shallow, or short. It defies logic. If life were fair, why don't we grow young?*

I am going to die.

I considered scientific alternatives to death. There are current medical advances that could drastically increase the duration of human life, and these advances could be available to us within our lifetime. But if we extend our lives to a point where death is no longer inevitable, we will need to adjust to a changing evolutionary process which previously relied on death.

There is room for speculation of an afterlife. Just because we can't measure what happens to our consciousness after death, doesn't mean existence ends. We just don't know. We don't know if we're living a *Matrix*-like simulation. We don't know if we possess some form of soul that floats elsewhere or if we try another opportunity for life in a different role. We don't know if the myriad of thoughts which comprise our consciousness disperse or shatter and rejoin with the oneness of the universe.

I read a lot of Sam Harris in 1 Post-Dogma. *Waking Up* was a significant influence on me. In one part, Sam talks about *split brain phenomenon*, where the fiber tracts which connect the left and right hemispheres are severed to treat epileptic seizures. The procedure also severs the conscious inputs to the two hemispheres. A patient would close one eye and only one side of the brain would receive an image. Researchers found they could ask questions to either side of the same brain independently and would receive different answers. Either side of the brain would have different desires and beliefs. One hemisphere could be religious and the other atheist.[211] Researchers were forced to concede that each hemisphere appeared independently conscious after the procedure, though such conclusions remain contested.

The concept of consciousness is core to belief in an afterlife. If our body dies, what else would move on, if not our consciousness? Sam's words opened an entire realm of possibilities. If there were two separate consciousnesses in the brain after the procedure, what if there were always two – they simply found a way to communicate? If it's possible there are two consciousness' within our brain, what if there are more? Many more. What if we live daily as a composite of harmonious, and sometimes competing consciousness?

If that were true, what if, as human individuals interacting with other individuals, we form a macro-personality where the culture of the group shows the personality of a collective consciousness? And if that's true, what if the whole earth: the rock, the flora and fauna, all things interacting with each other; form a large collective entity with its own personality and preferences? From there we could scale the concept to the solar system and then galaxies and beyond.

The last day of my father's life, as he struggled to speak; struggled to function; struggled to compose himself and present with his former dignity, he confided that he was done. *This is it.* He can't do it anymore. While his nurses and doctors were incapable of providing us with a timeline for his passing, my father knew. What changed for him was *acceptance.* He no longer feared death.

In previous months he had fought. But whatever those motivations were, they had become irrelevant on his last day. At a certain point, wishes and desires cease to be relevant. And that's ok. We can go kicking and screaming, or we can stand dauntless in the face of death. Like my dad.

I was moved by an episode of the Joe Rogan Experience where Joe interviewed the actor, Mike Smith. Mike talked about the calm feeling of acceptance he experienced when facing death – that what was going to happen was ok. It was good. Mike had spent his life fearing death, but when it was tangible and close, the fear dissolved. His concerns, his cares, and his responsibilities were no longer his burden to carry. And the peace resulting from that changed his view of death forever. The lifting of the weight of those responsibilities offered a welcomed relief. He doesn't invite death, but no longer lives in the grip of its fear.[212]

Having already watched that interview, I found myself staring into my father's eyes seeing exactly that sentiment. The concerns he had in prior months were no longer concerns. He wasn't burdened with thoughts of fairness or my well-being. And I'm glad that's true. Knowing I was watching his last few hours, I considered pouring out to him how I felt and ensuring he knew what a positive impact he had been. Instead I found myself paralyzed with the thought he had found his peace. He didn't need to be burdened with more sentiment and to feel motivated to live longer, suffering endlessly and needlessly. So I kept it to myself. Telling my father what he meant to me seemed an exercise that would benefit me, and only me.

I'm not sure that's true anymore. I'm not sure if I skirted a sacred opportunity in favor of what was easier. But that is what happened.

In the Journal of Personality and Social Psychology, Pelin Kesebir argues that death is not nearly as painful as the continuous agony some endure fearing it. What makes death painful is our refusal to accept it. What makes death hard is not being mentally prepared for it. Refusing to accept reality sets us out of alignment. Focusing on ourselves makes it unbearable. Death is hard to come to terms with when we think so highly of ourselves that the tragedy of our own demise plays in our minds as if the world must grind to a halt and mourn.[213]

But the ruthless truth is the world does not stop when we die. It doesn't stop when our loved ones die either. Death is most painful when we resist it, and fear it, and pretend it isn't real. That is why I have come to believe that promises of eternal life are more harmful than good because they prevent people from mentally preparing for the inevitability of nature.[214]

The fear that permeates the globe creates an eagerness to accept concepts which alleviate that fear. A Pew Research survey in 2015 showed that 72% of Americans believe in heaven.[215] While I understand the intent is to comfort those who have lost, what are the consequences of deviating from reality?

I submit that if we were meant to live with the hope of living forever, that hope would be made evident to each of us. Even if it were true that we would live on, the fact it has not been clearly expressed suggests we should view death as permanent.

Perhaps the mental anguish I endured coming to terms with death was not because of death. It was the anguish guaranteed to occur when a grown-ass adult realizes one of his fantasies was just that. While my hope in Paradise made me feel better in certain moments, it also led me to direct my energy and time like a slave, a human sacrifice for the interests of others, on the promise of another life.

I don't know if there is an afterlife. I want there to be an afterlife. I *do* know, on the other hand, that I have *this* life. And I know investments I poured into a stairway to heaven – the years dedicated to further the interest of religion – would assuredly have been better spent on a different cult, like my family, with greater return on investment.

Death and pain are not frightening, it's the fear of pain and death we need to fear. Which is why we praise the poet who wrote, 'Death is not fearful, but dying like a coward is.'

Every part of me then will be reduced by change into some part of the universe, and that again will change into another part of the universe, and so on forever.

Marcus Aurelius

INTEGRITY

3.

We hold these truths to be self-evident, that all men are created equal, that they are endowed by their Creator with certain unalienable Rights, that among these are Life, Liberty and the pursuit of Happiness.

AMERICAN DECLARATION OF INDEPENDENCE

Building a satisfying life is a noble pursuit. It was considered so vital the American founding fathers considered it an unalienable right for all humankind. That concept of liberty and independence indeed appears inseparable from happiness. Even if we condition our mind to find joy in any circumstance, slavery must be the least conducive to happiness.

> *The secret to happiness is freedom. And the secret to freedom is courage.*
>
> Thucydides

Slavery exists in the 21st century. In countries with antiquated governance it might exist in very much the same state it had in western nations before outlawed. Sexual slavery continues to stain humanity with its horrific existence. Slavery often takes the form of an abusive relationship where one person is incapable of honoring the self-determination of another. That relationship might be with an organization, a government, a corporation, or a partner.

I watched a discussion between psychologist Jordan Peterson and political pundit Ben Shapiro, both well-educated men and accomplished authors. Yet I was dismayed to hear these accomplished people attributing lofty intelligence to words I learned did not contain such. From my perspective they demonstrated a departure from reality while drawing connections between bible verses and auspicious philosophies.[216]

Peterson and Shapiro attributed meaning to the Bible story of Jacob. In Genesis 32, Jacob, carrying enormous wealth, meets an angel on a riverbank and wrestles with him through the night. When he eventually overpowered the angel, the angel told Jacob to let him go. But Jacob refused without a blessing. The angel told Jacob he would then be called

Israel because he contended with man and with God, and then blessed Jacob (Genesis 32:24-28).

Peterson is in awe of the story and ties it to some transcendent understanding where struggle and effort is rewarded. He makes the conclusion that anyone who works hard can lay claim to the name *Israelite* and therefore chosen by God.[217] And bless Jordan's heart. That is a wonderful insight and the best way to look at the chapter. But another person might learn a different lesson.

Jacob obtained his wealth in large part by defrauding his uncle Laban using a series of magical breeding schemes (Genesis 30:31-43). Jacob was earlier able to secure a blessing from God reserved for his older brother, Esau. Jacob lied to obtain this as well. (Genesis 27:6-29). One moral a person could glean from the story is the acquisition of great wealth through dishonesty. Adding that he is named for a struggle might add insult to injury for those who truly have struggled.

Peterson and Shapiro credit the Bible for influencing individual liberties, and the inspiration behind the Declaration of Independence. Their basis for this assertion is found in Genesis 1:27 which states: "God created mankind in his own image." They find within those words evidence all men are created equal because all are endowed with the qualities of God. I never extracted that in the numerous times I read the passage. Which in itself is meaningless, but surely those words were washed away with Paul's instructions: "slaves, be obedient to your human masters with fear and trembling (Ephesians 6:5$_{NWT}$)." Granted, Shapiro, being of Jewish faith, doesn't consider Paul *inspired of God.* But nowhere in the Bible can we find an individualist concept. The overreaching theme is obedience – to accept domination (Romans 13:1-7).

To grant the Bible with credit for equality seems to ignore how the institution of slavery is clearly expressed in both old and new testaments (Exodus 21:2-10; 1 Corinthians 7:21-24). In neither is it condemned. The Bible was used by Christian slave owners in America to resist abolition.[218]

Upon hearing such glowing accolades for the Bible I could imagine the reaction of Thomas Jefferson, the primary author of that declaration, and originator of the famous words "all men are created equal." If we could witness such a reaction we might learn of Jefferson's contempt for the Bible. Jefferson had his Bible torn apart so it only contained select portions of the gospels of Jesus and omitted any miracles or supernatural events.[219] It was the intent of the founding fathers to remove religion from the decision-making levers of the government – to separate Church from State. Objectively, should we not conclude the freedom offered by the Declaration of Independence is more-so attributed to a *distancing* from the Bible? I am perplexed as to how any person could gift the Bible with credit for individual rights when it appears nothing on Earth is more instrumental in removing them.

I mean no exaggeration with that statement either. The words of the Bible had been used to keep my friends, my family and myself in subjection. From warnings about eating from the tree of knowledge to Jeremiah's: "to earthling man his way does not belong," to Paul's: "Be in subjection," the theme is clear and effective. For centuries the book has been used to create a subservient crowd. When colonials overtook North America did they send first their armies or their priests?

Around 610 CE, a man named Muhammad encountered an entirely new means of control. He never credited the Bible, but he claimed to receive a series of revelations which strikingly resembled the stories of the Bible and contained many of the same characters and places. It's more than incredulous to think he could have produced such stories without access to the Bible. The bible had been compiled nearly 200 years prior and was circulating toward Muhammed by 610. After having scribes commit his revelations to a book known as the *Quran*, he would use the book to gather willing servants and assign them the Arabic word for *submissive one*: *Muslim*. A term often translated as *slave*. Could Muhammad have recognized the power of the Bible to remove the will of the populace, reduce their freedom, and access a new pool of slaves? I'm willing to offer such credit.

Without precisely *knowing* the historical circumstances, I am also willing to concede Shapiro and Peterson's position. Perhaps the Bible was indeed a critical influence in dismantling human oppression. If that *were* true, it would be difficult to say it remains true. Statistics showing the quality of life for Bible and Quran readers do not honor those books.[220] If the Bible were a positive catalyst for freedom, it deserves our accolades and a seat within the pantheon of mankind's greatest achievements. Yet, it would not be disrespectful to retire it to a position more in line with evidence – that it is a human creation, and easily weaponized for the enslavement of people.

Make Jehovah's thoughts your own.[221] This message should frighten Peterson. This is specific, bible-based instruction, weaponized to control the thoughts of individuals. It becomes the voice of God, and therefore God Himself. With the typing of a few words the scribe gains the authority to redirect values and motivations of readers. In the presence of this paper god, all humans are good for nothing slaves. *Make* our *thoughts your own. Think like we told you.*

That does not mean Jordan Peterson and Ben Shapiro were not highlighting real issues. I agree we can't bulldoze the constructs of religion and expect people will immediately behave in a socially acceptable manner. Some atheists think it simple to exit religion and find substance without. They are unaware of the loss of families, resources, and a reference point to build perspective from. They won't understand how the formerly faithful lack skills for individual thought, decision-making, and social adaptation. Our code of conduct and source of discipline is not easily replaced.

I can attest to the difficulty in attempting to build a life without those conventions. There is a sense of loneliness; of being disconnected; loss of direction compounded by a sense of meaninglessness. Some people find a life after religion unbearably empty. This is expected from those who recently shed bonds of slavery.

On the American day of emancipation in 1865, former slave and abolitionist Harriet Tubman is attributed with saying "I was free, but there was no one to welcome me to the land of freedom. I was a stranger in a strange land."[222]   Although the legality of slavery had been significantly resolved, the effects would persist.

Imagine the psychological differences between former slaves and former master. Both lived for generations with contrasting perspectives. Those generations incrementally cementing their position into their minds both through inherited neurological traits and generational adaptation. One group acquired wealth from the efforts of the other.

Slaves were uneducated academically and culturally. They were more susceptible to the economic fallout the southern states were to endure after abolition. They experienced a lack of identity, a loss of direction, and the defeat of a dream which had not materialized. Many found themselves forced to return to plantations under a repackaged form of slavery known as *sharecropping*.[223] Many found themselves in circumstances nearly identical to the former.

If a former slave asked you *what is the purpose of life without my former structure and direction from my former master?* What would you tell them? It's important to note their role and direction in life had been assigned to them. It provided the slave with their identity. The purpose of the slave was clearly outlined: *you are a harvester.* When first freed, that slave might be elated. But when faced with the myriad of opportunities and their first encounter with the risks of freedom, can you imagine their confusion, indecisiveness, and fear? They likely have no resources, no friends, and perhaps no family.

You might tell them there is no reason to confine themself to a single role. They need not be a harvester. They can be anything. They can choose whatever vocation they wish. But those choices would be impossible to imagine having only experienced harvesting. What career would they be familiar with? Those who never experienced slavery won't understand how alien the world seems to a slave; how little a slave understands their options.

They lack skills others take for granted like networking, job-search, self-discipline, life-planning, or basic conversation with free-folk.

If you are leaving the grasp of authoritarian thought control, you will find yourself in a similar mental condition as a freed slave. That is because you *were* a slave. You were not free to choose your own direction or even your own thoughts. You were taught to accept the ideals of others and to obey. That is a mental disposition which will not disappear overnight.

The emotional manipulation of *loyalty*, the continued enslavement of your family, and the voids left after having beliefs imposed upon you are powerful forces. But I'm confident they will fade to oblivion. You no longer need to be defined as you were. You do not need a purpose as if you were some sort of tool. I propose what you need is *meaning*, and from meaning, *direction*, and then *skills* to equip you in your pursuit of happiness.

I'm not a psychologist or a sociologist. I am barely educated. All I offer is my experience having been heavily indoctrinated and controlled by a dogma-dominated, authoritarian cult. Because of my lack of training, I recommend help from a professional - an accredited mental health care professional experienced in dealing with indoctrination. Though I can't pretend such a resource is accessible to everyone.

You're likely to find the experiences of others helpful. Talk to others. Journalize your journey. Let your words articulate your feelings the best they can. It was my experience that when they are expressed, they become an exhalation of bad air, an exorcism of demons. But when engaging in conversation or when reading, be keenly aware whether the other party is encouraging you to think, or if they're simply expecting you to memorize their opinions.

Modern slavery exists and is prevalent. I submit that being aware of our limitations and those of others is critical. As is knowing where our boundaries are, and insisting we retain the right to determine what is acceptable. Owning our morality and keeping it tuned is a critical component of liberty. Happiness depends upon that freedom. Our lives have little meaning when they belong to another. Our lives mean nothing to those who own us.

Equally important is ensuring we never impose such a thing on others. It would be hard to say we learned a lesson from slavery if we escaped only to impose it on others. One significant aspect to understanding our self-determination is understand how all others possess their own. Demanding others adopt our newest beliefs, failing to respect their boundaries, and insisting on what we *know* does little to improve our world.

I contend that no good parent raises their child to be dependent upon them. Neither would a God. Should there be a Creator, they would not enjoy our servitude. They would rejoice in the freedom of their creation. I am convinced God would hold deep appreciation for those who stand up for truth despite the repercussions. There is no reason any apostate from any faith should feel the shame that is imposed upon them. If ever there remains a doubt, you were never rejected by God. But you may have been rejected by a culture which could not subject you. That is something to be proud of.

In the following chapters I will share techniques I found to help in rebuilding a life post-dogma – after dangerous beliefs have been rendered ineffective and removed from our core. I found it important to piece together the fragments of our being, and to align with reality, with the present moment, with our minds, with our bodies, with the people around us, and with our environment. This form of integration is what I consider *wholeness*, or *integrity*.

The mind adapts and converts to its own purposes the obstacle to our acting. The impediment to action advances action. What stands in the way becomes the way.
Marcus Aurelius

3.1 CHARTS OF THE NAVIGATOR

One does not become enlightened by imaginary figures of light, but by making the darkness conscious.

Carl Jung

Imagine success. Unlimited resources. Freedom is yours. You're handed the keys to a 100' yacht. The sun is shining. The day is young. Everything is perfect. Except you're not familiar with the waters. You've never even sailed before.

After the initial excitement you find yourself drawn to the helm. You assess the cluster of controls and navigation instruments and realize *I have no idea how this thing works or where to go.* You might find a big button that says *autopilot.* That's easy. But not even the autopilot knows where you want to go. Maybe your life's ambition is to explore – and that's an exciting prospect. But if you're not sure even of that, you're just as likely to sit on a seat and let your cell phone tell you what you like.

This is the circumstance for those who lack direction in life. Addiction counsellor Steve Rose said, "Lacking a sense of direction is risky because it creates a mental vulnerability during times of transition. Losing direction means losing hope. Like getting lost in the forest and deciding to lie down in the grass and wait for the inevitable. Losing direction is a factor in suicidal risk."[224]

I found it difficult to find direction after a lifetime of slavery. After the initial excitement new freedom brings, I lost interest in the shiny parts of the world before struggling to take aim. This is where religion often boasts its usefulness. It does indeed offer meaning. Meaning of their design. Authoritarian religion has no problem giving people direction. Is it possible to find direction without it?

Unless we want to serve a slave master, we need to be the architects of our purpose. Finding purpose is determined by our values and interests, and our values and interests are developed through experience. Thus gaining life experience seems important.

The advice I wish I followed was simple: *Go out and live life. Experience things you would not have considered before – safely. Consciously attempt to be less averse to new experiences, new foods, new people, new places, new hobbies. Don't shrink back because you don't have the skills or feel embarrassed for lack of experience. Fear not to look stupid. View life as the adventure it is.*

> *Do the best you can until you know better. Then when you know better, do better.*
>
> Maya Angelou

I missed a lot of opportunities out of fear of other's opinions. This book, in one way, is me trying to overcome that by putting myself out there. By sharing what I learned. Within my profession I have been trained to develop extremely detailed plans. I have been able to transfer that ability into personal planning and thought it was important to share.

What is important to you? This is the key determinant. *Values* are our guiding force toward purpose. I could state a purpose and list a set of goals all I want. But if my purpose is not aligned with my values, I will never live up to that purpose. I will be pulled off course by the ever-powerful draw of those values. Identifying our values is crucial.[225]

Understanding our personal values might be more difficult than initially assessed. If you have lived as a slave, your values had been dictated to you and developing the skills to assess such a thing requires time. When I was first asked about my values, I didn't understand the question. It had to be explained slowly. *Values are the things most important to you. They are the driving force for motivations and actions.* When I felt I understood the question, I still struggled to respond. I started to regurgitate the value system imposed upon me. "Family, I guess" came my feeble response.

Family is a good answer when asked about values. It's what we're supposed to say. But if I had been honest with myself, I would have admitted *family* had not been the motivation behind most of my behaviors. Certainly, none of my selfish behaviors. In fact, had I been honest, I would have been surprised how low a priority I placed on family.

I was in the habit of lying to myself. I resisted aspects of myself I disliked. I became so accustomed to excusing myself I formed a protective barrier around those dark features of my personality, and around those hidden memories of my past. But that was not aligning with reality. That was not being honest. If I wanted to feel whole, if I want to accomplish anything of substance, if I wanted to find meaning and happiness, I needed to face those dark figures. I had to shine a light on my shadows.

I soon learned shadow work is an intense process which takes time. It is not fun. It is the awful-tasting medicine that only works when it hurts. It requires a depth of courage for which we may never again require. An article published in *The Qualitative Report* describes this well.

> *Our willingness to own and engage with our own vulnerability determines the depth of our courage and the clarity of our prose; the level to which we protect ourselves from being vulnerable is a measure of our fear and disconnection.*
>
> Dwayne Custer

The article discusses the merits of a process called *autoethnography*, which I found to be an essential life hack. In this process, a person journalizes their thoughts as a form of *self-therapy*. "Autoethnography is a style of autobiographical writing and qualitative research that explores an individual's unique life experiences in relationship to social and cultural institutions."[226]

In the *Handbook of Autoethnography*, Carolyn Ellis wrote: "Autoethnography is not simply a way of knowing about the world; it has become a way of being in the world, one that requires living consciously, emotionally, reflexively. It asks that we not only examine our lives but also consider how and why we think, act, and feel as we do. Autoethnography requires that we observe ourselves observing, that we interrogate what we think and believe, and that we challenge our own assumptions, asking over and over if we have penetrated as many layers of our own defenses, fears, and insecurities as our project requires. It asks that we rethink and revise our lives, making conscious decisions about who and how we want to be. And in the process, it seeks a story that is hopeful, where authors ultimately write themselves as survivors of the story they are living."[227]

The idea with this technique is to peel back the layers of our false front – of our mask, so we can accurately understand our values. It is the basic premise behind Jordan Peterson's *Self Authoring Program* where you, as a participant, write a version of your life. "You envision a meaningful, healthy and productive future, three to five years down the road, and [...] develop a detailed, implementable plan to make that future a reality."[i] I had earlier levelled criticism of Dr. Peterson, but my criticism ends abruptly with his religious views. As a clinical psychologist I found Peterson's theories worthy of consideration. And statistics showing the success of his Self-Authoring Program are astounding.

A person's sense of direction is almost always lost when leaving authoritarian rule. But understanding our values is only the first step in regaining it. Creating a plan encompasses the next steps. A plan ensures we make the best use of our time and prevents aimlessness. Having a direction in life is an important feature of mental health. It provides mental resilience. It fulfills a sense of meaning and it builds self-worth. It keeps us motivated and productive.

It took me years to gather a means of life-planning. And I was fortunate to choose a vocation where planning was an essential facet. The tricks and techniques I have gathered over years of managing projects can be adapted to our personal lives and I found notable success in doing so.

---

[i] www.selfauthoring.com

The process I developed runs as follows: I prepare my mind with a short *meditation*, I *brainstorm* my thoughts, I list my *values*, assign myself *goals*, identify the *tasks* which will achieve those goals, then break those tasks into fragmented *activities*. I fit the activities into a *schedule* and try my best to follow that schedule.

First I should point out it is critical to write these down. This exercise will not work if we attempt to keep the steps inside our head. Our brain is a poor ledger. Writing is vital for remaining on subject, knowing where to return a wandering mind, and staying motivated for each activity. Writing offers a unique perspective. When I commit thoughts to words I am often surprised how they sound. The emotional attachments tend to disconnect for those moments and my thoughts become visible for what they are.

Meditating sets the mind to the right condition for this exercise. If you're unfamiliar with meditative techniques I encourage listening to a guided meditation. A simple google search of "mindfulness meditation" should supply no shortage of material. Rest your neural networks and embrace a much-needed break from the noise of your cerebral circus. Embrace the sensual inputs from your body. This is the concept of mindfulness meditation. I have often tried to plan without meditating and the results are of far less quality.

The next phase of my process is to conduct a *Brain Dump*. This isn't much different from a *Brainstorm* if you're more familiar with that term. In this process I write down or sketch everything weighing on my mind. All my worries and wants, obstacles, and anxieties. I write what I'm grateful for. I write down my motivations if they concern me. I'll record injustices I perceived. I try to allow my emotions to flow without resisting them. That's where I find holes in my thought processes which sabotage goals.

Following the meditation and braindump my mind is in a better condition to consider my values. As previously mentioned, I found that determining values is not straight forward and they did not come into focus when I first started these exercises. I found it critical to be honest because I could easily lie through this exercise, and the process was thus of no benefit.

In reading about values I learned a few tricks to avoid self-deception. One of those is to list what I have afforded the most time and resources to the past month. What did I find most entertaining? What websites did I browse? To what did I navigate conversations toward? What interests me? Another trick is to take that list and for each item ask *why*? Then ask again. If I keep asking myself *why*, my values should eventually come into focus. Those values are the essential first step in planning.

When I first did this I was startled to find how I was directed by so many selfish values. I had to concede that I assigned too high a value on sex, glory, alcohol, and food. Animalistic desires. Dopamine-fueled tendencies. But if we can honestly assess them we can adjust them.

If I feel the need to adjust my values, I make a conscious decision to do so. I will cross out the unwanted values and write-in those more important. The physical act of crossing out and re-writing my values seems to be a powerful ritual. It makes it feel official – authorized – and with that I'm empowered to chart a new course. I take the helm. *This is my yacht, and I will not allow it to run on autopilot.*

After my values are identified, I will set goals. Here is where my purpose is identified. I set long range, midrange, and short-term goals. Long range goals are what I want to achieve in my life, or in the next few years. My midrange goals might be achieved within a few months. My short-term goals could be achieved within weeks or days or could be goals I set for myself as daily achievements. These goals should take into consideration the needs and wants of those closest to me. They should be clearly defined, and they should align with my values.

To accomplish a structured record of my values and goals, I'll use a pre-designed form known in the planning community as a *mission board* or *vision board*. After performing the brain dump, I'll sift through the thoughts from the brain dump and extract the values which lurk in the mess. I pick out the core components and list those on the vision board. I'll then organize those in order of importance. I then arrange goals around those values.

I use the vision board to draft specific activities for the following week or weeks. I use a project management technique called *decomposition*. It sounds morbid but if you find yourself in a situation where you know what needs to be done, but you haven't been able to accomplish it, that could indicate you haven't broken the task down into small-enough, more manageable pieces. We may have to deconstruct a task into ridiculously small fractions if we can't find a means to get from point A to point B. I have struggled with this often. Those times I've felt stuck, I've most likely over-estimated my attention span and left myself with tasks too large; tasks which require more thought than estimated. That leaves opportunity for my A.D.D. mind to wander off track. Tasks are best assigned when small enough they require little heavy thinking. That thinking should have been completed here in the planning session.

We can build resiliency into our plans by incorporating alternatives. A Plan B. It is inevitable that circumstances will render some plans impractical. If I have the time, and if following the plan is critical, building into it *if / then* features makes it stronger.

I then assign tasks an achievable allotment of time, then add them to a schedule. For the schedule, I use an app on my phone. You could use a day planner, a calendar, a notebook, sticky notes. But I am convinced you cannot rely on your memory. The key is committing those thoughts to writing so you have them in front of you.

Another trick is to pick the most important and most urgent activities and add them before adding those of lesser import. That doesn't mean they need to be placed in an earlier time slot. It means picking the most opportune times for the most important tasks and fitting the less important activities in what is left over. This is like trying to fill a jar with sand, pebbles, and rocks. To fit the most into the jar, place the largest rocks first, then the pebbles, then the sand. The best way to accomplish the most, is to schedule according to importance. (I first heard this analogy from a JW talk).

With the planning session complete I come away with two documents: A vision board to post at my desk. And a schedule on my phone.

Meditation, brain dump, vision board, schedule. Charting my vision, my goals, and providing myself with step-by-step instructions has a dramatic effect on the likelihood of accomplishing what I want. If I can keep disciplined to maintain this routine, I am never left feeling without direction.

I also found it provides an unexpected benefit. This exercise intentionally immerses me into my cerebral thoughts, so I don't need to the rest of the time. I accomplish my heavy thinking in these sessions and with a plan in hand, I'm not persistently worried I forgot something. I can remain present, trusting the big things are cared for. I can perform at a high level and do so thoughtlessly and proficiently. I can listen to my intuition. I can engage with other people attentively. My experiences flow.

Every living organism is fulfilled when it follows the right path for its own nature.
Marcus Aurelius

3.2 THE BASAL GANGLIA

He who cannot obey himself will be commanded.

Friedrich Nietzsche

One important consideration when transitioning from a dogmatic life is that of discipline. I feel the topic is often treated as *the elephant in the room* where post-dogmatic people shy from admitting the benefits they experienced with high-control discipline. I think discipline qualifies as a big thing and it would be a mistake not to admit so. I also think it's fair to keep in mind how that elephant in the room was tied to a post most of its life.

Discipline in itself is vital for a happy, sustainable, and productive life. In 1970 Mischel and Ebbesen published their famous marshmallow experiment where they left a marshmallow in front of children and promised they could have two if they could resist the one. Then they left the room. The average child could resist eating the marshmallow for six minutes before giving in to early gratification.[228] When researchers followed up with those children 20 years later, "those who could delay gratification had comparatively better academic performance and higher educational achievements than those who could not"[229]

Duckworth and Seligman found **"self-control to have a more significant positive impact on academic success than cognitive intelligence."**[230] Self-control has been shown to reduce risk of obesity, to correlate with better muscular and aerobic fitness, and closely linked to greater occupational and career achievement.[231]

Hofmann, Luhmann, Fisher, Vohs, and Baumeister conducted a series of studies examining happiness and well-being. "The key predictor was [trait self-control], with affective well-being and life satisfaction ratings as key outcomes. [...] Self-control positively contributes to happiness through avoiding and dealing with motivational conflict."[232]

With the measurable benefits of discipline could we conclude that high control groups offer a higher quality of life? Some people adapt to highly disciplined environments and find a life outside those confines a long series of failed attempts to control their inclinations. But if such is the case does that not suggest the group has *failed* to teach self-control? If their behaviors have been held together externally – in a little box – and if those behaviors are easily abandoned when leaving that little box, have they really developed self-control, or simply experienced *control?*

When self-determination is denied, the individual is denied the experience to test out methods of operation and develop skills for successful self-management. This could explain why some find themselves in situations like the Prodigal Son - or to children in *Rumspringa* facing the disastrous consequences of freedom without discipline.

How can we develop self-control without relinquishing it to others? This is a difficult subject for me. I would be hypocritical if I told you I knew anything about discipline. I failed miserably to develop my own. There have been years and situations where I maintained discipline – mostly in my work. But it seems when I get home those habits evaporate. So I won't be giving any advice here, other than, perhaps to myself.

In this chapter I'll discuss at a high-level my research about why we struggle with discipline. And I'll share the techniques which appear to rate highest from an academic standpoint and one or two which found success in terms of popularity. This is not an exhaustive consideration of self-discipline. There are better works for that.

Perhaps if we explore *why* people struggle to find motivation that might be enough to help someone push through. It might also help remove the nagging feeling some have that their difficult personal circumstances are evidence the high control group was right.

In doing so it would be helpful to understand the parts of our brain known as the basal ganglia. The basal ganglia are three areas of the central brain. They are vital for control of our movements, responsible for learning routine behaviors, and serve to control cognitive emotional functions. They do not have the capability of conscious thought. They are more like a program which executes pre-planned responses to stimuli. This is where our brain decides to release specific hormones like dopamine, severely impacting our motivations and actions, and where habits and addictions are formed.[233]

3.2.1 Autopilot

When you're living by default, you're automatically reacting to life in habitual ways, many of which may be limiting you and your life. In contrast, living deliberately means making more conscious and constructive life choices. When you're living deliberately, you're living from a position of responsibility; you're making choices with greater awareness. You've taken yourself off autopilot, so you're better prepared to align your actions with the results you want to achieve.

Lauren Mackler

The basal ganglia help us accomplish extraordinary tasks. This is the part of the brain which learned to ride our bicycle and elevated our species to walk AND chew gum. It learns to drive our car so well we don't need to be conscious. It memorizes complex pieces of music and can respond with *wow, crazy* when we've tuned out. It holds the capacity for specific forms of memory and is mostly known for how it guides motor control. More recent studies have explored its role in motivating our behavior, in decision-making, and controlling hormone levels.[234]

"The function of the basal ganglia is to fine-tune the voluntary movements. They do so by receiving impulses for the upcoming movement from the cerebral cortex, which they process and adjust. They convey their instructions to the thalamus, which then relays this information back to the cortex."[235]

If you've ever drifted off while driving a car, you might recall being surprised how far you travelled without remembering how you got there. The basal ganglia are fully capable of navigating the road without your conscious inputs. As long as your eyes remain open they can respond to changing traffic lights and obstacles. They can operate the turn signals as required, apply the brake with smooth control, and maintain the correct speed. They are "left with the autonomy to control nuances of the cortical activity, i.e. to modulate the movements."[236] I thought this was significant because it demonstrates how similar to a computerized autopilot they really are. They can drive. But without our conscious input they will drive right past our destination.

With the proliferation of cell phones and other electronic devices we are facing a pandemic of zombies – where people drift into autopilot mode attempting to perform simultaneous tasks. Because they learned they could rely on such a sophisticated feature they make the most use of it. People are in autopilot while walking. They're in autopilot trying to hold conversations. They risk other's lives in autopilot while driving.

We might have every reason to want to accomplish more. How many times have we thought *I wish there were two of me*? When the opportunity arises where we can engage in our online life whilst offering the task at hand our stand-in is there really a downside? Vehicles are becoming increasingly automated as are other apparatus. Are we remaining a step behind if we don't take full advantage?

In *Frontiers in Neuroscience* an article compares autopilot with a condition known as *out of the loop*. "The out of the loop performance problem arises when operators suffer from complacency and vigilance decrement; consequently, when automation does not behave as expected, understanding the system or taking back manual control may be difficult. Close to the out of the loop problem, mind wandering points to the propensity of the human mind to think about matters unrelated to the task at hand." The article explained: "an individual who is [mind wandering] is at least partly decoupled from his or her environment and show little to no reaction to external stimuli. In brain imaging studies, [mind wandering] is characterized by the activation of the Default Mode Network [...]. Even though [mind wandering] is thought to facilitate prospection, introspection and problem solving, performance-drops in numerous tasks has been observed during [mind wandering] episodes." It highlighted how the "phenomenon has been involved in many accidents in safety-critical industries."[237]

If we are not giving our full attention to what is in front of us, we can only expect issues to compound. The relationships we tried to maintain on autopilot are going to suffer. Our workmanship will not reach expectations, and we place ourselves at considerable risk.

What is interesting about this autopilot mode – or this *default of mind wandering* – is just how often we engage in it. In 2010, Matt Killingsworth and Daniel Gilbert published a study where they found, on average, the mind was wandering 46.9% of the time. Certain activities which required more presence, such as sex, brought the person out of this default mode and into a more conscious state. It was also found that people were measurably *less happy* when engaged in mind wandering.[238] So we have a reason, just in a measure of happiness, to be more present.

3.2.2 Presence

In the stillness of your presence, you can feel your own formless and timeless reality as the unmanifested life that animates your physical form. You can then feel the same life deep within every other human and every other creature. You look beyond the veil of form and separation. This is the realization of oneness. This is love.

Eckart Tolle

Living in our head and relinquishing our consciousness to autopilot is addictive. I often felt guilty if I wasn't trying to accomplish two things at once or if I neglected my cell phone. The urge to pick it up seemed ever present. How could a person resist those inclinations? How can we overcome distractions? How can we develop self-discipline?

Five major, over-reaching techniques have been identified to be most successful for attaining self-discipline. *Developing self-awareness, believing in our ability to increase self-discipline, developing useful habits, becoming comfortable with discomfort,* and *implementation intention.*

Implementation intention involves creating an if/then plan that specifies when, where, and how we will act to achieve a goal and was largely covered in the previous chapter. We will discuss beliefs related to discipline, as well as discomfort and habits a little later. The most effective means of taking control of our inclinations and actions has shown to be the development of awareness.

Self-awareness is the ability to assess and understand our thoughts and feelings. The idea being that if we accurately understand the multitude of signals flashing through our mind, we can avoid being swept away by them. We can process and prioritize those signals appropriately, determining which require our attention and which can be dismissed. It requires a higher level of cognitive processing and an effective perspective from which to gather information.[239]

Emotions are powerful enough to pull us off track. Part of developing self-awareness is taking an objective view of our feelings, and understanding why we experience those.[240] This requires a self-distanced, basically stoic perspective. A person would consciously examine their feelings when they rise. If you're angry, sad, anxious, jealous or disgusted, think how that physically feels in your body. Each time we analyze those feelings we gain awareness of our emotions. Awareness, in turn, allows the ability to control.

Journalizing emotions is often cited as an effective means to gain awareness of them. Taking the time to describe those feelings, and especially the physical sensations we experience, highlight how they operate. It offers a valuable perspective of the basal ganglia. A regular practice of journalizing emotions trains our mind to observe our feelings from an objective and conscious state. We thus have another reason for autoethnography.

Meditation is another. "The term 'meditation' refers to a variety of practices that focus on mind and body integration and are used to calm the mind and enhance overall well-being. Some types of meditation involve maintaining mental focus on a particular sensation, such as breathing, a sound, a visual image, or a mantra, which is a repeated word or phrase. Other forms of meditation include the practice of mindfulness, which involves maintaining attention or awareness on the present moment without making judgments" (National Center for Complementary and Integrative Health). The benefits of mindfulness meditation have been demonstrated in numerous studies and include lowered blood pressure, and effectiveness in treating substance abuse, anxiety, depression and post-traumatic stress.[241]

Maintaining focus on the present moment is often described as *emptying the mind*. Not because such a thing is possible but because it serves the purpose of removing the distractions of our thoughts. If a person were to concentrate only on the moment they would have gained control over thoughts which attempt to intrude. By recognizing those intrusions and ending them, we are left with our sensory inputs and remain in a purer form of awareness. We hear the light noises in the distance, we feel the clothes on our back, we feel our chest rising with each breath. But we don't judge those things. We don't allow our minds to meander into a narrative or wander off in any way. This is a practice of discipline in itself and could be the most effective.

Without practice, mindfulness is difficult. A regular routine of mindfulness meditation develops our awareness, making it stronger at all times. It conditions the neural pathways to find a state of heightened awareness, to do so with increasing ease, and to hold that awareness for increasing durations.

I was oblivious to mindfulness meditation while living dogmatic. That was no accident. Jehovah's Witnesses have a different take on meditation. The May 2014 Awake states: "The Bible puts a high value on meditation. The kind of meditation that it encourages, however, does not entail emptying the mind [...]. Rather, Biblical meditation involves purposeful thinking on wholesome topics, such as God's qualities, standards, and creations [...]. Yes, like a fire, meditation must be controlled! Otherwise, improper thoughts could nurture hurtful desires that might race out of control and lead to evil deeds." Warning taken. If the idea that emptying our minds is dangerous is not clearly outlined in the article, it was most certainly taught from the pulpit. We were warned if we empty our minds of thought the devil will fill them with his own thoughts. I have also heard this sentiment from mainstream Christians, so I suspect it is common among Bible-folk.

It is likely everyone who offered me those warnings were doing so with the best intentions. It might have been a mix up with "idle hands are the devil's playground," an adage only loosely taken from the Bible.[242] But it's hard not to think somewhere up the ladder there may have been a more nefarious intent. Especially when considering how it appears slavers in the 19th century were aware they could derive benefit from sabotaging the mental health of their slaves.[243]

> *Do not kill them, but put the FEAR of a God in them so they can be used for future breeding!*
>
> *Keep the slave physically strong but psychologically weak and dependent on the slave master.*
>
> *Keep the body, but take the mind.*
>
> Willie Lynch (attributed to)

Mindfulness is not the only form of meditation. The Awake did outline a legitimate form of meditation where a person concentrates on a singular subject.

One form of meditation which has worked to keep me present is where I imagine myself playing a video game of my life. An ultra-realistic 3D virtual reality game where I can feel each of my senses as inputs from the game and I consciously control my entire range of movements. Then I try to stay immersed in this mode, maintaining a sense of awe while controlling my human avatar. I try to feel every physical sensation, not allowing myself to become accustomed to what I see and smell; how my shirt feels as it touches my shoulders and back, the weight of my body on my feet. I'm especially conscious of each of my movements and the combination of muscular motions required. I found this meditation holds my presence longer and keeps me motivated for the mundane.

I developed another means to find awareness when needed. I remind myself *I am here*. This is more powerful than it might sound initially. Saying those words reminds me to climb out from under my thoughts and take active control. Like stepping up to a microphone, it helps me into presence. Into my body. Nothing else seems simple enough or effective enough to recite when circumstances demand immediate presence. *I am here*.

Instead of recording your child's school play, why not just be there? Why not soak in the sounds and speak with the people? This is true for vacations. Why miss the whole thing by seeing it through a viewfinder? The concept remains true for all aspects of life. If we consciously attempt to remain present – to be HERE – we are both exercising our awareness and soaking in the experiences. We nurture resilience, appreciation, gratitude, and relationships. *I am here.*

However presence of mind is accomplished, the key to sustainable improvement appears to be a regular routine of mental health exercises. Regular meditation makes a person happier, healthier, and grants us control of our minds. With that control we are equipped to inhibit certain thoughts, program our autopilot, and focus on subjects that matter most.

3.2.3 Addiction

The one thing that's worse than being a slave is being a slave that loves his chains.

Constance Friday

Besides autopilot, the basal ganglia mediate "other higher cortical functions as well, such as planning and modulation of movement, memory, eye movements, reward processing, and motivation."[244] *Reward processing and motivation? That is significant.* If you could control a person's motivations and reward processing, well... you could be a cult leader. Imagine how unstoppable you would be if you could control just your own motivations and reward processing.

Our autopilot mode may not possess conscious thought – the basal ganglia may not make decisions – but they have the power to *influence* decisions, and often irresistibly. They motivate us toward an action by creating an emotional response.

Emotional responses can be problematic. The temper tantrums of children are often caused by a flood of emotion-inducing chemicals. Children can become overwhelmed with those emotions and are incapable of understanding what is happening. Typically those tantrums taper off in frequency as children grow. But adults are just as likely to experience emotional break down when flooded by hormones. Testosterone, estrogen, cortisol, serotonin, and dopamine can fundamentally change how a person thinks. And the consequences for adult tantrums are considerably greater than those of children.

Dopamine is often described as a chemical of pleasure. But that isn't the only way it works. Dopamine often behaves as a reward-*promiser*. Our brain releases dopamine in *anticipation* of something. The emotional response motivates our actions toward a behavior. It creates a feeling of desire toward an object.

A computer can be programmed to self-destruct. If our autopilot is programmed incorrectly, it can attach itself to a harmful object. It can associate destructive behaviors with positive. The opportunity for self-destructive programming significantly increases when we are not present enough to recognize and avoid harmful behavior. When we persist within a state of non-presence, we allow numerous poor habits to establish through a combination of powerful chemicals.

This alteration of our brain chemistry is the principle behind addiction, and certainly addiction to stimulants like nicotine, crystal meth, or cocaine. Those stimulants release copious amounts of dopamine onto our neural network. That release is saved into the autopilot programming, which associates the drug with a positive event. Depressants such as alcohol and heroine similarly hijack our reward and desire systems using an opposite effect on the body chemistry. But the results usually play out the same: a dopamine insertion to inspire continued use. It offers dopamine as the carrot to incite your desire toward another dopamine release, and the cycle continues.[245]

Steve-O, a star of MTV's hit show *Jackass* made a video where he breaks down all the drugs he has done. When he gets to cocaine, it is perplexing to him. He can't remember a time he actually enjoyed cocaine, yet he was addicted for years.[246] The desire to continue using the drug was most certainly fueled by dopamine. As experiments have shown, rats will starve themselves pulling a lever to get more dopamine when the lever for food is easily accessible.[247]

I can relate to Steve-O. I have dealt with numerous addictions in my life and have watched friends and family struggle with them. I rid myself of nicotine dependency twice. I wrestled over control of alcohol each of my adult years. And more recently I found myself trapped in an addiction via prescription to treat attention deficit disorder – a narcotic chemically similar to methamphetamine.

People addicted to these stimulants find it impossible to be motivated by normal rewards after being exposed to such a rich flood of dopamine.[248]

Studies in previous decades understood addiction as a malfunction of the addict's neurotransmitter system. This gave rise to the theory certain individuals are born with the problem, and the concept of the *addictive personality* was born. There was hope addiction could be cured with pharmaceuticals which correct the neurotransmitter system. Both theories proved to be wrong.[249]

With physical dependence, our body is continuously trying to reach a state of homeostasis. Our chemical composition swings out of balance for the duration of intoxication. When the intended effects wear off, the chemicals of the body will swing like a pendulum to an opposite condition before eventually finding balance – or homeostasis. During that first inevitable pendulum swing away from the effects of a drug, the user will experience discomfort which can be difficult to endure. Some learn to combat the *come-down* by taking the drug again – a behavior that almost guarantees addiction. In doing this, they indicate to the basal ganglia the drug isn't just positive, but necessary to avoid illness. From there, continued use further strengthens the association between the basal ganglia and the sensation of the high. The autopilot has been programmed by the user. At least that's my theory.

Physical addiction is only one factor. Within our thoughts is a different beast. And this animal is fed both internally, and from external forces – forces which might be trying to help.

Allen Carr developed a commercially successful program for treating addictions. His program does not follow the patterns of Alcoholics Anonymous or similar 12-step programs. With his method a person simply reads one of his books, rids themselves of the thoughts which excuse their habits, sees things for what they are, and most people stop using the substance after finishing the book.[250] *Most people!* What other addiction treatment can boast a success rate better than 50%? In fact, Carr boasted a *90% success rate!* Unfortunately, those statistics were not backed by clinical trials.

"Public health doctors and psychiatrists dismissed the Carr method as being too intellectually demanding for many uneducated smokers. [Burn].

"In turn, some supporters of the Carr method painted a picture of a churlish medical profession, peeved that someone scientifically unqualified had provided such novel insights into such an important sphere of public health.

"Carr clashed with leading anti-smoking campaigners and even the government over their promotion of what he considered to be failed smoking cessation techniques. In particular, his uncompromising opposition to the use of nicotine replacement therapy, which he said merely prolonged addiction, put him on a collision course with conventional campaign groups such as Action on Smoking and Health (ASH)" (PubMed Central).[251]

His Easy Way brand expanded its reach to address addictions to alcohol, drugs, food, gambling and to overcome various phobias. Carr blasted the medical community for distributing a narrative which only strengthened addictions. In his books, he boldly claimed quitting was easy.[252]

Since his death in 2006, clinical trials were finally conducted to measure the effectiveness of Easy Way and to compare it to conventional methods. Easy Way did not reach the 90% success rate Carr boasted. But it did show superior efficacy over conventional methods.

In *Effectiveness of the Allen Carr smoking cessation training in companies tested in a quasi-experimental design*, 124 smokers were selected to use Carr's method and compared to a control group of 161 quitting smokers who shared similar characteristics. Success was determined when participants maintained abstinence from smoking for 13 months and CO tests were used to confirm. The results showed a success rate of 41.1% for those using Easy Way compared to 9.6% for the control group. "Smokers following the [Allen Carr method] in their company were about 6 times more likely to be abstinent."[253] Hmm, but to be fair, it was a small sample size and used the descriptor: *quasi-experimental design*. That doesn't sound like a clinical trial.

In 2019, the results of a clinical, randomized trial, comparing 300 smokers, showed a success rate of 22% for Easy Way and 11% for Quit.ie. It was concluded that "all [Allen Carr] quit rates were superior to Quit.ie, outcomes were comparable with established interventions."[254] *Outcomes were comparable with established interventions? But they didn't compare data for established interventions.*

Worry not. A clinical trial published in 2020 would compare Allen Carr's Easy Way to the UK National Institute for Health 1 on 1 counselling program. "A two-arm, parallel-group, blinded, randomised, controlled trial" was conducted on 620 participants and showed 19.4% success for Easy Way compared to 14.8% for the established intervention. Curiously, the report concluded: "There was no clear evidence of a difference in the efficacies of the Allen Carr's Easyway."[255]

No clear evidence of a difference? That seems bizarrely quick to dismiss. Each year since Carr's death the efficiency of his method seems to taper off. Could it really be said they were testing his method? He challenged the foundations of conventional approaches and by every account was shown more effective. Even if they are not sweeping this under the rug, they sure make themselves appear to. There is clear evidence of a difference in efficacy. And even if that is overstating the evidence, people's lives are at stake. Addiction affects a large proportion of the population. The powers that be won't even consider revisiting their approach?

It appears we have been fed a counter-productive narrative about addiction. When an addicted person gives into their cravings for 1000th time, they're bound to feel frustrated and wonder if it's possible to quit. The urging of dopamine is imperceptible. They simply *want* the drug. How could anyone fight something they *want? This must be a disease.*

As if to strengthen the fears of every addict, a Google search of addiction returned for me little more than pages saying quitting was hard. I never saw any references to dopamine. They state the obvious: *few people successfully quit their addiction without help from a professional,* but in those words suggest the help of a professional offered a significant difference. They're selling their solution, and they displace useful information.

One of the keys to self-discipline is believing that it is possible. It seems to me that when conventional methods start out saying people can't quite without professional help they remove that key.

Not to say I know the secret formula either, mind you. And I clearly oversimplified what addiction is by placing it all in the lap of dopamine. There are numerous other neural systems involved and factors which couldn't fit into this chapter. But it seems to me this is one corner of human knowledge which has not benefited by being explored almost exclusively by people who have not experienced it. I don't mean to dish on people trying to help, but within the profession of addiction therapy, there appears little understanding of what it is or how to treat it.

Whether the addiction is alcohol, nicotine, heroine, meth, cocaine, sex, or cell phones – the common public narrative toward addiction is not something we need to take as gospel. The notion that we are powerless without help combines with other factors to create a powerful mental addiction.

I assert that the hopelessness of dependence is a dangerous belief. Seeing things for what they are empowers us. Deciphering the difference between a *perceived* reward – like one synthesized by a chemical – and a *real* reward, helps us filter out poor motivators. Possessing the skills and presence of mind to step up and control those motivators is known as *self-discipline*. Self-discipline can be developed at any age.

3.2.4 Discipline

If you want to cultivate a habit, do it without any reservation, until it is firmly established. Until it is so confirmed, until it becomes a part of your character, let there be no exception, no relaxation of effort.

Mahavira

Excellence is achieved through discipline. Our goals will only be achieved through discipline. Lack of discipline is the cause of societal decay and personal problems. You might cringe when hearing the word *discipline*, but it is the key to achieving what you want. It is the key to good health, personal achievement, quality relationships, and overall happiness. Developing self-discipline is worth pushing through the cringe and spending time to develop. And of course, I'm saying all of this to myself.

I combined as many studies related to discipline I could find. Then I looked for recurring themes. I also compared this to what I experienced personally, being a professional of failed self-discipline. Who wants to listen to people who exhibit self-discipline? They wouldn't know what they're missing! They wouldn't know the direct consequences of such a lack. For those valuable insights one would need to hear from a pro.

I mentioned five major techniques for developing self-discipline. *Developing self-awareness, believing in our ability to increase self-discipline, developing useful habits, becoming comfortable with discomfort,* and *implementation intention.* These are what I have identified as a requirement, and these are what I am going to implement. I will explain why and how below, and then I am going to consciously attempt to follow these.

Awareness: I do meditate but it has become infrequent. When I was on my game I relished the opportunity to wait in line or sit in a waiting room because those were good opportunities to meditate. My mind was sharp, I felt alive and prepared for anything. Returning to a regular routine of meditation is something I know I will benefit from, so I will commit to meditating daily.

I will make a conscious effort to soak in every experience by being *here*. I will try to be present for every conversation I have, not allowing distractions like my cell phone or intrusive thoughts to take from the present moment. I will leave nothing for my autopilot to control. I will leave reminders for myself to say *I am here* – finding a way to return my mind to being present. Maybe a tattoo. *I am here*.

Believing: The theme of this book centers around belief – for the most part not to remain attached to beliefs. In this case, though, I intend to foster a belief. A convincing belief that I can improve my self-discipline. I think Allen Carr's books succeeded because they developed that belief. They allowed the reader the chance to see the truth of their situation and they nurtured a confidence of possibilities. Carr understood what the professionals did not. That there is another a gear down there somewhere. It just requires a motivation which has been missing. The trick is to find that motivation to propel a person toward their goals.

The question then is *how can I do that?* I haven't found much success in tricking my mind so this will have to be a genuine belief. I can look back at times where I clearly exhibited discipline and use those examples to shore up the possibility of repeating them. Perhaps I could draft a mantra to keep these beliefs in sight and on my lips.

I heard a therapist once say that we struggle with self-discipline because we have identified with the opposite. As such, regardless of our efforts to develop self-discipline, we will find those efforts fruitless because they conflict with our identity. To make such a change we would need to adjust our identity to include self-discipline. *Until it becomes part of our character.* I can't confirm the validity of this theory, but I am certain it would strengthen my belief if I identified with it. *I am self-disciplined.* I could imagine a self-disciplined version of me. How it would feel to be the self-disciplined. Because that is who I am. While I remind myself *I am here*, it wouldn't hurt to tack on *I am disciplined*.

Habits: I am not going to rid myself of poor habits if I don't have something to replace them with. Not having a purpose, not having something to do with my hands, not having a reason to get up in the morning is a sure way to sink into a quagmire.

One significant difference I notice between my personal life and my professional life is that in my professional life, I pride myself on taking care of details. Doing things right the first time. I do not do this when I get home. And I can think of countless times when that harmed me. So I will make it a habit to care for the details and refuse to take shortcuts.

One recurring theme I have heard from people who are well-motivated and from academic research is it is imperative to go back to basics. Perform those small activities you normally feel are beneath you. Clean up after yourself in all you do, even if you have people who do that for you. Make your bed each morning. Cook for yourself and for others. Take the time to organize each facet of your life. Keep your work area tidy. Find fulfillment in slugging through the mundane. This concept must become a way of life, or a mode of being. If you're anything like me who jumped ahead of each detail and chased the big achievements, you'll find this feels tedious, forced, and unnatural. But the silver lining to our efforts is reaching our goals.

The mechanics around how this works – or at least how I perceive this exercise to work – is by reprogramming the reward signals in our basal ganglia. The process of caring for each detail is where we reignite the spark in that reward system. Each completion of a small task releases dopamine. A steady release from small but productive tasks reprograms it for productive activity.

Most people become addicted to substances when normal dopamine levels no longer suffice to hold their interest. They have become accustomed to colossal rewards, and the small secretions offered by small achievements seems meaningless. An addict might say they are *bored*, and that is true. The motivating function of dopamine has been overused, and the mind requires another big hit to hold their attention. But with diligent reprogramming of the autopilot they can move beyond the continuous chasing. Performing those detailed tasks at every opportunity is the means to reprogram. This concept of re-tooling the basal ganglia is not only how addictions are treated, but how each bad habit can be re-written. It requires our conscious effort to push through without it feeling good. Until it does.

> *You will never change your life until you change something you do daily. The secret of your success is found in your daily routine.*
> John C. Maxwell

A skilled professional is a master of details. They take pride in the flawlessness of their work and that flawlessness is a result of meticulous care for the mundane. To build the largest company, the best app, a best-selling novel, or the next greatest invention, each of the smallest details must be arranged just so. So it seems with a successful human life. The care we demonstrate for our bodies, our habits, and our mental health, are the cornerstones of achievement. We must consciously care for each of them. We cannot delegate these.

I am a master of details.

Discomfort: If you have ever heard a Navy Seal talk or give advice, it seems they want everyone to suffer as they have. Kidding aside, they all seem to laud the benefits of being comfortable with discomfort. This is not an intuitive concept for me. I can get irritated when I'm not comfortable. But I can also understand the benefits. This is part of resilience, and I have no doubt that sitting in discomfort while I have a choice will offer considerably more benefit than being miserable over a condition I cannot affect.

I am comfortable.

Intention: I will maximize my use of time through regular personal planning. I will set aside time to declare for myself my intentions, to be honest about my values, and set achievable goals. My intentions and goals are not meaningless, and they are not impossible. They are important and I will do everything I can to achieve them. I will work diligently to follow my plans and I understand the gift that each moment offers. I will not allow this time to be wasted.

My goals are important.

How much would you enjoy seeing the smug look of *I told you so* on the faces of your former slave drivers? Does that work for motivation? It does for me.

I feel I have wasted enough time pursuing worthless things and spinning my tires with lack of discipline. And I invite you to join me as I apply genuine effort to make a change. If any of these tactics seem reasonable and you can find a way to personalize them, or if you would like to add tactics you found to work, I would like to hear from you. I will start a *Discipline* conversation on the Dogmablog page at postdogma.org. If I commit to sharing my journey I think that too will add to my motivation and I feel the need to put everything into this. Please join me.

You must build up your life action by action, and be content if each one achieves its goal as far as possible and no one can keep you from this. But there will be some external obstacle! Perhaps, but no obstacle to acting with justice, self-control, and wisdom. But what if some other area of my action is thwarted? Well, gladly accept the obstacle for what it is and shift your attention to what is given, and another action will immediately take its place, one that better fits the life you are building.

Marcus Aurelius

3.3 REALITY AND SPIRITUALITY

To develop a complete mind: study the science of art;
study the art of science. Learn how to see. Realize that
everything connects to everything else.

Leonardo Da Vinci

It is hard to imagine exploring the concept of spirituality without some form of unverified belief. Our cultures have programmed us to associate spirituality with the stories and images of their choosing. Those images can find themselves planted in our mind like archetypes of specific personalities. We might conjure images of a person meditating amidst the stars with chakras aglow, or an indigenous shaman wearing a ceremonial headdress. Perhaps spirituality conjures within you the sound of an Islamic Salah, a prayerful memory, a story from the Bible, or a near-death experience.

If taking the time to search for the meaning of *spirituality*, you might find there is little consensus on the definition. There seems to be no consistent determination of what it might be, or where to find it.

In my early post dogmatic years, the word *spirituality* triggered feelings of abhorrence and embarrassment. In my head, the word was linked to the biblical *holy spirit*. That holy spirit served as a catch-all force which enabled biblical miracles, powered the creation of the universe, and explained how certain privileged individuals could assert they know things.

I remember driving down a highway on a long trip from home, alone with my thoughts. I had already attended my last meeting as one of Jehovah's Witnesses. I had read the Shepherds Book which alerted to me the leadership was not to be trusted. But something was holding me back from complete disconnection with the religion. On this drive I was desperately trying to sort through my thoughts about what this religion was. *The elders are guided by holy spirit yet conduct themselves with such cold contempt for people who sinned.*

There on a highway in northern Alberta, surrounded by a featureless landscape came the most simple and obvious answer. *They have no holy spirit.* **Boom**! It was the moment the elephant realizes the rope can be broken. In that moment, my view of spirituality changed forever. I awoke from my dogmatic coma, broke down the walls of my mental prison and stepped out of that little box. This would later lead to complete disbelief in God.

I would soon find myself disgusted even by the sound of the word. I felt cheated. Lied to. I was ashamed of having been fooled by the illusory glimmer of Jehovah's invisible force. I started to look woefully upon those who used the word *spirituality*. To me they were clueless about the topic. They were equating a drip of chemicals in their brain – feelings – with some mystical, transcendent force.

But despite being dismissive, I could not ignore how feelings described by the *non-spiritual* followed a strikingly consistent pattern. Regardless of the variations of belief in spirituality, a *lack* of spirituality is described unmistakably consistent – as a disconnection.

In the months following this road trip I wanted a form of spirituality to be true. There had to be a truth that didn't require fanciful beliefs or the strong arm of religious authority. And that search continued, until it didn't. The endeavor simply faded from my mind without success.

A few years down the road, while researching for this project, I intentionally sought beliefs empirically shown to be valuable. *Are there any good beliefs?* It was a daunting task. After an inordinate time digging, I couldn't find any reason to think belief was a useful feature. I was ready to close the case on the subject, a prospect which would allow me to present a clean and simple conclusion. *Don't believe anything.* This was an appealing prospect given it would save significant time.

ONENESS

Just before I closed the door and moved on with my life, I stumbled upon a study published in the American Psychological Association in 2019 by Laura Marie Edinger-Schons of the University of Mannheim. The article was entitled *Oneness Beliefs and their Effect on Life Satisfaction,* and it has completely changed my personal view and attitudes toward the world. In the moments it took to read the study, I had become immediately happier and more aware of myself. I felt more connected with my family and with my position in the universe. [256] I credit her work, and the work of those whose shoulders she stood upon, because for this chapter, I will shamelessly appropriate that work.

Oneness is a feeling that we are connected with every person, with the physical world around us, and with the frequency of time with which we live. It is a realization we are not separate or compartmentalized. We are in no way immune to our environment. We are intrinsically linked. Our actions and attitudes have a direct effect on the people around us, and theirs on us.

Oneness has been described as "the zone," a mindset where time collapses away, distractions melt, and we can perform at the top of our ability – in a state of heightened focus – where mind and body are fully integrated. It is the opposite of dissociative disorder.

> *A sense of being one with all of creation, being one with the ocean, being one with the heavens. . . there's a feeling of completeness.*
> Anona Napoleon—Surfing for Life

Oneness was a concept taught by the Stoic philosophers, including Marcus Aurelius, who wrote "All things are linked with one another, and this oneness is sacred." It is thought oneness had been a prevailing belief among early followers of Jesus. It is a fundamental principle in Hinduism and Taoism.

The term *oneness* can also mean something entirely unrelated. Many faith groups enmesh the concept with their beliefs in a Creator. The term describes a variant to the trinitarian ideology when read as *Catholic Oneness* or *Pentecostal Oneness*. Other entities distort the concept to such a degree they function to *remove* oneness from the believer, despite the outward suggestion. Because the word is attached to so many variant concepts, I find myself reluctant to use it for fear there may be no way of separating the term from those beliefs.

This isn't to say other beliefs are wrong. I haven't explored them all in detail, and quite frankly I don't see how that would be a good use of my time. While those beliefs could prove true, I don't see a need to add elements when in its purest form, oneness functions well without further belief. If however a person is inclined to ponder and examine those ideologies, or to expand the theory, the opportunities exist in quantity. Oneness lends itself to every religious teaching yet requires none.

Research from a wide variety of psychological and physiological disciplines point to the positive effects of the belief. This would include the feeling of connectivity with others, the feeling of connectivity with nature, life satisfaction, and overall well-being. Roman Rolland coined the term "oceanic feeling" when writing to Sigmund Freud in 1927 and used the term to refer to a sense of *oneness with the Universe* which Rolland attributed to religious energy.[257] Freud was initially dismissive of the concept, but was later inspired by Hindu meditation techniques, describing the results as a feeling of "oneness with the universe."

A Study by Kenneth Parker in 1982 showed a positive correlation between oneness or *subconscious symbiosis* using the effect of the word "mother" in student exams.[258] In 1982 Schurtman, Palmatier and Martin drew a correlation for the same symbiotic feeling in recovery of alcoholics,[259] and a study in 1987 saw a decrease in use of heroin among addicts exposed to feelings of oneness.[260]

Social Connectedness is a field of study which has showed positive correlations between our social bonds and every aspect of psychological and physiological health. Social connectivity being a foundational element of oneness.

In 2006, Doris Hill published findings with her studies on American indigenous peoples where she highlighted that a lack of connectivity spurned a host of destructive behaviors. Passive-aggressiveness, compulsive gambling, alcohol addiction, drug abuse, and suicide were causally linked to a lack of oneness – feelings of separation, and abandonment.[261]

A sense of oneness with other people was shown to be a driving force for empathy, where subjects were more willing to help a person, or more neurologically responsive to the errors of a person when they perceived that person as similar, at one, or "of ourselves."[262]

In his article *The Feeling of Being,* Matthew Ratcliffe argues for the existence of what he calls "existential feelings." A group of feelings not found on a standard list of emotions but in his eyes make a considerable contribution to the structure of experience, thought, and action. These feelings are related to a general relationship toward the world. "The world can sometimes appear unfamiliar, unreal, distant, or close. It can be something that one feels apart from or at one with [...] One can feel like a participant in the world or like a detached, estranged observer, staring at objects that do not feel quite 'there.'" Thus, he explains, that in cases of anxiety the "hold on things" or the sense of "being there" can be lost. He describes this feeling as a "total loss of relatedness" or as "disconnectedness from the world."[263]

This relationship of oneness is not restricted to our human connections. Repeated studies over the last two decades provide us with strong evidence that psychological well-being, meaningfulness, and vitality, are found to be robustly correlated with connectedness to *nature* – a sense of oneness with our environment.

Oneness of time or *situational oneness* is another feature that fits alongside our relationship with both people and nature. Oneness with time or *the now* has been documented in art, religion, and literature. It is shown as healthy, progressive, and life-enhancing components of human experience, vitality, and integration. The *progressive oneness experience* is, according to clinical sports psychologist Sharon Chirban, marked by a deeper integration of the self, catalyzed by timelessness, being in the present moment, absence of self-consciousness, and experience of unity with others.[264]

In the 1970s, Mihály Csíkszentmihályi introduced the concept of *flow experiences* to describe a state of absorption in an activity. He observed this intense immersion with people successfully engaging in risky sports activities when their skills match the challenge; when they are neither bored nor overstrained. Csíkszentmihályi described that in this state the activity and the consciousness become one. Worries as well as the sense of time vanish and a feeling of effortlessness and control over the activity leads to satisfaction and happiness.[265]

The 2019 study by Edinger-Schons, which initially sent me down this path, took advantage of a large sample size and was able to extrapolate data across a wide range of subjects. Her findings showed that oneness beliefs significantly enhanced adaption, or life-satisfaction, regardless of religious affiliation. She also found atheists were the least likely to experience oneness.

A paper in the Journal of Scientific Study of Religion describes oneness as "a belief in the spiritual interconnectedness and essential oneness of all phenomena, both living and non-living; and a belief that happiness depends on living in accord with this understanding." The authors report oneness beliefs are more strongly related to mystical experiences and spirituality than to traditional religiosity.[266] I once set about an exploration of spirituality without dogma, without dangerous beliefs, without a basis in pseudoscientific constructs. In reading this study, it appeared oneness could very well be that. *A belief in the spiritual interconnectedness and essential oneness of all phenomena.*

SPIRITUAL CONNECTION

Having read the benefits of oneness, I tried searching more for what it was – how such a belief could be formulated, and why it would work. *Does a person require an additional belief – perhaps in a creator – to develop a proper belief in oneness? Is seeking out oneness too vague a pursuit? What level of conviction would I require to experience flow? Could our interconnectedness ever be proven?*

How could spatial harmony be proven? That answer became obvious and required little stretch of the imagination. We already know we're connected. We understand how the subtle changes in our attitude are shown to transmit non-verbal clues and how our unconscious thoughts are affected without our being aware. We know we affect the space around us. We displace the air and change its pattern of flow. Our body disperses microscopic material into the air which changes the behavior of plants and animals. We have an odor, we release pheromones. Our actions and even our existence have consequences for other people and the environment we occupy. In turn we are affected by waves of physical materials in the air, the measurable energy around us and the objects which fill the landscape. When we join a group, the attitude of the whole group is affected by our own.

Beyond the measurable world of classical mechanics, we could take steps even further and venture into theoretical models. Studies in the quantum world have revealed the empty space between us is not empty at all, but alive with various forms of energy.[267] Quantum field theory suggests subatomic particles affect those around them without being in contact. They transmit a field we can't measure with existing technology. Some have theorized this *unified field* provides the scientific explanation for consciousness. Particles able to communicate over impossible distances combine to form a vast communication network. "The Universe is constructed of fundamental forces or fields, resembling an invisible nervous system, which stretches throughout space and is continuously vibrating, becoming, and transforming trillions of times per second" wrote author Joseph Rain.

Modern physics is increasingly aligning with the concept of invisible connections and previously immeasurable forces. Quantum biology appears to offer the explanation for how living organisms sense invisible phenomena like magnetic fields. It is thought the interaction between entangled electron pairs is the mechanism behind the sensory perception of Earth's magnetic field. I had known that birds use the magnetic pull of Earth's poles to navigate. But I hadn't stopped to consider how those birds perceive magnetism. Birds don't have metal magnets in their brains. It appears that a quantum explanation is most reasonable.[268]

Whether or not spirituality can be explained by quantum mechanics, it isn't rational to think we are disconnected from the world. Not only are we connected by obvious means such as speech and technology, but we are also made of the same Earth. Living beings are a growth of earthly materials which have bubbled forth from the crust, have become animated through some form of complexity, and rather than infect our planet, they constitute our planet. We are *of* the Earth. We *are* the Earth.

Paraphrasing an analogy from Eckhart Tolle: the feeling of disconnection with the world is like feeling as a ripple on the ocean, separate from the ocean. If one part of the ocean does not feel connected with the ocean, it will face a difficult assessment of itself. If a ripple on the ocean thinks it is alone, it is likely to notice the differences among ripples and feel that loneliness within a massive cold and dark expanse of different pieces. Or it could accept it is part of the ocean; an essential part; an intrinsic part. It could realize it *is* the ocean. This becomes a wonderfully freeing perspective. Because not only does the ripple feel connected and complete, but that short life-expectancy it had is also an illusion. As the ripple nears the shore, it is not destroyed. It flows back, and the cycle continues. Though the ripples come and go, the ocean lasts forever. The ripple is not temporary at all. It does not have to worry other ripples are larger, wider, or shaped differently. It is perfect just the way it is. The others are perfect the way they are. They are connected. The uniqueness of their individuality is precious and worthwhile – a necessary part of the whole.[269]

Eventually, as our research into these phenomena increases, we will have a broader understanding of those connections. Perhaps our consciousness and the interconnections with everything could be explained in detail by quantum mechanics and how the quirks and quarks of the universe function within us and around us and communicate across distances like a universal internet of things – a vast neural network of which our thoughts are added. We don't need to understand how it works to know that it does. This part of recognizing the limits of our comprehension is critical. It's also exciting. We get to pioneer the unknown. Whatever little box we have climbed out of, pales in comparison to the adventure that is the true pursuit of knowledge.

ALIGNING THE MIND

I found benefit in pondering how oneness was active in my life and how to harness the belief. What forces could be at play to facilitate this interaction and what are the implications? How could I benefit from this knowledge as those who were positively affected in the various studies? In performing this thought process, I found immediate and overwhelmingly positive improvements in my social connections. I will speak at length about those later.

Aside from human connections, I found oneness connected the dots with other healthy aspects of what it is. For example oneness of time allows us to live in this moment. Sometimes people get caught up trying to speed their thoughts ahead toward future events. They leave their presence of mind to anticipate circumstances which may or may not happen, thus operating on a frequency not in harmony with the flow of time. They're misaligned with our natural frequency, and that misalignment makes them anxious.

Likewise, for those attempting to slow time down, wishing it would not move forward or failing to recognize that it is – they could be in love with, angry with, or in mourning for their past. They too are misaligned with the pace of time, and they feel depressed.

Knowing what causes those misalignments is key. We could eliminate the need for invasive drug therapies and help people address the root of their problem instead of ineffectively treating symptoms. Oneness can heal. Our psychological structure is suited to live in harmony with what is. Misaligning ourselves with the frequency of reality appears to be the cause of many mental health disorders. It stands to reason the best form of treatment is *realignment with reality*. It could also explain why techniques and mental exercises like mindfulness meditation have proven effective in treating anxiety and depression.

Before I get any deeper into my thoughts regarding mental health, it's important that I'm clear that I know nothing. I am not trained in any mental health field and everything I say is only my opinion, and that opinion is not shored up with any qualifications from any field of mental health. I defer then to those who are qualified in these fields.

An article posted by the Mayo Clinic says "meditation has been studied in many clinical trials. The overall evidence supports the effectiveness of meditation for various conditions, including stress, anxiety, pain, depression, insomnia, and high blood pressure... Meditation can help you experience thoughts and emotions with greater balance and acceptance."[270] A Stanford study published by the American Psychological Association showed meditation techniques increased connectedness and helped people connect with strangers. Even just a few minutes of meditation increased feelings of social connection among the subjects.[271]

Meditation performs a double duty. It helps us align with the moment, but its most important feature is helping us become aware. Those two conditions appear to be fundamentally linked. Being in tune with time, fully aware of our senses, our thoughts, and without distraction from background concerns could be two sides of the same coin.

Honesty too is intrinsically linked. Honesty is an element of spirituality. An integration with oneness. An honest person is aligned with reality. They are here. They needn't construct false fantasies or live in an artificial reconstruction of universe. They are liberated from mental imprisonment. They are empowered by the truth. Their fear of others, their weaknesses, and their position in the Universe melts away. They are the Universe. This perception is a powerful means for feeling whole, for being in tune with reality, seeing things for what they are, for awareness.

I have come to realize awareness is a vital component of spirituality, if not the definition. Those in tune with their spiritual side are not dreamy, disconnected people who fail to see reality around them. People in touch with their spirituality are acutely aware of the world, attune to their senses, and intuitively aware of other forces at play. Spirituality is a clarity obtained by aligning with reality, and therefore we could say that *spirituality, awareness, honesty,* and *oneness,* are varying descriptions of the same phenomenon.

Whether the universe is a concourse of atoms, or nature is a system, let this first be established: that I am a part of the whole that is governed by nature; next, that I stand in some intimate connection with other kindred parts.
Marcus Aurelius

3.4 INCUBATOR OF SUCCESS

The way you help heal the world is you start with your own family.

Mother Teresa

After coming to terms with oneness and developing mental exercises to integrate with this process, my life immediately improved. My perception of myself and others was the first noticeable change. It was a monumental shift toward positivity and unity.

For over a year I had been desperate to reach out to my daughter who was 11 at the time. It had been evident to me that we were similar in our cerebral approach to the world. I sense from her reclusiveness and from her responses to social life that we shared a similar self-image. But I had never known how to reach out to her. My attempts had always been met with resistance and her default to disconnect. When you're worried your daughter isn't healthy and she won't talk to you, few things could present a more haunting and helpless feeling.

In just one day of coming to terms with oneness I found a way to connect with her and ask questions she was happy to answer. We sorted out awkward barriers to our communication and what our interests and worries had been. We validated our existence and shared our hopes. Our time spent in valuable communication and warm proximity are the most valuable I've experienced.

Social connections with other people are among the most important aspects of human existence. They shape humanity – making us the unique species we are. Our best-running hypothesis for how humans developed such large brains is causally linked to social connectivity.

Research over the course of the last 20 years has offered unmistakable correlations between human social bonds and our well-being – our physical health, our mental health, and longevity. A study, published in the Proceedings of the National Academy of Sciences illustrated how strong social relationships have the power to reduce health risks at each life stage, starting with adolescence and continuing through young, middle, and late adulthood. [272] Behavioral patterns including alcohol intake, drug use, diet and exercise are significant factors in longevity -and all those are heavily influenced by our social network. In Matthew Lieberman's book, *Social*, he makes the case that our need to connect is as fundamental as our need for food and water.[273]

The same parts of our brain which register pain also show similar indicators in response to social rejection. We associate physical pain with social pain. A *broken heart*, or *hurt feelings* convey those connections. These associations are not an accident nor are they misplaced. Pain and pleasure are hardwired into our operating system and these features motivate us toward connections with other people.

In secular employment I take a special interest in *culture*. When I was younger, I was privileged to work on teams operating with powerfully motivating cultures. I observed them performing to their best abilities – individuals would work those extra few minutes to complete a task and without the need for recognition. They would assist and defend teammates, openly sharing information instead of hoarding it. Their happy and positive demeanor was infectious, even toward those who were being difficult or for whom they would not normally assist.

When working within teams which did not have a good culture, I watched team members spend more time gossiping and complaining than accomplishing objectives. They expended only the minimum effort and some even stole from the company. It was impressed upon me how incredibly powerful the culture of a group was to influence such a wide spectrum of behaviors and attitudes. There are no policies or procedures a company could impose which would approach the effectiveness *culture* has on productivity, safety, quality, and retention.

It shouldn't come as a surprise if we consider the Stanley Milgram experiment regarding authority, or when we think how easily a student could be pressured to give a false answer when other students are doing so. The attitudes and habits of those within close proximity have a profound effect. Even if we are unaware of it, we begin to subconsciously mimic the human behaviors we see. *Monkey see. Monkey do.* Our attitudes align with those around us. Our speech patterns are affected by contagion, as is our work ethic, our vocabulary, attitude, success, inclinations, and overall morale. We cannot escape the influence of people who are close. From a social psychological point of view, we are tightly interconnected. We are one.

We may lack social skills or fail to see the value of social connections. Both of those conditions tend to feed into each other and produce a snowball effect toward loneliness. This is a condition we are likely to see increase as advances in technology preclude the requirement for in-person contact. We don't need to gather at a market. We don't need to stand face-to-face to communicate. If the Covid-19 pandemic taught us anything, it's that we don't need physical contact to share materials or ideas. And from a cerebral perspective, why would anyone want to? Why would anyone want to lay bare their faults for others to see? Why would we want to smell their body odor, touch their sweat, get their hair caught in our mouth or breathe in their infectious diseases and farts?

The reason we're moved to take such risks can be attributed to four hundred million years of evolution. During that time humanoids who cooperated socially found the strength to ward off predators and competing groups. If they could defend their territory, they could acquire more resources and live longer and reproduce. Those who kept to themselves could not acquire the same resources and died off without passing their genes to following generations. Those were not our ancestors.

Our ancestors remained socially unified and human intelligence can be attributed to this. As groups enlarged, the need for more sophisticated social customs brought success to those possessing social intelligence. With such a thing posted high on the list of desired traits, our brains grew larger from the need for social connection.[274] With each passing generation, our need for social interaction became further engrained.

As the dangers of predators subsided for our early ancestors, their need for coordination did not diminish. It increased. Other people emerged as the greater threat. Groups would then have to increase in size from families to communities, then cities, then nations. Larger groups required increasingly sophisticated social systems, and that in turn favored people who had greater social intelligence. Social status would form as hierarchies became the default method for coordination. The study, *Evolution of Human Parental Behavior and the Human Family* says, "Competition within and between these communities was analogous to climbing a ladder, with each step up resulting in greater access to and control of essential resources. During population crashes, those on the bottom rungs of the ladder suffered disproportionate mortality."[275]

KEY TO HUMAN SUCCESS

The success and survival of humanity depends on our ability to engage with other people. Describing the means for successful human characteristics, the study quoted above contends that social characteristics are so valuable to people they should be considered along with resources like money. Some of those characteristics are internal. Others are external, like the value of good parental guidance, inherited wealth, or a stable environment. "Humans form complex kinship networks that cooperate to control social dynamics and gain access to material resources in the wider community."

Kinship networks are the key to human success. A study published by the Gerontological Society of America says "family relationships play a central role in shaping an individual's well-being across the life course [...] Family members are linked in important ways through each stage of life, and these relationships are an important source of social connection and social influence for individuals throughout their lives. Family connections can provide a greater sense of meaning and purpose as well as social and tangible resources that benefit well-being."[276]

Bonds of trust among family members allow for increased communication, the sharing of ideas and the exchange of resources. From this, strongly connected families benefit from confidence, tenacity, and a motivation to strive for higher education and increased income capacity. Strong families also accumulate wealth generationally, which amplifies opportunities for following generations.

Society benefits from strong families. The fabric of our culture is strengthened when families are strong. This is due both to strong economic benefits, and because people from strong families behave in a cooperative manner. This as opposed to behaviors detrimental to the group, like criminal activity. Adversely, the breakdown of families accounts for the lion's share of poverty in the western world. It is responsible for the disintegration of formerly successful empires.

Accolades for families are hard words to hear when you're not able to connect with your family. And there are too many reasons for such a disconnection. Some have lost family members in death. A social or emotional barrier might separate you. For others it is distance, sickness, abuse, or hurt feelings. Is it possible there might be one barrier you can overcome? The key to your success lays within your relationship with your family. Whatever remains in your power to overcome those barriers is an effort worth investing. It's good to have people to trust. It's good to have people compelled to trust you. It's good to have the confidence knowing someone will love you regardless of your failures. It is a critical resource to have some*one* or some *cult,* who loves you unconditionally.

I was taught Jehovah was the originator of the human family. But families predate Jehovah by millions of years. From an anthropological view, families have existed for hundreds of millions of years.

For the last 30,000 years or more, human families have consisted of about 30 people, led by a group of men, and supported by females which were shared by those men. The first recorded marriage comes from Mesopotamia and dates back 4300 years. Religion doesn't appear to take a central role in marriage or families until 1563 CE.[277] Claims that religion is the originator of the family are simply ungrounded.

I'm not saying religion has played no positive role on the family. Religion has provided, in many cases an imperative structure. A grounding of values and a discipline of the hands. I have watched people improve their lives while becoming Jehovah's Witnesses. I know many wonderful people and families who attribute their family happiness and well-being to their religion. Because religion shapes our values, a religion which genuinely promotes the family is accomplishing something important and positive.

An article in the Journal for the Scientific Study for Religion posits that while many studies indicate religious families are more likely to stay together, few studies have found an increase in the quality of those bonds. Religious families may be less likely to end in divorce, but they come with other social costs. Parents who are religious have a higher rate of stress and this affects the family in a negative way. Religious families tend to be less inclusive of their community, and more likely to cut ties with family members if the member's behaviors do not fit within the moral confines of that religion. With conditions set on family bonds, family members feel a lack of substance. They might not be able to articulate it, but if a child is only loved if they share their parent's belief, those family bonds are perceived as weaker, and this results in less confidence in the family unit.[278]

Since shifting to a post-dogmatic life, it has become painfully clear that I undervalued family. Religion didn't *make* me devalue family, but it did reinforce that family was merely a secondary consideration.

Conditions within my childhood home, and specifically the generational repercussions of war followed by decades of abuse, failed to provide a strong familial foundation. Following patterns of violence and neglect from their own respective childhoods, my mother and stepfather did not form a cohesive bond. Their entire means of communication was conflict. They fought each other daily for over a decade until they finally divorced.

Conflict didn't exist only within my home. My extended family consistently spoke negatively about each other and were quick to cut ties when relationships appeared to offer more conflict than benefits. Before I was brought on to the scene, religion was introduced to my mother's side, which created a further chasm. My great grandparents became Jehovah's Witnesses and since that time, religion served as a line in the sand effectively dividing the family between JWs and non-JWs. The Jehovah's Witnesses in my family were quick to amputate Worldy family, and to shun family who left the faith.

LOYALTY

From my perspective, the Bible might have a strong claim for strengthening socially beneficial structures. But it fails to do so for the best reasons and therefore fails to maintain those structures appropriately; just like it fails to maintain morality. Successful religions have succeeded because they evolved to do some of the successful things. But their dogma precludes them from exploring *why* they are successful.

Such a feat could only be accomplished by valuing honesty over popularity. But honesty is rarely popular. Yet another reason to place a high value on honesty. Loyalty has been weaponized as an agent for harm instead of good. The Stanford Encyclopedia of Philosophy points out, "loyalty is usually seen as a virtue, albeit a problematic one." Being loyal for the sake of being loyal allows an individual to attach themselves to people, groups or beliefs which deserve no such loyalty. Nazis were loyal to Hitler – that could hardly be counted as a virtue.

The encyclopedia explains: "The strong feelings and devotion often associated with loyalty have led some to assert that loyalty is only or primarily a feeling or sentiment." Feelings are not rational entities. This leaves people who rely on their feelings open to manipulation and harm. "The loyal person acts for or stays with or remains committed to the object of loyalty even when it is likely to be disadvantageous or costly to the loyal person to do so."[279] Such is the case with those who remain loyal to abusive partners.

You might think a person committed to a strangely different religion has misplaced loyalty, and you might have a good point. Loyalty has the potential to exclude people, groups, or ideals which may be more valuable. Excluding others because of a blanket policy is not a virtue. In R.E. Ewin's submission to Philosophical Quarterly, he argues that because loyalty can be misplaced and because it often requires us to suspend our personal judgment, loyalty shouldn't fit within the category of *virtue*.[280]

Seeing things for what they are is a virtue. Honesty is a virtue. Using skillful personal judgment is imperative. But believing we owe loyalty to a fake representation of God helps nobody. Believing that a handful of men somewhere disconnected from real human struggle are representatives of the Divine, and it is they whom God intended to reveal truth, simply isn't being honest. I would contend any human governing body who would place their opinions as a higher value than your family is sending you down a dangerous road.

Until just a couple years before writing this I didn't know unconditional love was a good thing or even if it were a thing at all. I thought there were always strings attached to relationships and family relationships were expendable. I thought unconditional love was the stuff of fairy tales – little more than a catch phrase for movies. *A mother doesn't love a son who becomes a serial killer, right?*

It appears the biological tendency for humans is to love. We were very much born with it. Leading up to and during childbirth, high amounts of oxytocin are released by the mother and can reach the fetus via the placenta. Dopamine and oxytocin also increase when women look at their babies, or hear their babies' coos and cries, or snuggle with them. The result is an overwhelming feeling of love, of fierce protectiveness, a desire to nest, and to constantly worry. In other words, we are forcefully induced to love our children by means of a cocktail of chemicals. From this, we care for their needs instead of discarding them and looking out for personal interests.[281]

This cocktail of drugs is the basis for our emotions, and produce a desire to seek out social interaction, to recognize others and to be more generous and attentive to their needs. That condition doesn't end at childbirth. We have evolved the function to release dopamine, oxytocin, and serotonin with increased human interaction – when we develop trust and learn to cooperate. We're then rewarded emotionally for these interactions and these rewards serve to promote our survival in nature. We are naturally wired toward loving our family members. It's written in our DNA. A mother *can* love a serial killer son. Within strong familial bonds, unconditional love does exist. And it is a powerful aid for the confidence a person requires to set out and make a mark on this world.

Early interaction with children makes them happier and more fulfilled. They develop better social and cognitive skills, are better at regulating emotion, developing beneficial habits, and enjoy increased self-esteem. Studies consistently show children who grow up with both biological parents have a considerable advantage over children who did not. Kids with both parents have more time to interact with their parents and are more economically stable.

In Liebermann's book we learn there are two distinct neurological networks, one that supports social thinking, and another that supports non-social thinking. As one network increases its activity, the other tends to quiet down. What's interesting is that whenever we finish non-social thinking, the network for social thinking lights up like a reflex – almost instantly. This reflex prepares us to walk into the next moment of our lives set to encounter other people. Evolution has placed a bet that the best thing for our brain to do in any moment is to get ready to see the world socially. This is our cognitive default mode.

Loyalty to family is a valuable trait handed down over many generations. Loyalty is a precious commodity which bolsters the confidence of each family member. But when people demand or expect loyalty, that should serve as a red flag. Loyalty is natural, not compulsory. Nobody should need to ask you for loyalty. Faith groups who have imprinted through repetition a need to be loyal to God, and by proxy the group, equip themselves with power when a family member dissents from their control. The family then becomes a hostage mark for the group who lay claim to its origins. Like slave masters they reserve for themselves the right to reconstruct and separate families as they see fit.

To demonstrate how religion has held the human family ransom I'll share with you a story from a father who was faced with a crisis of conscience. He had learned like I had that his religious beliefs were false. He became one of Jehovah's Witnesses as a young adult and had since married a woman who was a generational Witness. Together, they had two children. When he spoke to one of his congregation elders about his doubts, the elder responded by reading from the book of Exodus. In the 21st chapter, God gives regulations for the management of slaves.

> *If you buy a Hebrew slave, he will serve as a slave for six years, but in the seventh year, he will be set free without paying anything. If he came by himself, he will go out by himself. If he is the husband of a wife, then his wife must go out with him. If his master gives him a wife and she bear him sons or daughters, the wife and her children will become her master's, and he will go out by himself. But if the slave should insist and say, 'I love my master, my wife, and my sons; I do not want to be set free,' his master must bring him before the true God. Then he will bring him up against the door or the doorpost, and his master will pierce his ear through with an awl, and he will be his slave for life.*
>
> Genesis 21:2-6

The point was made to the young father: *you dedicated yourself to Jehovah, and you will either remain one of Jehovah's Witnesses, or you will leave* **without** *your wife and children.* This common view of the family among Jehovah's Witnesses demonstrates perhaps why my personal views of the family were of less importance than they should have been.

SAVING JWs

A frequent question in EXJW support groups is *how can I get my (relative or friend) to understand they're being manipulated?* And the short answer is *you can't.* You can't make anyone believe anything. That's what the Faithful Slave does, and it isn't ethical.

Since the moment JWs start to study, they are trained to resist criticism of their beliefs. Life-long JWs have spent their whole life resisting frontal opposition. JW rote training is designed to equip them with canned responses for defense. That's where their armor is the strongest, that's where their shields are up. No amount of reasoning or logic will penetrate that heart.

Another reason logic won't work is because their attachment isn't logical. It's emotional. Emotional trigger words like *loyalty* are strategically built into their studies and songs to foster an effective, visceral reaction to any notion contrary to the Faithful Slave.

But we aren't powerless to help people who are emotionally attached. Logical arguments are powerless. But a simple strategy shift might work. That person's emotions are misaligned and so perhaps that should be our focus. Help them realign their emotions. Find the values behind their beliefs and a means to redirect them. If *loyalty to Jehovah* is the biggest value, would it not show loyalty to think critically? To be honest? *Adopt* their value and make it personal. "I feel Jehovah would think I was disloyal if I didn't thoroughly analyze this." And be patient when they have a lame response for every argument. This is a long game.

SAVING JWS CONT'D

Jehovah's Witnesses are told apostates can't say the name Jehovah, they're angry, and they lie. It will not help your cause to prove them right. Don't lie. Stay positive. I like to say *Jehovah* often and to articulate it well.

Every JW holds certain reservations about their beliefs and for the Organization. In each of your interactions refrain from challenging the religion. If they are going to confide in someone about their doubts, it will not be with an apostate. You would be better off showering JWs with praises until the loved one gets sick of hearing it and wants to confide in you the reality.

If they want to talk to you about their religion, show genuine interest and use the opportunity to ask questions which get them thinking critically. But don't accept a study - that will only excite and encourage them.

Be the breath of fresh air they need. Provide a safe place where they can finally relax and feel free from judgment. Keep all conversations positive especially when referring to specific Witnesses. End each conversation before they want to. This entices them for more and prevents overload.

IMPLEMENTING ONENESS

I needed an adjustment to my concept of family. For that I am thankful for Edinger-Schon's study. The influence we trade among people is significant. We mimic the behavior of others and are molded by every human interaction. This has enormous implications. I set about to develop a strategy to derive the most benefit. I considered how simply being in proximity to successful people increases our chance of success. We therefore have a vested interest in the success of people around us. Our partner, our immediate family members, our friends, workmates, and those we merely walk past – if they are happier and enjoying life, we are more likely to be happier and enjoy life. I let that point sink in. I imagined how that should affect my decisions and how I use my time. Thrusting forward toward personal success is fruitless if done alone. It's ineffective and when it comes at the cost of time from our families, that is a net loss.

On the other hand, our material sacrifices for our family – the opportunities for financial gain we abandoned in their favor – are not lost. They are well-invested. They will pay back in dividends throughout our lives. They offer financial returns because we ensured the people surrounding us are successful. Even if those financial returns don't fully recover, the confidence we gain knowing we have our family behind us is profound. This is how we derive meaning and embrace oneness; our integration with reality.

Because the investment is so crucial, I concluded that I should concentrate my purpose on the success of others. I would focus on those I spend the most time with. This is where those conversations with my daughter started. I would ensure interactions with any person would be positive and with a mind for helping them succeed. I would keep myself clean and presentable, but it would not be my intent to benefit myself during this extended time. My intent would have to remain selfless, and I would prove true to this ethic.

It might seem paradoxical that I would attempt to derive benefit by not attempting to derive benefit, and the irony of that was not lost on me. Just the same, it was a tangible motivation, and I reasoned it would only work if I had the success of others genuinely at heart. If a selfish desire was required to act unselfishly, it was better than one which was not effective.

I've read self-help books telling us to surround ourselves with successful people if we want to be successful. But if you're not successful, why would they want to spend time with you? It appeared more practical to create the success in others. It's certainly a more genuine motivation. And it works. It became my engrossing mission to make everyone I encountered succeed. Like igniting a massive wildfire, I would set the world aglow with positivity, kindling it with small actions among those closest. I would create a culture of happiness. An incubator of success with my family at the epicenter. I would then work to benefit workmates and extended family, friends, all of which became closer.

This proved difficult on several occasions, especially with my employment. I was forced to realize I did not like certain individuals. This concept then served a double duty in teaching me where I still cast judgment. I came to understand how difficult it is to help a person succeed when their success doesn't make you happy; when you don't feel they deserve the success they have, or when their success is likely to reduce your own. I realized I had to dig deep and chase those bugs out.

I imagined worst-case scenarios. If there were a hate-filled person wielding a machete and screaming how he wished me harm, would the ethos of helping others succeed still apply? I decided it would. The best way for me to find safety in such a circumstance is to help that person succeed. It would not help them succeed to murder me. Something is misaligned and if I can correct that, perhaps their hate could be ventilated toward something more productive. And how disarming for the crazy machete man when I approached and asked, "how can I help you?"

It was difficult when assisting a workmate obtain honor with our superiors. His promotion would eliminate any chance for my own. I found myself hesitating to help. Eventually I realized my greatest chance for long-term success was with his success. So I recommitted to the concept. I went out of my way to help him. I rescued him from a situation which could have severely damaged his reputation. My rescue attempt did not position me for advancement. Not immediately. But all my relationships at work improved. My standing with our superiors could not have improved more, or by any other means.

None of these concepts would work if I approached them insincerely. I had to genuinely care for their success and when you're genuine, that reality is evident. You appear more attractive and approachable. You radiate with harmony.

I took this a step further and included the cleaning of my environment as a quality of oneness. This meant making my bed regularly, cleaning my vehicle, and doing things right the first time – avoiding short cuts. It required patience, because I tend to get ahead of the moment, leaving myself misaligned and anxious. I had to help others who did not make it easy.

It was a simple formula: Give compliments. Offer help in any way. Make it a practice to say, "how can I help you?" Extend this to every person I encounter. If it seemed it might repel them, I wouldn't do it. Aggravating or repelling people was not the idea. When I needed to triage my time, I did so for my family.

But there is a tragic turn: At some point I lost that ethos. After a couple months I fell out of practice despite experiencing the benefits. I was scheduled for a legal matter and when that was over I wasn't interested in other people's success. I have tried somewhat to get back to that mindset, but it has been two years and I haven't fully embraced it. I'm not sure why that is. But because the benefits were so profound I am determined to redevelop and retain this wildfire of positivity. I think it would fit in conjunction with my pledge to strengthen self-discipline. With this, too, you are welcomed to join me.

In a sense, people are our proper occupation. Our job is to do them good and put up with them.
Marcus Aurelius

3.5 WHOLENESS

Tell me, what is it you plan to do with your one wild and precious life?

Mary Oliver

The evolution of our civilization is built upon a foundation of human groups uniting themselves around a common cause. Individuals who have not worked within civilization simply haven't survived. We have evolved to work together. We owe the size of our brains to the complexities of social interaction.

Within this evolution of civilization, religion has assumed a prominent role. The oldest and most widespread of religious entities are worth examining. Their longevity and reach are evidence of their success and that could provide vital intelligence for forming modern organizations.

With the information humanity now has available, we can begin to structure ourselves socially for the right reasons. But we owe religion a debt of gratitude for getting us here. Without religion's scaffold concepts, and the beliefs which held it together, it's hard to imagine how we could have advanced as a civilization.

It's hard, but not impossible.

Religion has often discarded people and used them as slaves. For this they must either evolve or fade away. Critical theorists in sociology recognize the value contained within individual welfare. The basic requirements of individuals should be of higher concern than the maintenance of the structure itself.[282] There lies the faults of communism or any social structure which showed more concern for the structure than the person.

Some might look to a more anarchist or libertarian approach, and the freedoms those concepts promise are intriguing. But large groups of people require systems of governance. Anarchist societies would need to be small. And small groups hold no chance against an organized attack.

Efficient complexes produce better than the sum of their individual members. Within these complexes, humans can trade and therefore not confined to basic survival methods and endless hunting and gathering. When not spending each waking hour in the search for food people can specialize in science, economics, or construction, and play to their natural strengths. The organization of human beings is a tremendous advantage over the individual. Individuals simply cannot compete with cooperatives.

Unfortunately when humans group together there appears to be a charismatic few who succeed in evangelizing their opinions. When people become attached to beliefs and stubbornly insist there is no other possibility, those beliefs become dogma. Being of such a rigid material, dogma guarantees conflict and a stifling of new ideas. We can defeat dogma, at least in our minds, simply by understanding our conclusions are tentative. This makes room for new information and invites peace. *I know nothing* is the cure for religious dogma.

There is an optimism that grows with each detachment from a dangerous belief. As I grow into my feelings of connection with this world and with the people around me, I am also careful to remember we are not the first to be freed from the bonds of dogma. And yet despite earlier advancements, others have found a way to sink back into it.

Enlightenment periods have failed in the past. The monumental works of Socrates, Plato and Aristotle indicated a deep understanding of the world and humanity. As the Greek empire peaked, it seems to have developed the first steam engine, known as the *Aeolipile*. It looked as though they were advancing into the industrial revolution. But that industrial revolution would not materialize. The Alexandrian Library would fade out of relevance and burn to the ground. The light of enlightenment flickered into dark ages.

The United States of America was founded upon principles of freedom and separation of church and state. Only 70 years ago it held the admiration of the world and boasted the wealthiest middle class the world had ever seen. Neither of those are true anymore. How could that happen?

> *Men fight for liberty and win it with hard knocks. Their children, brought up easy, let it slip away again, poor fools. And their grandchildren are once more slaves.*
>
> D. H. Lawrence

When we lose our consciousness, we want that little box again. We want to be told what to do. We crave the booming voice overhead which tells us how to think and directs our steps. We seek out the constructs that organize us and make us useful. If a slave considers himself a slave he will search endlessly for a master, and there is always someone willing to fill that void – if not a person, an organization. Religion along with its dangerous beliefs are doomed to follow us so long as we crave them. And so long as we support the organizations which thrive on dominance.

With that said, we have seen powerful bodies like the Catholic Church evolve to relax many of their dangerous dogmas and adopt a more inclusive approach toward humanity. We see the application of Islam in many western cultures where the violent, conquering styles of its founder are retired to history. These forms of Islam offer a genuine service to their community. I assert the difference between their past and now being the absence of dogma. People who were not clouded with erroneous beliefs felt it was important to demand the organization hold a higher value for individuals. Without dogma, is religion anything more than a social club? There's nothing wrong with social clubs. Social clubs benefit the world.

I like to think Jehovah's Witnesses, as individuals, could make a brave stand within their organization and refuse to believe or to support the absurdities of dogma. They don't need to believe the word *generation* is some open-ended concept that unfolds infinitely, or that we are still living in the same generation as 1914. They needn't believe that lions will literally only ever eat straw. They could admit they don't know how God created the Earth. They could embrace evolution as a genuine possibility, that it violates no part of the Bible. They needn't believe the *two-witness rule* is the only permissible means to investigate child sexual abuse when local authorities could serve as an effective resource. They don't have to think God hates everyone in the LGBTQ community. I hope they can come to the realization that they are allowed, in fact they are expected, to stand up against authoritarian thought-control and take Jesus' example by protecting truth (Matthew 12:1-7). I hope they make the best use of God's gift of self-determination.

Unfortunately, though, the trend is not in that direction. The oversight of the Watchtower seems increasingly intrusive, and the Faithful Slave insists on imposing their opinions on all aspects of Jehovah's Witness's lives. Independent thought continues to be discouraged and punished. A tighter grip appears to close around the behaviors of individual JWs as the Watchtower seeks to maintain an image of purity and good conduct.

They're not achieving this image by improving people. They accomplish this by deleting people. Deleting people who struggle under the heavy weight of their restrictions. The 33% retention rate of Jehovah's Witnesses is an indication that their behavioral controls are not working.[283] People denied the opportunity to exercise freewill are not improving their self-discipline. They don't have the opportunity to learn from the consequences of their actions. They're not encouraged to think for themselves, and they don't benefit from multiple viewpoints.

Instead of admitting and redressing the policies and procedures which led to the sexual assault of thousands of children, the Faithful Slave have taken a more defiant and brazen stand, insisting their rules are right,[284] refusing to admit wrong, and releasing themselves from the obligation of reparation.[285]

"Who really is the faithful and discreet slave whom his master appointed over his domestics, to give them food at the proper time?" (Mat 24:45NWT) It would be hard to describe the governing body of Jehovah's Witnesses as faithful, discreet, or as slaves. It appears they got mixed up about who in Matthew's account is to provide whom with food. They have lived lavishly on the backs of millions of *domestics* – those who more accurately could be described as slaves. Meanwhile they keep their fold intellectually starved.

The governing body does fit the later description offered in Matthew's account: "But if ever that evil slave says in his heart, 'My master is delaying,' and he starts to beat his fellow slaves and to eat and drink with the confirmed drunkards, the master of that slave will come on a day that he does not expect and in an hour that he does not know, and he will punish him with the greatest severity and will assign him his place with the hypocrites. There is where his weeping and the gnashing of his teeth will be" (Mat 24:48-51$_{NWT}$). I'm not one to point out fulfilled prophecy these days, but it's hard not to see how the governing body really took to their role. *Did they know Jesus called them evil?* There's the beating of slaves, eating and drinking, hypocrisy, I might have seen one gnashing their teeth while condemning apostates recently. Rumor has it the original text in Matthew described the Faithful Slave as organizing a pedophile ring so... maybe there's more to the Bible than I thought.

It's hard to imagine how the influence of rank-and-file devotees could improve upon a system with such a tightly controlled hierarchy. But despite the odds, that is the only way I think that religion is going to survive. There simply are no other options. There is no room in the world for authoritarian rulership. There is no room for those who presume to speak for God. There is no room in this world for the callous disregard of human individuality. There is no room in this world for slavery.

I might be an optimist concerning humanity, but on a path toward harming other people, they cannot find success in the direction they are heading. They won't find the satisfying life they had hoped for and were promised. When the pleas of an innocent child haunt the dreams of an elder for the remaining years of his life; when he can remember the look on her face when he turned her away because she couldn't muster two witnesses; when he can't sleep knowing he forced that child to reunite with her abuser;

when he can relive the sound his voice made when he announced she was no longer one of Jehovah's Witnesses; how he knew those words condemned her to shunning from every person the child had ever known; when he recalls the agony knowing that shunning occurred for no other reason than she had shown the courage to stand for what was right; when he understands her courage was something he could never muster. When those memories haunt that elder, what quality of life could he enjoy?

What quality of life is there for a family who lost their father because he refused a blood transfusion? What quality of life is there for a mother who shuns her son because she thinks God wants her to? What quality of life is there for anyone not allowed to determine their own beliefs? However it may prove to be, I want them to succeed. Each one of them.

Jehovah's Witnesses are not the only people who hold dangerous beliefs. I'm empathetic to the pleas of Scientologists and Muslims forced to adhere to dangerous beliefs. I'm empathetic to Mormons, Christian Scientists and every little spurious cult that decides it must interpret for its people what God thinks and what morals are. I'm empathetic to those who find themselves believing politicians who make promises they cannot keep and who divide humanity in to opposing tribes. I'm empathetic to anyone who has been imprisoned by poverty or who have been denied access to education. I want every human on this planet to succeed. I believe there is room for everyone to succeed, and in a world buzzing with success and respect it would be impossible not to find oneself infected with those qualities.

Further to that I believe without social structures, without an organization of people around a set of values and objectives, that there are few options for advancement and no protection from the hordes. No stash of firearms will protect from invading armies.

I believe we can build useful social structures which elevate our species, reduce conflict, and promote harmony with all things. I believe if we founded organizations on values and not on opinions we would find more success and longevity. Why don't we vote for values? And hold the people in positions of authority accountable when they don't perform to uphold those values? Why don't we build appropriate incentives into government structures? Why don't we construct policies based on careful research? Why don't we disconnect big money from the levers of power by eliminating political campaigning? We have the internet. It seriously doesn't need to be a thing.

We could collectively determine our morals. But we don't. We could proliferate education and support others in times of need. But we don't. We could experiment with ways to improve family structures and offer relief from the struggles of single parenting. But we don't. We could come together to coordinate, compile, and protect the human body of knowledge. But we don't do that either. *Why don't we?*

Perhaps *we* don't. This book was never about changing the world. This book is about increasing the quality of life for those people who have survived dogmatic control. In our first steps to achieving our life of substance, there is little advantage in worrying about the world outside our immediate environment. We can work on the world when we have conquered ourselves.

With that objective in mind it is critical to find a sense of wholeness. It is the sense of wholeness we often lose when leaving behind a religion. Our foundations have crumbled, our families shattered, our sense of purpose left askew. We're not sure what the future holds or what is right or wrong. It feels like large pieces of the puzzle are missing. It is not an enviable condition.

But those pieces can be replaced. Those pieces *will* be replaced, and when complete, that puzzle will be better than it was. The pieces you thought were wholesome were never the right fit. You were forced to mash in the wrong ones and make them look right. But they didn't. The edges had to be bent and frayed. There were gaps where there shouldn't have been. It wasn't real. It wasn't whole. Now you're faced with the opportunity to find what is real. You will be whole. And you will be whole on your own terms.

To make the steps toward being whole I have had to learn the importance of humility, honesty, and I had to learn what made me whole. Integrity. I had to learn the importance of everything. I also had to learn what was less important.

I know nothing. It had to start there. As long as I knew the things I knew, I wasn't going to learn anything. I read a lot, post-dogma. I highly recommend it. I was so impressed with so many authors. It's amazing how deep and intelligent thoughts can be when they are not spoon-fed to hypnotize you.

It was important to learn the art of listening to everyone and believing no one. Another highly recommended balance of skills.

I ended up studying the Bible from truly amazing people who did not present their work as if to condescend. I was so impressed with the works of Bart Ehrman, Richard Friedman, John Cossan, James Tabor and the many others. The one who really stood out was Julius Wellhausen – what an impressive sleuth. What a difference to the form of study I was used to.

That doesn't mean I recommend studying the Bible. For that I would say cut your losses and run. Maybe I judge it too harshly, but it has been such an enormous time-sink. Worse than that, it effectively removes the will of the reader and serves as a yoke of slavery. It provides for those who represent its God, a clean slate of servitude. And it isn't honest.

Honesty arrived only at the tail end of a very difficult lesson. I had to face the fact I had been lied to about everything, and by everyone. Harder still was realizing that most of those lies were my own. And later still that it was ok to sit in that. Better to learn late, than never. Honesty has been a monumental shift in my mindset, and I'm not sure there is a way to fully express its import.

Learning not to judge is important and it's been tricky for me. Because, like honesty, I always think I'm on the right side of the bell-curve, until I cross it. I learned the philosophy of not judging early, but I still find myself surprised where I made a moral determination. Maybe those aren't all bad – like determining slavery is immoral. Still though, there's evidence that routing even those out would benefit.

Slavery is a sensitive issue for me. So much so that I have found it difficult – near impossible – to be employed while continuously noting and rejecting employers as behaving like they own me. Maybe that is because I judge it.

I spoke about self-discipline and though I couldn't speak from personal experience, the data on discipline is remarkable and clear. We need to get a handle on ourselves if we're going to find success and this seems one of those areas where exJWs struggle. I am committed to developing mine and I will post my progress as promised.

Edinger-Schon's study on oneness blows my mind. And warms my heart. That is something worth exploring more. The people around us are so important and having perceived, on a worldwide scale, lowered levels of empathy following Covid-19 lockdowns, I don't think our society will take much more. We need to find a way to remain connected, to talk about the big things, and we need to reach inside for empathy – understand why others believe what they do. I am convinced our only chance at opposing authoritative government, behemoth corporations, or charismatic cults is banding together.

If we think with humility, we can learn. If we value the truth, we might just find it. If we maintain unity, we could access powers we never thought possible.

Frequently consider the connection of all things in the Universe. ... Reflect upon the multitude of bodily and mental events taking place in the same brief time, simultaneously in every one of us and so you will not be surprised that many more events, or rather all things that come to pass, exist simultaneously in the one and entire unity, which we call the Universe. ... We should not say 'I am an Athenian' or 'I am a Roman' but 'I am a Citizen of the Universe.'

Marcus Aurelius

GRATITUDE

Forgiving myself for my many failings made room for gratefulness.

I can no longer find blame for those who affected me. Not only were they doing their best, but it needed to be that way so I could be who I am. All the pain I resented has proven to be the tool that improved me.

I owe everything to everyone I have ever encountered. My wife, Stacey, my daughter, Winter, and my son, Cale. I'll even squeak a thought of gratitude to my granddaughter who was recently brought into this world. I thank my Nana for caring and guiding me throughout my life. I thank Joe for being an instrumental help with this work. I'm grateful for the support of the Post Dogma group who helped me as a sounding board for thoughts and enduring my rants and shocking opinions. For the EXJW communities for being my testing ground and for supporting me while I struggled to find wholeness. For my sisters, cousins, nephew, and nieces. For my father and grandfather who both passed during the writing of this.

I owe everything to the incredible planet that I live on and that I am connected to. I'm grateful for living in this time, in this part of the world with the precise circumstances that are around me. I am precisely where I want to be.

Because of this I must also thank Jehovah's Witnesses. I must thank those who taught me that religion. The very same who trained me like an elephant. I know you meant well. And it went well. Nothing has shaped my life more.

Before I studied the Bible and before I felt I understood religion, it was my mother who taught me who God was. Further down the road that image would evolve, but the sense of a loving creator allowed me to see when it wasn't so – when what I was being taught no longer lived up to the standard set for God. That provided me the courage to stand up when those teachings fell short of that standard. So of all people I must thank my mother.

Jehovah doesn't exist – not in the manner in which I had thought. But there is a universe. And that universe is perfect and beautiful. And if that universe embodies the character and power which I had projected upon God than it wouldn't be appropriate at all to say there is no God.. Perhaps it would be more appropriate to express gratitude.

Thank you, Jehovah.

All you need are these: certainty of judgment in the present moment; action for the common good in the present moment; and an attitude of gratitude in the present moment for anything that comes your way.
Marcus Aurelius

APPENDICES

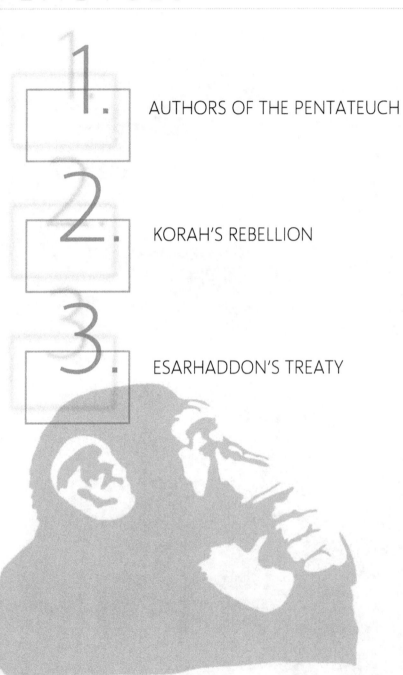

A. AUTHORS OF THE PENTATEUCH

GENESIS	J	E	P	R
Creation	2:4b–25		1:1–2:3	
Generations of heaven and earth				2:4a
Garden of Eden	3:1–24			
Cain and Abel	4:1–16			
Cain genealogy	4:17–26			
Generations of man	5:29			*5:1–28, 30–32
Sons of God and human women	6:1–4			
The flood	6:5–8; 7:1–5, 7, 10, 12, 16b–20, 22–23; 8:2b–3a, 6, 8–12, 13b, 20–22		6:9–22; 7:8–9, 11, 13–16a, 21, 24; 8:1–2a, 3b–5, 7, 13a, 14–19; 9:1–17	
Noah's drunkenness	9:18–27			
Noah's age				*7:6; 9:28–29
Generations of Noah's sons	10:8–19, 21, 24–30		10:1b–7, 20, 22–23, 31, 32	10:1a
The tower of Babel	11:1–9			
Generations of Shem				11:10a, *10b–26
Generations of Terah			11:27b–31; 12:4b–5	11:27a, *32
Abraham's migration	12:1–4a			
Promise to Abraham	12:6–9			
Wife/sister	12:10–20			
Abraham and Lot	13:1–5, 7–11a, 12b–18 [*14:1–24]		13:6, 11b–12a	
Abraham's covenant	*15:1–21		17:1–27	
Hagar and Ishmael	16:1–2, 4–14		16:3, 15–16	
The three visitors	18:1–33			
Sodom and Gomorrah	19:1–28, 30–38		19:29	
Wife/sister		20:1–18		
Birth of Isaac	21:1a, 2a, 7	21:6	21:1b, 2b–5	

Hagar and Ishmael		21:8–21	
Abraham and Abimelek		21:22–34	
The binding of Isaac		22:1–10, 16b–19 *22:11–16a	
Abraham's kin	22:20–24		23:1–20
The cave of Machpelah	24:1–67		25:5–6
Rebekah			25:20
The sons of Keturah		25:1–4	
The death of Abraham	25:8a		*25:7, 8b–11
Generations of Ishmael			25:13–18 25:12
Generations of Isaac			25:19
Jacob and Esau	25:11b, 21–34; 27:1–45		26:34–35; 27:46; 28:1–9
Wife/sister	26:1–11		
Isaac and Abimelek	26:12–33		
Jacob at Beth-El	28:10–11a, 13–16, 19	28:11b–12, 17–18, 20–22	
Jacob, Leah, and Rachel	29:1–30		
Jacob's children	29:31–35 30:1a, 4a, 24b	30:1b–3, 4b–24a	35:23–26
Jacob and Laban	30:25–43; 31:49	31:1–2, 4–16, 19–48, 50–54 32:1–3	
Jacob's return	31:3, 17, 18a; *32:4–13; 28b, 31–35	32:14–24 33:1–17	31:18b; 35:27
Jacob becomes Israel	32:25–33		35:9–15
Shechem	34:1–31	33:18–20	*33:18
Return to Beth-El	35:1–8		
Rachel dies in childbirth	35:16–20		
Reuben takes Jacob's concubine	35:21–22		
The death of Isaac		35:28–29	
Generations of Esau	36:31–43	*36:2–30	36:1
Joseph and his brothers	37:2b, 3b, 5–11, 19–20, 23, 25b–27, 28b, 31–35	37:3a, 4, 12–18, 21–22, 24, 25a, 28a, 29, 30, 36	37:1 37:2a
Judah and Tamar	38:1–30		
Joseph and Potiphar's wife	39:1–23		
The butler and the baker	40:1–23		

Joseph and the Pharaoh	41:1–45a, 46b–57		41:45b–46a	
Jacob's sons in Egypt	42:1–4, 8–20, 26–34, 38; 43:1–13, 15–17, 24–34; 44:1–34; 45:1–2, 4–28; *49:1–27; 50:1–11, 14–23	42:5–7, 21–25, 35–37; 43:14, 18–23; 45:3		
Jacob in Egypt	46:5b, 28–34; 47:1–6, 11–27a, 29–31; *49:1–27; 50:1–11, 14–23	46:1–5a; 47:7–10; 48:1–2, 8–22; 50:23–26	46:6–27; 47:27b; 48:3–6; 49:29–33; 50:12–13	*48:7; 49:28

EXODUS	J	E	P	R
Those who come to Egypt				1:1-5
The new generation	1:6		1:7	
The enslavement		1:8-12	1:13-14	
Killing the male infants	1:22	1:15-21		
Moses' birth and youth	2:1-23a			
God hears Israel's cry			2:23b-25	
Yahweh summons Moses	3:2-4a, 5, 7-8, 19-22; 4:19-20a, 24-26	3:1, 4b, 6, 9-18; 4:1-18, 20b, 21a, 22-23, 27-31	6:2-12, 14-25; 7:1-9 4:21b; 6:13, 26-30	
Moses and Pharaoh		5:1-2	5:3-6:1; 7:14-18, 20b-21a, 23-29; 8:3b-11a, 16-28; 9:1-7,	7:10-13 19-20a, 21b, 22; 8:1-3a, 12-15; 9:8-12
The Exodus	8:11b; 9:35; 10:20, 27; 11:9-10	13-34; 10:1-19, 21-26, 28-29; 11:1-8	12:1-20, 28, 40-49	12:37a, 50-51
The Red Sea	13:21-22; *14:5-7, 9a, 10b, 13-14, 19b, 20b, 21b, 24, 25b, 27b, 30-31; *15:1-18	12:21-23, *24-27, 29-36, 37b-39; *13:1-16 13:17-19; 14:11-12, 19a, 20a, 25a; 15:20-21	14:1-4, 8, 9b, 10a, 10c, 15-18, 21a, 21c, 22-23, 26-27a, 28-29	13:20; 15:19
Water in the wilderness	15:22b-25a			15:22a, 27
Commandments		15:25b-26		
Food in the wilderness	16:4-5, 35b		16:2-3, 6-35a, 36	16:1
Water in the wilderness		17:2-7		17:1
Amalek		17:8-16		
Jethro	18:1-27			
Horeb/Sinai	19:10-16a, 18, 20-25	19:2b-9, 16b-17, 19; 20:18-26	19:1	19:2a
The Ten Commandments			*20:1-17	
The Covenant Code		*21:1-27; 22:1-30; 23:1-33		
Horeb/Sinai (continued)	24:1-15a; 18b	24:15b-18a		
Tabernacle instruction			25:1-31:11	
Sabbath command			31:12-17	
The tablets			31:18	
The golden calf		32:1-33:11		
Theophany to Moses	34:1a, 2-13	33:12-23		34:1b

	J	E	P	R
The Ten Commandments		34:14-28		
The skin of Moses' face				34:29-35
Execution of the Tabernacle instruction				35-40

LEVITICUS	J	E	P	R
Entire book			1-27	
Except:				
Booths on Sukkot				23:39-43
Restoration from exile				26:39-45

NUMBERS	J	E	P	R
The last days at Mt. Sinai			1:1–2:34; 3:2–9:14; 10:1–10	3:1; 9:15–23
Departure from Mt. Sinai	10:29–36		10:11–12, 14–27	10:13, 28
Taberah		11:1–3		
Food in the wilderness		11:4–35		
Moses' Cushite wife		12:1–16		
The spies	13:17–20, 23–24, 27–31, 33; 14:1b, 4, 11–25, 39–45		13:1–16, 21–22, 25–26, 32; 14:1a, 2–3, 5–10, 26–39	
Additional sacrificial law				15:1–31
A sabbath violation			15:32–36	
Fringes on apparel			15:37–41	
Korah, Dathan, & Abiram	16:1b–2a, 12–14, 25, 27b–32a, 33–34		16:1a, 2b–11, 15–24, 26, 27a, 32b, 35	[*16:24, 27]
Aaronids and Levites			17:1–18:32	
The red heifer			19:1–22	
Water in the wilderness			20:1b–13	20:1a
Israel and Edom	20:14–21			*21:4a?
The death of Aaron			20:23–29 20:22	
Israel and Arad	21:1–3			
The bronze serpent		21:4b–9		
Journeys				21:10–11, [*12–20]
Sihon and Og	21:21–35			
Balaam		22:2–24:25		22:1
The heresy of Peor	25:1–5		25:6–19	
Census			26:1–8, 12–65	26:9–11
The daughters of Zelophehad			27:1–11	
The appointment of Joshua			27:12–23	
Additional sacrificial law				28:1–31; 29:1–39
Laws on annulling women's vows			30:1–17	
The defeat of the Midianites			31:1–54	
Tribal portions			*32:1–42; 33:50–56; 34:1–29; 35:1–34; 36:1–13	
The stations list			*33:1–49	

DEUTERONOMY	DTR1	DTR2	OTHER	I	E	P
Moses' introduction	1:1–4:24, 32–49; 5:1–8:18; 9:1–11:32	4:25–31; 8:19–20				
Law code	26:16–19; 27:1–10		12:1–26:15			
Covenant ceremony	27:11–26					
Blessings and curses	28:1–35, 38–62	28:36–37, 63–68				
Moses' conclusion	28:69; 29:1–20, 28; 30:11–13; 31:1–8	29:21–27; 30:1–10, 14–20				
The appointment of Joshua					31:14–15, 23	
The torah	31:9–13, 24–27					
The Song of Moses		31:16–22, 28–30; 32:44	32:1–43			
Moses' last words	32:45–47		33:2–27			
The Blessing of Moses	33:1			34:5–7		
The death of Moses	34:1–4, 10–12		32:48–52 (R)	34:5–7		34:8–9

B. KORAH'S REBELLION

NUMBERS 16 ACCORDING TO:

JE   P

¹ And Korah son of Izhar son of Kohath son of Levi
and Dathan and Abiram, sons of Eliab, and On son
of Peleth, sons of Reuben, ² rose up before Moses.

And two hundred fifty people from the children of Israel, princes of the congregation, known in assembly, people of stature ³ assembled against Moses and against Aaron and said to them: "You have a great deal! For all of the congregation, all of them are holy—and Yahweh is in their midst. And why do you lift yourselves up over Yahweh's community?" ⁴ and Moses listened, and he fell on his face. ⁵ And he spoke to Korah and to all of his congregation, saying, "in the morning Yahweh will make known who is his and who is holy and whom he will bring close to him. He will bring close to him the one whom he chooses. ⁶ Do this: Take yourselves incense burners, Korah and his congregation, ⁷ and put fire in them, and set incense on them before Yahweh tomorrow. And it will be that the man whom Yahweh will choose, he will be the holy. You have a great deal, sons of Levi!" ⁸ And Moses said to Korah, "listen, sons of Levi, ⁹ is it too small a thing for you that the God of Israel has separated you from the congregation to bring you close to him, to do the service of the tabernacle of Yahweh and to stand before the congregation to serve them, ¹⁰ and that he has brought you and all your brothers the sons of Levi with you close to him? And you seek the priesthood as well?! ¹¹ Therefore you and all your congregation who are gathering are against Yahweh. And Aaron, what is he that you complain against him?"

¹² And Moses sent to call Dathan and Abiram, sons of Eliab, and they said, "we will not come up. ¹³ Is it a small thing that you brought us up from a land flowing with milk and honey to kill us in the wilderness, that you lord it over us as well? ¹⁴ Besides, you have not brought us to a land flowing with milk and honey or given us possession of field or vineyard. Will you put out those people's eyes? We will not come up." ¹⁵ And Moses was very angry, and he said to Yahweh, "do not incline to their offering. Not one ass of theirs have I taken away, and I have not wronged one of them."

¹⁶ And Moses said to Korah, "you and all your congregation, be before Yahweh—you and they and Aaron—tomorrow. ¹⁷ And each man take his incense burner, and put incense on them, and each man bring his incense burner close before Yahweh, two hundred fifty incense burners, and you and Aaron, each man, his incense burner." ¹⁸ And each man took his incense burner, and they put fire on them and set incense on them, and they stood at the entrance of the tent of meeting, and Moses and Aaron. ¹⁹ And Korah assembled all the congregation against them, to the entrance of the tent of meeting. And the glory of Yahweh appeared to the whole congregation. ²⁰ And Yahweh spoke to Moses and to Aaron, saying, ²¹ "separate from the midst of this congregation, and I shall consume them in an instant." ²² And they fell on their faces, and they said, "God, the god of the spirits of all flesh, will one man sin and you be furious at the whole congregation?" ²³ And Yahweh spoke to Moses, saying, ²⁴ "speak to the congregation, saying, 'get up from around the tabernacle of Korah, [Dathan, and Abiram].'"

²⁵ And Moses rose and went to Dathan and Abiram, and the elders of Israel went after him.

²⁶ And he spoke to the congregation, saying, "turn away from the tents of these wicked men and do not touch anything that is theirs, lest you be destroyed in all their sins." ²⁷ And they got up from around the tabernacle of Korah, [Dathan, and Abiram].

And Dathan and Abiram went out, standing at the entrance of their tents, and their wives and their sons and their infants. [28] And Moses said, "by this you will know that Yahweh sent me to do all these things, for it is not from my own heart. [29] If these die like the death of every human, and the event of every human happens to them, then Yahweh has not sent me. [30] But if Yahweh will create something, and the ground opens its mouth and swallows them and all that is theirs, and they go down alive to sheol, then you will know that these men have provoked Yahweh." [31] And it was as he was finishing to speak all these things; and the ground under them was split. [32] And the earth opened its mouth and swallowed them and their houses.

And all the people who were with Korah, and all the property.

[33] And they and all they had went down alive to Sheol. And the earth covered them over, and they perished from the midst of the community. [34] And all Israel that was around them fled at the sound of them; for they said, "lest the earth swallow us."

[35] And fire went out from Yahweh and consumed the two hundred fifty people offering the incense.

from
WHO WROTE THE BIBLE?
by
RICHARD ELLIOTT FRIEDMAN

C. ESARHADDON'S TREATY

Esarhaddon's Treaty	Lines	Topic	Deut. Chapter	Verse
4 First Commandment	41-61	Do not change or alter the word of Esarhaddon, king of Assyria; To loyally help Ashurbanipal as the successor of Esarhaddon	13	1 do not add or take away from it
Stipulations				
10 Stipulation	108-122	Not to pay attention to, or conceal anything against Ashurbanipal, (abutu la dug`ga`tu la sig5 -tu la banitu)	13	2-12
12 Stipulation	130-146	Lynching	13	10
14 Stipulation	162-172	To assist in suppression of revolts, let Ashurbanipal flee (ea~bu-S)	-	-
25 Admonition	283-301	To Repeat the ade to their sons with the warning of deportation:'Do not set any other king before you!'	17; 28	14f; 36
Curses				
38A Anu	-	Mesopotamian god of the heaven: illness	28	21-24?
39 Sin	-	Mesopotamian god of the moon: skin disease	28	27,35?
40 Samas	-	Mesopotamian god of the sun: blindness, injustice	28	28-34?
41 Ninurta	-	Mesopotamian god of war: defeat	28	25-26?
42 Dilbat	-	Mesopotamian god of Venus: being plundered	28	36-42?
52 Gula	-	Mesopotamian goddess of healing	28	35?
53 Sebetti	-	Left out of the manuscript of Tell Tayinat	-	
54 Aramis	-	Qarnaim, east of the Lake of Tiberias (Palestine)	-	
54A Adad and Sala of Kurba'il	-	Kurba'il, Northgeastern Mesopotamia (Kurdistan)	-	
54B Sarrat-Ekron	-	Ekron, Mediterranean coast (Palestine)	-	
54 Bethel and Anat-Bethel	-	Bethel (Palestine)	-	
55 Kubaba	-	Charchemish (Syria)	-	
56 Curse	472-493	Great Gods of heaven and earth	28	20-44
	476-479	Hunger (ezabu-G)		20b21
		Deportation of the king you have set over you		36
Oath				
57	494-511; 501,502; [cf.10]	sa amat sal.hul la du`g'ga'tu la banitu dabab surate la kinate	13	6 (dbr sarah)
Ceremonial Curses				
58-106	63	Earth turned into iron, sky of bronze	28	23

Data from Hans Steymans 2012[286]

REFERENCES

1 Karen Armstrong, *Fields of Blood: Religion and the History of Violence*, 2014, London the Bodley Head

2 Asad, Talal. *Formations of the Secular: Christianity, Islam, Modernity*. Stanford University Press, 2014, p.100, 187-190.

3 Ciesielski, Krzystof, *Set Theory for the Working Mathematician*, 1997, Cambridge University Press

4 PMI, *The Guide to the Project Management Body of Knowledge*, 4th Edition 2008, Project Management Institute. p.148, 287

5 Robert Butts, John Davis, *The Methodological Heritage of Newton*, 1970, University of Toronto Press, Original English Translation by Motte 1729, Original Work by Newton 1687

6 TheraminTrees and Qualiasoup, *How Dogma Pollutes Discourse*, March 31, 2018, YouTube channel TheraminTrees, https://www.youtube.com/watch?v=o6-Htscvf4k

7 Leon Miller and Gordon Anderson, *Religion's Role in Creating National Unity*, March 2009, International Journal on World Peace, 26(1) p.91

8 Rupert Sheldrake, *The Science Delusion: Freeing the Spirit of Enquiry*, 2012, Coronet Books

9 D. L. Chambless, T. H. Ollendick, *Empirically Supported Psychological Interventions: Controversies and Evidence*, 2001, Annual Review of Psychology, 52(1), p.685-716

10 Cesare Pavese, *This Business of Living*, English 1st Edition, March 30 2009, Routledge

11 Michael Roth, *Safe Enough Spaces*, August 2019, Yale University Press

12 Flemming Rose, *Safe Spaces On College Campuses Are Creating Intolerant Students Ideological safe spaces make those on the left and the right more extreme*, Interview with Van Jones, HuffPost.com 2017, updated June 12 2017, Verizon Media, Huffington Post

13 Liz Stillwaggon Swan, *Safe Spaces Can Be Dangerous*, March 20 2017, Psychology Today

14 Barbara Gayle, Derek Cortez, Raymond Preiss, *Safe Places, Difficult Dialogues, and Critical Thinking*, 2013, International Journal for the Scholarship of Teaching and Learning, (7)2, p.9

15 Chris Bail, *Breaking the Social Media Prism: How to Make Our Platforms Less Polarizing*, 2021, Princeton University Press

16 Jane Jacobs, Paul Kuhne, C.J. Peek, *Better Angels Participant-Identified Effects of Better Angels Experiences*, Oct 2019, Better Angels, p.1

17 Andrew Sherman, *Difficult Conversations: As Important to Teach as Math or Science*, 2017, Childhood Education, 93(4), p. 292-294

18 Hanibal Goitom, *Laws Criminalizing Apostasy in Selected Jurisdictions,* May 2014, Global Legal Research Center, The Law Library of Congress

19 US House of Representatives Permanent Select Committee on Intelligence, *Exposing Russia's Effort to Sow Discord Online: The Internet Research Agency and Advertisements*, Retrieved Feb 19 2022, https://intelligence.house.gov/social-media-content/

20 Arthur Brooks, *Love Your Enemies: How Decent People Can Save America from the Culture of Contempt*, 2019, Broadside Books

21 James Richardson, *Definitions of Cult: From Sociological-Technical to Popular-Negative*, Review of Religious Research, June 1993, (34)4, Springer, p.348-356

22 Pew Research Center, *Religion's Relationship to Happiness, Civic Engagement and Health Around the World*, Jan 31 2019 https://www.pewforum.org/wp-content/uploads/sites/7/2019/01/Wellbeing-report-1-25-19-FULL-REPORT-FOR-WEB.pdf

23 Chaeyoon Lim and Robert D. Putnam, *Religion, Social Networks, and Life Satisfaction*, American Sociological Review 75(6) Dec 2010, p.914-933

24 Beth Azar, *A Reason to Believe*, Dec 2010, Monitor on Psychology, (41)10, American Psychological Association, p.52

25 Steve Crabtree, *Religiosity Highest in World's Poorest Nations*, Aug 31, 2010 Gallup, Inc. https://news.gallup.com/poll/142727/religiosity-highest-world-poorest-nations.aspx

26 David Masci, *How income varies among U.S. religious groups*, Oct 11, 2016, Pew Research Center, https://www.pewresearch.org/fact-tank/2016/10/11/how-income-varies-among-u-s-religious-groups/

27 Michael Lipka, *A Closer Look at Jehovah's Witnesses Living in the U.S.*, Apr 26 2016, Pew Research Center, https://www.pewresearch.org/fact-tank/2016/04/26/a-closer-look-at-jehovahs-witnesses-living-in-the-u-s/

28 Casimir Nwaoga, *Religion, Violence, Poverty and Underdevelopment in West Africa: Issues and Challenges of Boko Haram Phenomenon in Nigeria*, Feb 2014, Open Journal of Philosophy, (4)1, SCIRP, p.59-67

29 Don Locke, *Beliefs, Desires and Reasons for Action*, Jul 3, 1982, American Philosophical Quarterly (19)3, pp. 241

30 Alan Baker, *Simplicity*, The Stanford Encyclopedia of Philosophy, Winter 2016 Edition, The Metaphysical Research Lab, Center for the Study of Language and Information. https://plato.stanford.edu/archives/win2016/entries/simplicity/

31 Loyd Swenson Jr, *The Ethereal Aether: A History of the Michelson-Morley-Miller Aether-drift Experiments*, 1880-1930, 2013, University of Texas Press

32 *COVID-19 Cases, Hospitalizations, Deaths by Vaccination Status*, Jan 26 2022, Washington State Department of Health Publication No. 420-010

33 J. L. Schellenberg, *How to Make Faith a Virtue, from Religious Faith and Intellectual Virtue*, 2014, Oxford Scholarship Online, Ch 6. Quote taken from abstract

34 Richard M. Ryan, Edward L. Deci, *Self-determination theory and the facilitation of intrinsic motivation, social development, and well-being*, 2000, American Psychologist

35 Edward L. Deci, Richard M. Ryan, *Human Autonomy: The basis for true self-esteem*, Jan 1995, Plenum Press, P. 31

36 Watchtower, *Organized to Do Jehovah's Will*, Aug 2019, Watchtower Bible and Tract Society, ch3 p.17-23

37 Watchtower, *How to Remain in God's Love*, Jan 2018, Watchtower Bible and Tract Society, ch.5

38 Watchtower, *Letter to the Body of Elders*, Mar 6, 2012, a-E, Christian Congregation of Jehovah's Witnesses

39 Joe Pompeo, *Did You Know The Most Widely Circulated Magazine In The World Is The Monthly Publication Of Jehovah's Witnesses?*, Sep 30 2010, Business Insider

40 Andrew Holden, *Jehovah's Witnesses: Portrait of a Contemporary Religious Movement*, 2002, Routledge, p. 67

41 Watchtower, *How Can Sisters Reach Out?*, Our Christian Life and Ministry, Nov-Dec 2021, 6(11) p.7 https://www.jw.org/en/library/jw-meeting-workbook/november-december-2021-mwb/Life-and-Ministry-Meeting-Schedule-for-November-29-December-5-2021/How-Can-Sisters-Reach-Out/

42 Watchtower, www.jw.org, *2019 Service Year Report of Jehovah's Witnesses*, 2019, Watchtower Bible and Tract Society

43 Watchtower, *"Do Not Lean On Your Own Understanding,"* Nov 15 2011, Watchtower Bible and Tract Society, p.6-10

44 Watchtower, Jan 15 1983, *Exposing the Devil's Subtle Designs*, p.22

45 Watchtower, *Firmly Uphold Godly Teaching*, May 1 2000, p.11 par.14

46 Watchtower, *"Let Your Kingdom" Come But When?* Jan 15 2014, Study Edition, p.30,31 par.14-19

47 Watchtower, *Insight on the Scriptures* (1), 2018, Watch Tower Bible and Tract Society, p.114

48 Watchtower, *Shepherd the Flock of God*, Oct 2019, Watchtower Bible and Tract Society, ch.12,15,16

49 Watchtower, *Shepherd the Flock of God*, Oct 2019, Watchtower Bible and Tract Society, ch.18

50 Watchtower, *Seven Shepherds, Eight Dukes – What They Mean For Us Today*, Nov 15 2013, Watchtower Bible and Tract Society, p.20, par.17

51 Marisa Kwiatkowski, *Jehovah's Witnesses Reportedly Under Investigation by Pennsylvania Attorney General*, Feb 8 2020, USA Today

52 Steve Hassan, *The BITE Model and Jehovah's Witnesses*, Aug 2 2018, Freedom of Mind Resource Center, https://freedomofmind.com/the-bite-model-and-jehovahs-witnesses/

53 Donald Kraybill, *The Riddle of Amish Culture*, 2001, John Hopkins University Press, p.119,145

54 Rumspringa: *Amish Teens Venture into Modern Vices*, Jun 7 2006, NPR;

55 Donald B. Kraybill, James P. Hurd, *Horse-and-Buggy Mennonites: Hoofbeats of humility in a postmodern world*, 2006, Penn State Press, p.169-173, 244

56 Gwen Dewar, *Teaching Critical Thinking: An Evidence-Based Guide*, 2012, Parenting Science, www.parentingscience.com/teaching-critical-thinking.html

57 Steve Hassan, *Combatting Cult Mind Control*, 2018, Freedom of Mind Press

58 Theramintrees, *Debunking Prophets – Part One*, Sep 6 2017, YouTube, https://www.youtube.com/watch?v=opx8iDvR_nU&t=463s

59 *Use Theocratic War Strategy*, Watchtower, May 1, 1957

60 Lorne Dawson, When Prophecy Fails and Faith Persists: A Theoretical Overview, 1993, Nova Religio 3(1), p.60-82

61 Peter Facione, *Critical Thinking: A Statement of Expert Consensus for Purposes of Educational Assessment and Instruction,* 1990, American Philosophical Association, The California Academic Press, Millbrae CA

62 Olivier Serrat, *The Five Whys Technique,* 2017, Knowledge Solutions, Springer, p.307-310

63 Douglas KM, Sutton RM, Callan MJ, et al. *Someone is pulling the strings: Hypersensitive agency detection and belief in conspiracy theories,* Thinking & Reasoning, 2016, 22:57-77.

64 Eli Pariser, *The Filter Bubble: What the Internet Is Hiding from You,* May 2011, Penguin Press, MoveOn.org

65 Christopher Wylie, *Mindf*ck: Cambridge Analytica and the Plot to Break America,* 2019, Random House

66 Shoshana Zuboff, *The Age of Surveillance Capitalism: The Fight for a Human Future at the New Frontier of Power,* 2019, Hachette Book Group Inc.

67 H. Sidky, *The War on Science, Anti-Intellectualism, and 'Alternative Ways of Knowing' in 21st-Century America,* Skeptical Inquirer. 42(2) p.38–43. Archived from the original on 2018-06-06, Retrieved 6 June 2018

68 Anne Applebaum, *Holodomor,* November 12 2019, Encyclopædia Britannica, inc. https://www.britannica.com/event/Holodomor

69 Eric Weitz, "*Racial Communism: Cambodia under the Khmer Rouge." A Century of Genocide: Utopias of Race and Nation,* 2005, Princeton University Press, p.156-157, 162-164, 171-172.

70 Lisa Bero, *Tobacco Industry Manipulation of Research,* 2005, Public Health Chronicles, 120(200); Leemon McHenry, Mellad Khoshnood, *Blood Money: Bayer's Inventory of HIV-Contaminated Blood Products and Third World Hemophiliacs,* 2014, National Library of Medicine, 21(6) P.389-400;

Thomas Sowell, *Intellectuals and Society,* 2009, Basic Books, p.296

71 James Cargill, *On the burden of proof,* 1997, Philosophy, Cambridge University Press 72(279), p.59–83

72 Joseph Weiss, *The Role of Pathogenic Beliefs in Psychic Reality,* Psychoanalytic Psychology, 1997, 14(3), p.427-434

73 Ben Affleck, *Real Time with Bill Maher,* Oct 3 2014

74 Amanat, Abbas, *In Abbas Amanat; Frank Griffel (eds.). Shari'a: Islamic Law in the Contemporary Context,* 2009, Preface, Stanford University Press (Kindle Edition)

75 Waqar Akbar Cheema, *Prophet Muhammad's Marriage with Nine-Year Old Aisha: A Review of Contentions,* Nov 28 2019, Islamic Center for Research and Academics, https://www.icraa.org/prophet-muhammad-marriage-with-nine-year-old-aisha-a-review-of-contentions/

76 Sondre Risholm Liverød (Ed), *The Problem with Obedience,* Aug 15 2014, Webpsychologist.net, http://www.webpsychologist.net/the-problem-with-obedience/

77 https://www.jwfacts.com/watchtower/medical.php#transplants

78 Proverbs 3:5, *New World Translation (Study Edition),* 2020, Watch Tower Bible and Tract Society

79 Watchtower, November 2018, Study Edition, p.13-27

80 https://freedomofmind.com/cult-mind-control/bite-model/

81 Stanley Milgram, *The Perils of Obedience*, 1974, Harper's Magazine, Dec 16 2010, Abridged and adapted from the original

82 D. Pence, C Wilson, U.*S. Department of Health and Human Services, The Role of Law Enforcement in the Response to Child Abuse and Neglect,*. 2002, Child Welfare Information Gateway, https://www.childwelfare.gov/pubs/usermanuals/law/

83 Australian Royal Commission into Institutional Responses to Child Sexual Abuses, *Findings Report*, Oct 2016, Commonwealth of Australia, P. 10

84 Kaya Burgess, *Jehovah's Witness child abuse victims told 'not to go to police,'* The Times, May 11 2007, retrieved May 11 2007

   Australian Royal Commission into Institutional Responses to Child Sexual Abuses, Findings Report, Oct 2016, Commonwealth of Australia, P. 55

85 David Splane, *Put Up a Hard Fight for the Faith!*, 2021 Powerful by Faith! Convention, video co-r21-137.v, Watchtower Bible and Tract Society, retrieved May 18 2022

   M. Stephen Lett, *Maintain the Oneness of the Spirit*, 2015, JW Morning Worship, video jwbmw.201502-5.v, Watchtower Bible and Tract Society, https://www.jw.org/en/library/videos/#en/mediaitems/VODPgmEvtMorningWorship/pub-jwbmw_201502_5_VIDEO , retrieved May 18 2022, 7:35-8:10

   Vanessa Brown, Tara, *Tara was abused by the man she was taught to trust most – now she wants justice*, News.com.au, Dec 9 2016, https://www.news.com.au/lifestyle/real-life/true-stories/tara-was-abused-by-the-man-she-was-taught-to-trust-most-now-she-wants-justice/news-story/50cf9dbf12e650ec22b9157e65e12db2 , Retrieved May 18 2022

86 Australian Royal Commission into Institutional Responses to Child Sexual Abuses, *Findings Report*, Oct 2016, Commonwealth of Australia, P. 60

87 Australian Royal Commission into Institutional Responses to Child Sexual Abuses, *Findings Report*, Oct 2016, Commonwealth of Australia, P. 77

88 Watchtower Bible and Tract Society of New York Inc v. J.W., a minor, July 5 2019, Supreme Court of the United States, https://www.supremecourt.gov/search.aspx?filename=/docket/docketfiles/html/public/19-40.html

   Caroline St. Pierre, *Quebec class action alleging sexual abuse in Jehovah's Witnesses can proceed*, Mar 5 2019, CBC News Montreal, https://www.cbc.ca/news/canada/montreal/jehovahs-witness-watchtower-canada-sexual-abuse-lawsuit-1.5044157 , Retrieved May 18 2022

   Jehovah's Witnesses face £1m legal bill after young girl was sexually abused by one of its members, Leicester Mercury, July 8 2016, Archived from the original Sep 26 2016, and retrieved May 18 2022, https://web.archive.org/web/20160926173418/http://www.leicestermercury.co.uk/jehovah-s-witnesses-face-1m-legal-bill-after-young-girl-was-sexually-abused-by-one-of-its-members/story-29491614-detail/story.html

89 *Shepherd the Flock of God*, Apr 2020, Christian Congregation of Jehovah's Witnesses, ch.14(8)

90 Douglas Quenqua, *The Jehovah's Witness Database of Child Abuse*, April 5, 2019 update, original March 22, 2019, The Atlantic, https://www.theatlantic.com/family/archive/2019/03/the-secret-jehovahs-witness-database-of-child-molesters/584311/

91 Michael Clarke, *Did Leaders of Jehovah's Witnesses Cover up Child Sex Abuse?* Feb 16 2015, PBS Newshour https://www.pbs.org/newshour/show/leaders-jehovahs-witnesses-cover-child-sex-abuse

92 Watchtower, *Statement to The Project regarding the National Redress Scheme and the sales of Kingdom Halls and properties*, The Project, Jul 10 2020, Network 10, https://10play.com.au/theproject/articles/statement-from-the-jehovahs-witnesses/tpa200621ycelq

93 American Society for the Positive Care of Children, *Child Abuse Statistics,* 2020, https://americanspcc.org/child-abuse-statistics/

94 Australian Royal Commission into Institutional Responses to Child Sexual Abuses, *Findings Report,* Oct 2016, Commonwealth of Australia, P.22

95 Watchtower, "*You Were Bought With a Price,*" Mar 15 2005, p.15-20, Watchtower Bible and Tract Society

96 *Five Groups Fail to Join Australia's National Child Abuse Redress Scheme,* 1 Jul 2020, The Guardian International Edition, https://www.theguardian.com/australia-news/2020/jul/01/six-groups-fail-to-join-australias-national-child-abuse-redress-scheme, Retrieved Oct 23, 2022

97 Rachel Browne, *Jehovah's Witnesses destroyed evidence, Royal Commission hears,* July 27 2015, The Sydney Morning Herald, https://www.smh.com.au/national/jehovahs-witnesses-destroyed-evidence-royal-commission-hears-20150727-gilgk6.html , Retrieved May 18, 2022

98 Watchtower, *Jehovah's Witnesses' Scripturally Based Position on Child Protection*, Jan 19 2019, Watchtower Bible and Tract Society, p.1

99 Max Henning, *Jehovah Proved to Be With Me*, Watchtower, Jun 1 1996, p.22,23

100 Lee Elder, *Jehovah's Witnesses and Blood – Tens of Thousands Dead in Hidden Tragedy*, Advocates for Jehovah's Witness Reform on Blood, Aug 9 2017, AJWRB.org

101 Watchtower, *Are You Making Jehovah's Thoughts Your Own?* Nov 2018 Study Edition, p.24 par. 6

102 Watchtower, VIDEO: *Avoid What Erodes Loyalty*, 2016, jwbcov.201605-8.v, Watch Tower Bible and Tract Society
VIDEO: *Pursue What Builds Loyalty*, 2016, jwbcov.201605-9.v, Watch Tower Bible and Tract Society

103 Steve Sauvé, "*Parents of Jehovah's Witnesses preferred to abandon their child because she had had a blood transfusion*", - Manon Boyer, VIVA MÉDIA, https://www.viva-media.ca/la-voix-regionale-beauharnois-salaberry-haut-saint-laurent/actualite-bshsl/communaute-bshsl/des-parents-temoins-de-jehovah-ont-prefere-abandonner-leur-enfant-car-elle-avait-eu-une-transfusion-sanguine-manon-boyer/?fbclid=IwAR1iCrFGSjRUapazUhM3NGaEzsW5E7b-E2NpJMwhlbqgsowmWIFr9OVZwMs

104 Awake! *To Trust or Not to Trust*, Nov 2007, Watchtower Bible and Tract Society of Pennsylvania

105 Paul S. Braterman, *How Science Figured Out the Age of Earth*, Oct 20 2013, Scientific American, Springer

106 Gary Nichols, *Sedimentology and Statigraphy,* 2nd Edition, 2009, Wiley-Blackwell

107 Seth Borenstein, *Oldest Fossil Found: Meet Your Microbial Mom*, Nov 13 2013, Excite, Associated Press

108 *The National Academy of Sciences and The Institute of Medicine, Science, Evolution, and Creationism,* 2008, The National Academies Press, Washington DC, p. xiii

109 John G. Swallow, Theodore Garland Jr. *Selection Experiments as a Tool in Evolutionary and Comparative Physiology: Insights into Complex Traits—an Introduction to the Symposium,* 2005, University of South Dakota, University of California

110 Brian K. Hall, Benedict Hallgrimsson, *Strickberger's Evolution,* 2008, 4th Edition, Jones and Bartlett Publishers, LLC, p.52-58, 287-290

111 Watchtower, *Was Life Created?* Oct 2010, Watchtower Bible and Tract Society of New York Inc, p.27,28

112 Benjamin Radford, *Noah's Ark discovered. Again.* Apr 28 2010, The Christian Science Monitor, https://www.csmonitor.com/Science/2010/0428/Noah-s-Ark-discovered.-Again.

113 Ashley S. Hammond, Danielle F. Royer, John G. Fleagle, *The Omo-Kibish* I Pelvis, July 2017, Journal of Human Evolution, 108, p. 199-219;

   Henshilwood et al, *Emergence of Modern Human Behavior: Middle Stone Age Engravings From South Africa,* 2002, Science, 295, p.1278-1280;

   Anna-Sapfo Malaspinas, *A Genomic History of Aboriginal Australia,* Oct 13 2016, Nature, 538, MacMillan Publishers, p.207-228,

114 Megan Brenan, *40% of Americans Believe in Creationism,* July 26 2019, Gallup

115 Awake!, The Radiocarbon Clock, Sept 22 1986, Watchtower Bible and Tract Society of Pennsylvania, p.22-23

116 Watchtower, *When Was Ancient Jerusalem Destroyed Part Two*, Nov 2011, Watchtower Bible and Tract Society of Pennsylvania, P.27

117 Awake!, *Reasons to Trust the Bible,* Nov 2007, Watchtower Bible and Tract Society of Pennsylvania, p.5

118 Israel Finkelstein, *The Forgotten Kingdom: The Archaeology and History of Northern Israel,* 2013, Society of Biblical Literature, p.17

119 Richard Taylor, Richard Phillips, *Address to the Geological Society, delivered on the Evening of the 18th of February 1831, by the Rev. Professor Sedgwick, M.A. F.R.S. &c. on retiring from the President's chair,* April 1831, Philisophical Magazine, 9, p.312-315

120 Israel Finkelstein, Amihay Mazar, *The Quest for Historical Israel,* 2007, Society of Biblical Literature, Quote attributed to William Albright, p.42

121 Thomas Holland, *Jericho,* 1997, The Oxford Encyclopedia of Archaeology in the Near East, Oxford University Press, p.220,224

122 Kathleen Kenyon, *Digging Up Jericho:The Results of the Jericho Excavations 1952-1956, 1957,* Praeger, p.229;
   Piotr Bienkowski, *Jericho in the Late Bronze Age,* 1986, Warminster, p.120-125

123 Ze'ev Herzog, *Deconstructing the Walls of Jerusalem Biblical Myth And Archaeological Reality,* Oct 29 1999, Ha'aretz
   https://web.archive.org/web/20011110114548/http://lib1.library.cornell.edu/colldev/mideast/jerqu es.htm p.74

124 *Israel Finkelstein,* Dan David Prize Laureates, Archived from the original Aug 29 2014,
   http://www.dandavidprize.org/laureates/2005/77-past-archaeology/173-prof-israel-finkelstein

125 Israel Finkelstein, Neil Silberman, *The Bible Unearthed: Archaeology's New Vision of Ancient Israel and the Origin of Its Sacred Texts,* 2002, Free Press, p.37-40, 66, 67

126 Zahi Hawass, *Did the Red Sea Part? No Evidence, Archeologists Say,* Apr 2007, The New York Times

127 Thomas Thompson, *The Bible in History: How Writers Create a Past,* 2000, Pimlico

128 William Dever, *What Did the Biblical Writers Know, and When Did They Know It?: What Archaeology Can Tell Us about the Reality of Ancient Israel,* 2001, Wm. B. Eerdmans, p.98

129 William Dever, *The Bible's Buried Secrets,* NOVA, 2007, PBS

130 Philip Davies, *Beyond Labels: What Comes Next?* Apr 2010, The Bible and Interpretation

131 Watchtower, *All Scripture is Inspired of God and Beneficial,* 1990, Watchtower Bible and Tract Society of New York, p.11

132 Watchtower, *All Scripture is Inspired of God and Beneficial,* 1990, Watchtower Bible and Tract Society of New York, p.37 par.9

133 Henrey Halley, *Halley's Bible Handbook,* 1988, Zondervan, P.56

134 Tim Callahan, *Secret Origins of the Bible,* 2002, Millenium Press, p.9

135 Richard Elliot Friedman, *Who Wrote the Bible?,* 2019, Simon and Schuster, p.18-21

136 Britannica, The Ed., *Julius Wellhausen,* May 13 2021, Encyclopedia Britannica.
   https://www.britannica.com/biography/Julius-Wellhausen

137 Richard Elliot Friedman, *Who Wrote the Bible?,* 2019, Simon and Schuster, p.24

138 Richard Elliot Friedman, *Who Wrote the Bible?,* 2019, Simon and Schuster, p.61

139 Israel Finkelstein, *The Forgotten Kingdom: The Archaeology and History of Northern Israel,* 2013, Society of Biblical Literature, p.154,155

140 Richard Elliot Friedman, *Who Wrote the Bible?,* 2019, Simon and Schuster, p.197,200

141 Richard Elliot Friedman, *Who Wrote the Bible?,* 2019, Simon and Schuster, p.60

142 Bernard Levinson, *Esarhaddon's succession treaty as the source for the canon formula in Deuteronomy 13:1,* 2012, Journal of the American Oriental Society, 130(3), p.337-347.

143 Bernard Levinson, *Esarhaddon's succession treaty as the source for the canon formula in Deuteronomy 13:1,* 2012, Journal of the American Oriental Society, 130(3), p.337-347.

144 C. Walker, *Reading the Past Cuneiform,* 1989, British Museum Press p.7-9

145 F. Simons, *Proto-Sinaitic – Progenitor of the Alphabet*, 2011, Rosetta, (9) p.16-40

146 Israel Finkelstein, *The Forgotten Kingdom: The Archaeology and History of Northern Israel*, 2013, Society of Biblical Literature, p.162

147 M. Bar-Ilan, *Illiteracy in the Land of Israel in the First Centuries CE*, 1992, Essays in the Social Scientific Study of Judaism and Jewish Society, Ktav, p.61

148 Avraham Ben-Yosef, *Introduction to the History of the Hebrew Language*, 1981, Tel-Aviv, p.38

149 Rachel Feldman, *Most Ancient Hebrew Biblical Inscription Deciphered*, Jan 7 2010, AAAS, University of Haifa

150 Jan Joosten, *The Distinction Between Classical and Late Biblical Hebrew as Reflected in Syntax, Hebrew Studies*, 2005, National Association of Professors of Hebrew, p.327-339

151 Charles Boutfower, *The Chaldeans of the Book of Daniel*, April 1904, Journal of the Royal Asiatic Society, 36(2), p. 188-189

152 Boutfower, 1904 p. 189-192

153 Francesca Rochberg, *The Heavenly Writing: Divination, Horoscopy and Astronomy in Mesopotamian Culture*, 2004, Bulletin of the School of Oriental and African Studies, 69(3), p.459-460

154 Watchtower, *Baruch—Jeremiah's Faithful Secretary*, Aug 15 2006, Watchtower Bible and Tract Society, p.19

155 Aaron Demsky, *A Proto-Canaanite Abecedary Dating from the Period of the Judges and Its Implications for the History of the Alphabet*, 1977, Tel Aviv (4) p.24

156 Martin Noth, *The Deuteronomistic History*, 1981, University of Sheffield, p.1-110

157 Antony Campbell, Sources of the Pentateuch: Texts, Introductions, Annotations, 1993, Fortress Press, p.11

   J. Van Seters, *Abraham in History and Tradition*, 1975, Yale University Press

   J. Van Seters, *In Search of History: Historiography in the Ancient World and the Origins of Biblical History*, 1983, Yale University Press

   J. Van Seters, *In the Shelter of Elyan: Essays on Ancient Palestinian Life and Literature*, 1984, JSOT, p.139-158

158 George Smith, *The Chaldean Account of Genesis*, 1880, Revision by A. H. Sayce, Sampson, Low, Marston, Searle, and Rivington

159 L. Petterson, *Priestly Source of the Pentateuch*, 2013, Encyclopedia of Hebrew Language and Linguistics, Brill Academic Publishers, p.230

160 Richard Elliot Friedman, *Who Wrote the Bible?*, 2019, Simon and Schuster, p.197

161 Julius Wellhausen, *Prolegomena to the History of Israel*, 1885, A&C Black, p. 124, translated from the original German, *Geschichte Israels*, 1878

162 G. I. Davies, *Introduction to the Pentateuch*, 2013, The Oxford Bible Commentary, Oxford University Press, ch. 3, Original quote from Abraham Kuenen

163 Wellhausen, 1885, p. 404-410, attributed to Abraham Kuenen

164 Davies, 2013, ch. 3, p.15

165 Lester L. Grabbe, *A History of the Jews and Judaism in the Second Temple Period* Volume 1, 2004, T&T Clark International, p.225-228

166 Davies, 2013, ch. 3, p.15

167 Timeline: *Greco-Persian Wars*, 2012, Oxford Reference, Oxford University Press, https://www.oxfordreference.com/view/10.1093/acref/9780191737824.timeline.0001

168 Kenneth G. Hoglund, *Achaemenid Imperial Administration in Syria-Palestine and the Missions of Ezra and Nehemiah*, 1992, Scholars Press, p.125

169 Christopher Tuplin, *Xenophon and the Garrisons of the Achaemenid Empire: History, Pedagogy and the Persian Solution to Greek Problems*, 2018, Political Affinities and Literary Interactions, Trends in Classics 10.1, p.13-55

170 Henry .W.F.Saggs, *Babylon*, Oct 19 2022, Encyclopedia Britannica, https://www.britannica.com/place/Babylon-ancient-city-Mesopotamia-Asia

171 Oded Lipschits, *Demographic Changes in Judah Between the Seventh and the Fifth Centuries B.C.E.*, 2003, Judah and the Judeans in the Neo-Babylonian Period, Winona-Lake p. 323-376
    Grabbe, 2004, p. 297

172 Richard Elliot Friedman, *Who Wrote the Bible?*, 2019, Simon and Schuster, p.159

173 Grabbe, 2004, p.80

174 Anne Killebrew, *Biblical Peoples and Ethnicity: An Archaeological Study of Egyptians, Canaanites, Philistines, and Early Israel, 1300-1100 BCE*, 2005, Society of Biblical Literature, p.230

175 Grabbe, 2004, p.78

176 Grabbe, 2004, p.270

177 John J. McDermott, *Reading the Pentateuch: A Historical Introduction*, 2002, Paulist Press, p.21

178 Catherine Strong, *Grunge: Music and Memory*, 2016, Routledge, p.18
    Rick Martin, *Grunge: A Success Story*, Nov 15 1992, The New York Times

179 James D. Tabor, *Paul and Jesus: How the Apostle Transformed Christianity*, 2012, Simon and Schuster, p.114

180 Robert H. Eisenman, *James the Brother of Jesus: The Key to Unlocking the Secrets of Early Christianity and the Dead Sea Scrolls*, March 1998, Penguin Books, p.154

181 Watchtower, *"Now You Are God's People,"* Nov 2014 Study Ed, Watchtower Bible and Tract Society, p.23,24

182 Shaye J. D. Cohen, *From the Maccabees to the Mishnah*, 3rd Ed., Jan 06 2016, World History Encyclopedia, p.228, https://www.worldhistory.org/review/97/from-the-maccabees-to-the-mishnah-3rd-edition/

183 James D. Tabor, *Paul and Jesus: How the Apostle Transformed Christianity*, 2012, Simon and Schuster, p. 21

184 Frederick J Cwiekowski, *The Beginnings of the Church*, 1988, Paulist Press, p.79,80

185 James D. Tabor, *Paul and Jesus: How the Apostle Transformed Christianity*, 2012, Simon and Schuster, p. 21

186 Robert E. Van Voorst, *The Ascents of James, 1989*, Scholars Press, p.59

187 Britannica, The Editors of Encyclopaedia, *Ebionite*, Encyclopedia Britannica, Jan 4 2007, https://www.britannica.com/topic/Ebionites, Accessed 6 September 2022.

188 Robert H. Eisenman, *James the Brother of Jesus: The Key to Unlocking the Secrets of Early Christianity and the Dead Sea Scrolls*, March 1998, Penguin Books, p.156

189 Bart Ehrman, *Lost Christianities: The Battles for Scripture and the Faiths We Never Knew*, 2003, Oxford University Press P.118-122

190 James D. Tabor, *Paul and Jesus: How the Apostle Transformed Christianity*, 2012, Simon and Schuster, p. 21

191 P. Brown, *St. Augustine's Attitude to Religious Coercion*, 1964, Journal of Roman Studies, 54(1-2), p.107-116, doi:10.2307/298656

192 Raymond E. Brown, *An Introduction to the New Testament*, 2010, The Anchor Yale Bible Reference Library, Yale University Press

193 Shlomo Pines, *The Jewish Christians of the Early Centuries of Christianity According to a New Source*, 1966, The Israel Academy of Sciences and Humanities, v12(13) pp.44-48

194 Jeremy Daniel, Margaret Haberman, *Clinical Potential of Psilocybin as a Treatment for Mental Health Conditions,* Jan 2017, Mental Health Clin, 1, p.24-28 https://www.ncbi.nlm.nih.gov/pmc/articles/PMC6007659/

195 Gregory Hays translation and introduction, Original work by Marcus Aurelius, *Meditation*, 2002, Modern Library

196 Steve Crabtree, *Religiosity Highest in World's Poorest Nations*, Aug 31, 2010 Gallup, Inc. https://news.gallup.com/poll/142727/religiosity-highest-world-poorest-nations.aspx

197 John J. Collins, *Daniel: With an Introduction to Apocalyptic Literature*, 1984, Eerdmans, p.34-36

198 Britannica, The Editors of Encyclopaedia, *Ten Commandments,* Encyclopedia Britannica, https://www.britannica.com/topic/Ten-Commandments. Accessed 9 September 2022.

199 Ben Shapiro, *The Right Side of History, How Reason and Moral Purpose Made the West Great,* 2019, Broadside Books, p.70 e-book

200 Ben Shapiro, *The Right Side of History, How Reason and Moral Purpose Made the West Great,* 2019, Broadside Books, p.56 e-book

201 David Kyle Johnson, *Say Goodbye to the Santa Claus Lie, Can Lying to Your Children About Santa be Excused in the Name of Imagination?* Dec 17 2012, Psychology Today

202 Albert Einstein, *Religion and Science*, 1930, New York Times

203 Watchtower, *You Can Live Forever in Paradise on Earth,* 1989, Watchtower Bible and Tract Society, p.20, par.12

204 Watchtower, *Shepherd the Flock of God*, 2019, Watchtower Bible and Tract Society, ch.19

205 Viktor Frankl, *Man's Search for Meaning: An Introduction to Logotherapy*, 1959, Beacon Press, Translated from German by Ilse Lasche (Part One), Original 1946 by Verlag für Jugend und Volk

206 Watchtower, *You Can Be God's Friend!,* Jan 2017 printing, Watchtower Bible and Tract Society of Pennsylvania, (14) p.22

207 Anthony Morris III, *Jehovah Will Carry It Out,* Morning Worship, Sep 2020, jwb.202009-11.v

208 Watchtower, *Shepherd the Flock of God*, 2019, Watchtower Bible and Tract Society, ch.16

209 Ralph Lewis, *Finding Purpose in a Godless World: Why We Care Even if the Universe Doesn't*, 2018, Prometheus Books, p.263

210 John W. Kimball, *Apoptosis*, Mar 8 2014, Kimball's Biology Pages, https://www.biology-pages.info/A/Apoptosis.html

211 Sam Harris, *Waking Up*, 2014, Simon and Schuster, p.63-68

212 Joe Rogan, Mike Smith, *The Joe Rogan Experience* #883, Dec 7 2016

213 Pelin Kesebir, *A Quiet Ego Quiets Death Anxiety: Humility as an Existential Anxiety Buffer*, 2014, Journal of Personality and Social Psychology, 106(4), p.610-623

214 Jesse Bering, *The End? Why So Many of Us Think Our Minds Continue On After We Die*, Oct/Nov 2008, Scientific American Mind, Scientific American p.34-41,

215 Carlyle Murphy, *Most Americans Believe in Heaven ... and Hell*, Nov 10 2015, Pew Research Center

216 Jordan Peterson, Ben Shapiro, *Religious Belief and the Enlightenment with Ben Shapiro*, Jul 21 2019, YouTube, Jordan B Peterson, https://www.youtube.com/watch?v=6LIR2zQ-jvQ&t=2968s

217 *Religious Belief and the Enlightenment with Ben Shapiro*, 38:43 – 40:50

218 John R. McKivigan, Mitchell Snay, *Religion and the Antebellum Debate Over Slavery*, 1998, University of Georgia Press

219 R.P. Nettelhorst, *Notes on the Founding Fathers and the Separation of Church and State*, Quartz School of Theology

220 Steve Crabtree, *Religiosity Highest in World's Poorest Nations*, Aug 31 2010 Gallup, Inc. https://news.gallup.com/poll/142727/religiosity-highest-world-poorest-nations.aspx

221 Watchtower, *Are you Making Jehovah's Thoughts Your Own?*, Nov 2018, The Watchtower Study Ed., Watch Tower Bible and Tract Society of Pennsylvania, https://wol.jw.org/en/wol/d/r1/lp-e/2018643

222 Sarah Bradford, *Scenes in the Life of Harriet Tubman, 1869*, 2000, University of North Carolina, p. 20

223 W.E.B. Du Bois, *Black Reconstruction: 1860-1880*, 1935, Harcourt, Brace & Co

224 Steve Rose, *The Importance of Having Direction in Life*, 2020, Steve Rose, PhD, https://steverosephd.com/the-importance-of-having-direction-in-life/

225 Neil Levy, *The Importance of Awareness*, 2013 Australasian Journal of Philosophy, 91:2, 211-229,

226 Dwayne Custer, *Autoethnography as a Transformative Research Method*, Sep 15, 2014, The Qualitative Report, 19(37) p. 4, Retrieved from https://nsuworks.nova.edu/tqr/vol19/iss37/3 Nov 12 2021

227 S. Jones, T. Adams, C. Ellis, *Handbook of Autoethnography*, 2013, Left Coast Press, p.10

228 W. Mischel, E.B. Ebbesen, 1970, *Attention in delay of gratification*. Journal of Personality and Social Psychology, 16(2), 329

229 Catherine Moore, *17 Self-Discipline Exercises to Help Build Self -Control*, Feb 1 2020, Positive Psychology.com, retrieved Oct 13, 2022, https://positivepsychology.com/self-discipline-exercises/

Y. Shoda, W. Mischel W, P.K. Peake, *Predicting adolescent cognitive and self-regulatory competencies from preschool delay of gratification: Identifying diagnostic conditions*, 1990, Developmental Psychology, 26(6), 978–986.

230 A.L. Duckworth, M.E. Seligman, *Self-discipline gives girls the edge: Gender in self-discipline, grades, and achievement test scores*, 2006, Journal of Educational Psychology, 98(1), 198–208

Quote from Moore 2020

231 E. Tsukayama, et al, *Self-control as a protective factor against overweight status in the transition from childhood to adolescence*, 2010, Archives of Pediatrics & Adolescent Medicine, 164(7), 631–635

K.M. King, et al, *Changes in self-control problems and attention problems during middle school predict alcohol, tobacco, and marijuana use during high school*, 2011, Psychology of Addictive Behaviors, 25(1), 69–79.

P.D. Converse, K.A. Piccone, M.C. Tocci, *Childhood self-control, adolescent behavior, and career success*, 2014, Personality and Individual Differences, 59, 65–70.

A. Unger, et al, *The revising of the Tangney Self-Control Scale for Chinese students*, 2016 PsyCh Journal, 5(2), 101–116.

232 Wilhelm Hofmann, et al, *Yes, But Are They Happy? Effects of Trait Self-Control on Affective Well-Being and Life Satisfaction*, Jun 11 2013, Journal of Personality 82(4) p.265-277

233 A. Stocco, C. Lebiere, J. Anderson, *Conditional Routing of Information to the Cortex: A Model of the Basal Ganglia's Role in Cognitive Coordination*, Apr 2010, Psychology Review, 117(2), p. 541

234 Karin Foerde, Daphna Shohamy, *The Role of the Basal Ganglia in Learning and Memory: Insight from Parkinson's Disease*, Nov 2011, Neurobiol Learn Mem 96(4) p. 624-636

235 Alexandru Andrusca, *Basal Ganglia*, Aug 1 2022, KenHub.com, https://www.kenhub.com/en/library/anatomy/basal-ganglia, retrieved Oct 13 2022

236 Andrusca 2022

237 J. Gouraud, A. Delorme, B. Berberian, *Autopilot, Mind Wandering, and the Out of the Loop Performance Problem*, Oct 5 2017, Frontiers of Neuroscience, 541(11)

238 Matthew Killingsworth, Daniel Gilbert, *A Wandering Mind is an Unhappy Mind*, Nov 12 2010, Science, American Association for the Advancement of Science, 330(6006), p.932

239 Goleman et al, *Self-Awareness (HBR Emotional Intelligent Series)*, 2018, Harvard Business Review

240 E. Kross, O. Ayduk, W. Mischel, *When Asking "Why" Does Not Hurt: Distinguishing Rumination from Reflective Processing of Negative Emotions*, 2005, Psychology Science 16(9), 709-715

241 National Center for Complementary and Integrative Health, *Meditation and Mindfulness: What You Need to Know*, Last Updated June 2022, https://www.nccih.nih.gov/health/meditation-and-mindfulness-what-you-need-to-know, retrieved Oct 14 2022

242 Clarence L. Haynes, *5 Ways an Idle Mind is the Devil;s Workshop*, Jul 2 2020, https://www.crosswalk.com/faith/spiritual-life/ways-an-idle-mind-is-the-devils-workshop.html, retrieved Oct 14 2022

243 Frederick Douglass, *Narrative of the Life of Frederick Douglass*, 1845, Yale University Press (2001)

244 Andrusca, 2022

245 K Berridge, T Robinson, J Aldridge, *Dissecting Components of Reward: 'Liking,' "Wanting," and Learning,* Feb 2009, Current Opinion in Pharmacology, 9(1), p.65-73

246 Stephen Glover, *Breaking Down Every Drug I Ever Did,* Sep 12 2019, YouTube Channel Steve-O, www.youtube.com/watch?v=SbTfJB-vfpc&t=521s, 7:27-8:41

247 J. Olds, P. Milner, *Positive reinforcement produced by electrical stimulation of septal area and other regions of rat brain,* 1954, Journal of Comparative and Physiological Psychology, 47(6), 419–427. https://doi.org/10.1037/h0058775

248 Terry Robinson, Kent Berridge, *The Neural Basis of Drug Craving: An Incentive-Sensitization Theory of Addiction,* Sep 1993, Brain Research Reviews, Elsevier 18(3) p.247-291,

249 Nutt, Lingford-Hughes, Erritzoe, Stokes, *The Dopamine Theory of Addiction: 40 Years of Highs and Lows,* 2015, Nature Reviews Neuroscience, 16, p.305-312

250 Allen Carr, *Allen Carr's Easy Way to Quit Smoking,* 2015, Arcturus Publishing

251 Michael Day, Allen Carr, Dec 14 2006, BMJ, (333)1273, https://doi.org/10.1136/bmj.39059.581123.FA

252 Allen Carr, *The Easy Way to Control Alcohol,* 2014, Arcturus, P.224

253 Dijstra et al, *The effectiveness of the Allen Carr smoking cessation training in companies tested in a quasi-experimental design,* Sep 13 2014, BMC Public Health, DOI: 10.1186/1471-2458-14-952

254 Sheila Keogan, Shasha Li, Luke Clancy, *Allen Carr's Easyway to Stop Smoking - A randomised clinical trial,* Jul 2019, Tob Control, 28(4) p. 414-419 doi: 10.1136/tobaccocontrol-2018-054243

255 Frings et al, *Comparison of Allen Carr's Easyway programme with a specialist behavioural and pharmacological smoking cessation support service: a randomized controlled trial,* 2020, Addiction, 115(5), p. 977-985, DOI: 10.1111/add.14897

256 Laura Marie Edinger-Schons, *Oneness Beliefs and Their Effect on Life Satisfaction,* Apr 11, 2019, Psychology of Religion and Spirituality, www.apa.org/pubs/journals/releases/rel-rel0000259.pdf

257 Sigmund Freud, translated by James Strachey, *Civilization and its Discontents,* Originally written in 1929, translated in 2018, CreateSpace Independent Publishing, p.5

258 Kenneth Parker, *Effects of Subliminal Symbiotic Stimulation on Academic Performance: Further Evidence on the Adaptation-Enhancing Effects of Oneness Fantasies,* 1982, Journal of Counseling Psychology (29) p.19-28

259 R. Schurtman, J. R. Palmatier and E. S. Martin, *On the Activation of Symbiotic Gratification Fantasies as an Aid in the Treatment of Alcoholic,* 1982, International Journal of the Addictions (17) p.1157-1174

260 P. Thornton, H. Igleheart, L. Silverman, *Subliminal Stimulation of Symbiotic Fantasies as an Aid in the Treatment Drug Abusers,* 1987, The International Journal of the Addictions, (22) p.751-765

261 Doris Hill, *Sense of Belonging as Connectedness,* American Indian Worldview, and Mental Health, Oct 2006, Archives of Psychiatric Nursing (20) p.210-216

262 L. Uddin et al, *The Self and Social Cognition: The Role of Cortical Midline Structures and Mirror Neurons,* 2007, Trends in Cognitive Sciences, (11) p.153-157

263 Matthew Ratcliffe, *The Feeling of Being,* Journal of Consciousness Studies, (12), No.8-10, p.45

264 Sharon Chirban, *Oneness Experience: Looking Through Multiple Lenses*, 2000, Journal of Applied Psychoanalytic Studies, 2(3), p.249

265 Mihály Csíkszentmihályi, *Beyond Boredom and Anxiety: Experiencing Flow in Work and Play*, 1975, Jossey-Bass

266 A. M. Garfield et al, *The Oneness Beliefs Scale: Connecting Spirituality with Pro-environmental Behavior*, 2014, Journal for the Scientific Study of Religion, (53) p.357

267 C. Riek, et al, *Direct Sampling of Electric-field Vacuum Fluctuations*, Oct 23 2015, Science, 350(6259), American Association for the Advancement of Science, p.420-423

268 J. Woodward, *Radical Pairs in Solution, Progress in Reaction and Mechanism*, 27(3), p.165-207

269 Eckhart Tolle, *Presence Beyond Form*, June 6 2020, Eckhart Tolle YouTube, https://www.youtube.com/watch?v=VwfTve6M0kk

270 Mayo Clinic Staff, *Mindfulness Exercises, Consumer Health*, Sep 15 2020, Mayo Foundation for Medical Education and Research, https://www.mayoclinic.org/healthy-lifestyle/consumer-health/in-depth/mindfulness-exercises/art-20046356

271 C. Hutcherson, E. Seppala, J. Gross, *Loving-Kindness Meditation Increases Social Connectedness*, 2008, Emotion, The American Psychological Association, (8)5, p.720-724

272 Yang Claire Yang, et al, *Social relationships and physiological determinants of longevity across the human life span*, Jan 2016, Proceedings of the National Academy of Sciences of the United States of American, 113(3) p.578-583

273 Matthew D. Lieberman, *Social: Why Our Brains Are Wired to Connect*, 2013, Crown

274 R. Dunbar, *The Social Brain Hypothesis, Evolutionary Anthropology*, 1998, 6, p.178-190

275 David Geary, Mark Flinn, *Evolution of Human Parental Behavior and the Human Family*, 2001, Parenting: Science and Practice, 1(1), Lawrence Erlbaum p.8-28

276 Patricia Thomas, Hui Liu, Debra Umberson, *Family Relationships and Well-Being*, Nov 2017, Innovation in Aging, 1(3), Oxford Press

277 John W. O'Malley, *Trent: What Happened at the Council*, Jan 15 2013, Harvard University Press, p.225

278 William V. D'Antonio, William M. Newman and Stuart A. Wright, *Religion and Family Life: How Social Scientists View the Relationship*, Sep 1982, Journal for the Scientific Study of Religion 21(3), Wiley, p.218-225

279 John Kleinig, *Loyalty*, The Stanford Encyclopedia of Philosophy, Winter 2020 Edition, Edward N. Zalta (ed.)

280 R.E. Ewin, *Loyalty and Virtues*, Philosophical Quarterly, 1992, 42(169), 403, 411

281 Ed Yong, *Maternal hormone shuts down baby's brain cells during birth*, Oct 7, 2008, Not Exactly Rocket Science, National Geographic Society www.nationalgeographic.com/science/phenomena/2008/10/07/maternal-hormone-shuts-down-babys-brain-cells-during-birth/

282 D. P. Johnson, *Critical Theory: Social System Requirements Versus Human Needs*, 2008, Contemporary Sociological Theory, Springer Science and Business Media, p.397-425

283 Michael Lipka, *A Closer Look at Jehovah's Witnesses Living in the U.S.*, Apr 26 2016, Pew Research Center, https://www.pewresearch.org/fact-tank/2016/04/26/a-closer-look-at-jehovahs-witnesses-living-in-the-u-s/

284 Gary Breaux, *JW Broadcasting*, Nov 2017, JW.org, Watchtower Bible and Tract Society, 53:27-55:44

285 Natalie O'Brien, *Jehovah's Witnesses Accused of Stashing Cash to Avoid Compo*, Jun 13 2020, The Daily Telegraph, News Corp Australia

286 Hans Steymans, *Deuteronomy 28 and Tell Taynat*. 2012, Verbum et Ecclesia, 34 p.1-13 10.4102/ve.v34i2.870.